Northborough
Through Time

Ellen Racine

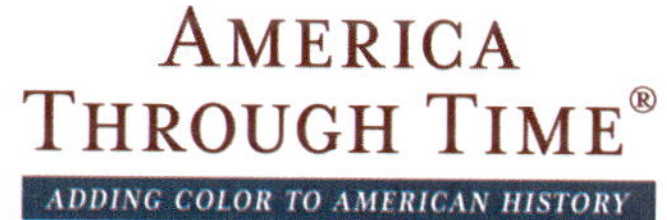

America Through Time is an imprint of Fonthill Media LLC

Fonthill Media LLC
www.fonthillmedia.com
office@fonthillmedia.com

First published 2015

ISBN 978-1-63500-025-2

Typeset in Mrs Eaves XL Serif Narrow
Printed and bound in England

Connect with us:
www.twitter.com/usathroughtime
www.facebook.com/AmericaThroughTime

Change was also evident in the countryside. Originally heavily forested, by the 1800s Northborough's landscape was mostly open space with sweeping views of farms and orchards. It is difficult to find similar views today, and not just because of modern construction. With a few notable exceptions, the old farm lands are once again forested. The rustic photograph included in this introduction is of Hudson Street, possibly in the 1880s, with Wallace Pond out of sight to the left. It depicts the picturesque quality of life in Northborough even though this area had two textile mills and a comb shop further to the east.

Still, there are some constants. Education has long been important to Northborough. The town had a network of four elementary schools and later a high school that were well supported. Building and expanding schools is a frequent event in our history. Another constant is the people of Northborough. The town has long benefited from those with the ability to start and operate businesses. We have also been blessed with a population that maintained a small town orientation and willingness to help neighbors.

Evidence of the changes, those of long ago and some more recent, are captured in our photographic history some of which is included in this book. This visual record is hopefully both educational and entertaining and will bring back fond memories to our long-time residents. Enjoy our history.

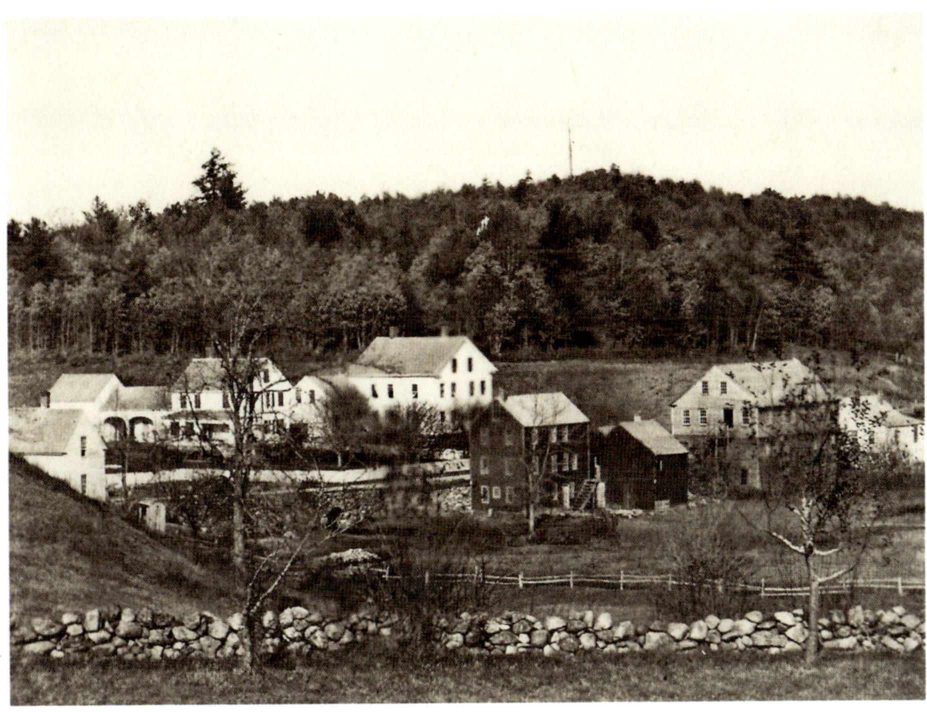

Introduction

The Town of Northborough was incorporated in 1766, motivated by the very practical consideration that residents of this northern outpost of Westborough found traveling the long distance to meeting house for Sunday worship a hardship.

Changes in the town have continued to be driven by pragmatic interests of providing life's necessities, supporting one's family, and improving the condition of life. Small shops and mills were initially built along the banks of our waterways to produce the goods needed locally for construction and transportation such as bricks, lumber, nails, and wagon wheels. Traveling any distance was slow and required overnight stops. Since Northborough was along the highly frequented routes, inns sprung up to meet the need such as the Elm Tree Inn on West Main and the Munroe Tavern that was pushed back on Blake Street to make room for the Town Hall in 1868.

As transportation improved, dependence on locally created goods lessened and it became easier to both import needed items and ship products to other markets. Horse and carriage roads were supplemented by the railroad coming to town in 1856. Practical entrepreneurs took advantage and began creating broader markets for Northborough products, notably horn goods, textiles, milk and produce. More comfortable hotels were built with features that attracted locals as well as distant travelers.

Resilient and never wasteful, the town residents adapted to changing economics. Buildings too small to meet growing needs were moved to other locations and repurposed. Seth Grout's Gospel Shop was moved and used as an addition to a home. Others were renovated or relocated to accommodate new construction. Anson Rice's house was moved a short distance off Main Street to make way for a gas station. Demolition took place when other approaches were not practical or economic and fires always demanded rebuilding. The south side of downtown West Main Street has changed dramatically over the years due to fires and commercial enterprises.

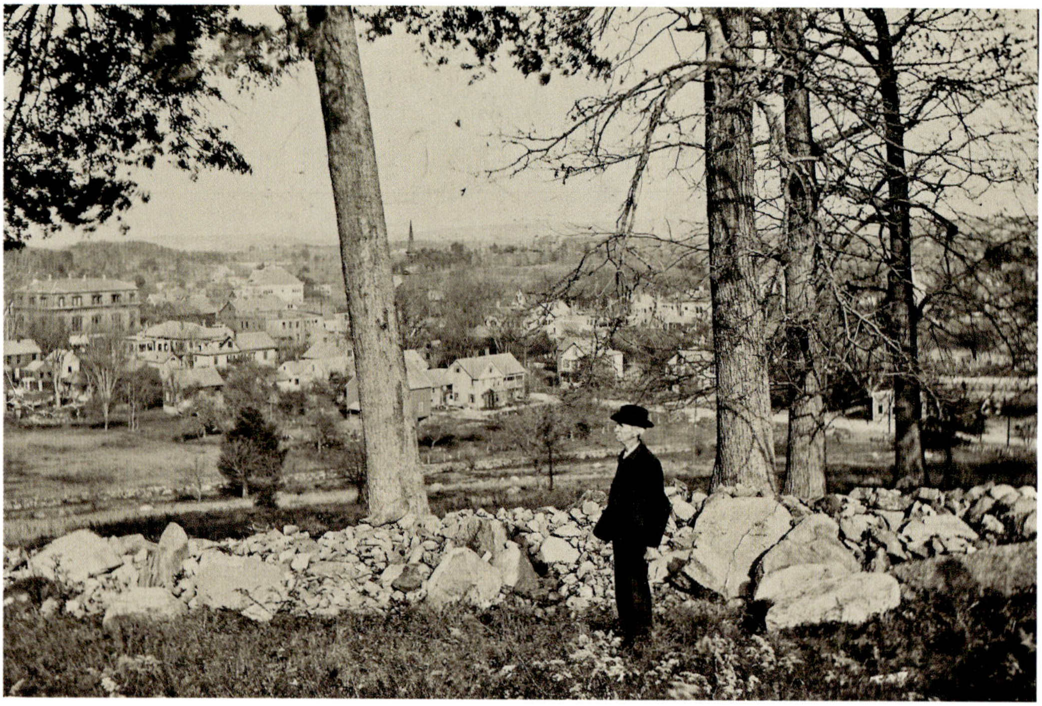

DOWNTOWN FROM HILL AND CHURCH: About 1895 Henry Lawrence strolled on the lower part of a hill once known as Liquor Hill but then as Assabet Hill. The hill offered a good view of town. By 2006, with Assabet Hill tree-covered, Trinity Church steeple, a few hundred yards to the northeast, provided Skip Doyle a better view of the downtown area.

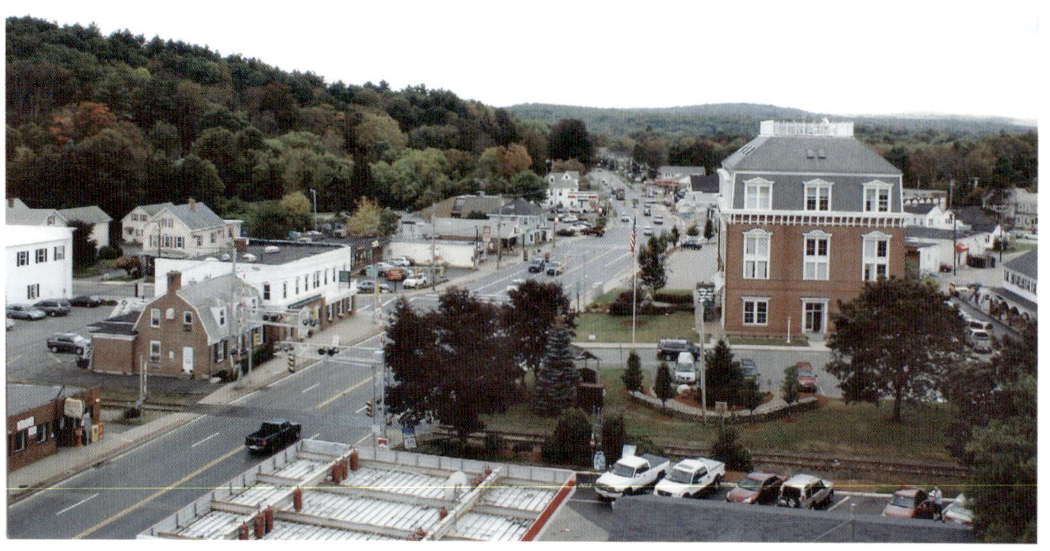

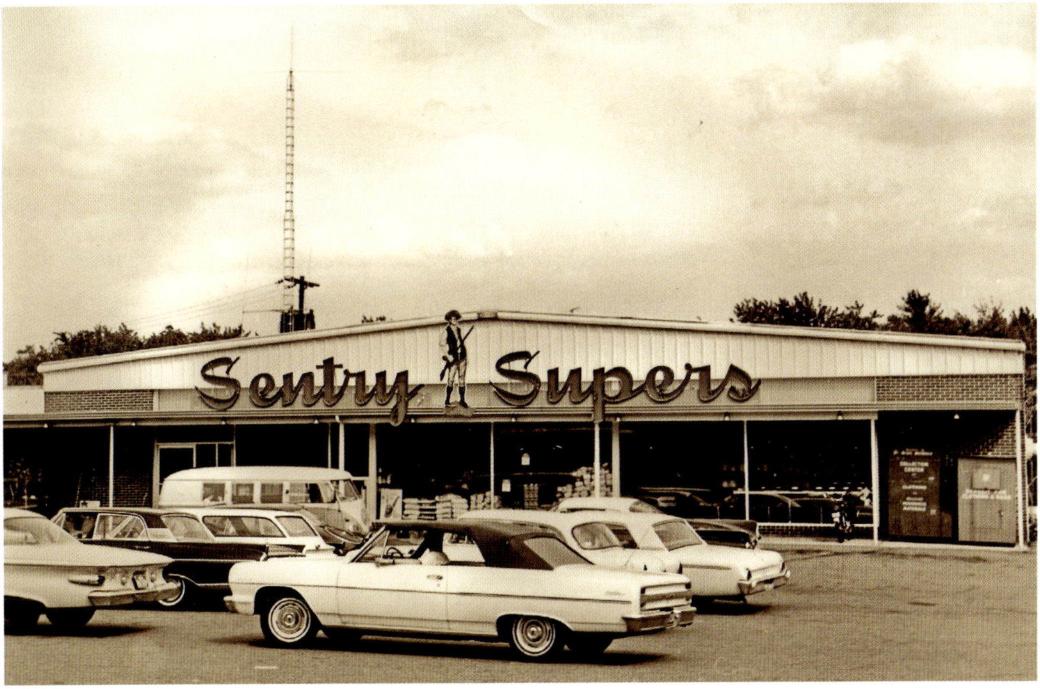

MORE PRODUCTS, MORE SPACE: In 1966 a supermarket occupied the largest space in what is the Northborough Shopping Center in 2015, on West Main Street. More recently such stores require more space for their rapidly growing inventories, and markets generally must become more "super." Hardware stores, such as the one pictured elsewhere in this volume, faced the same problem, although on a less gigantic scale, a few decades later. The former Sentry Super was big enough to provide the answer.

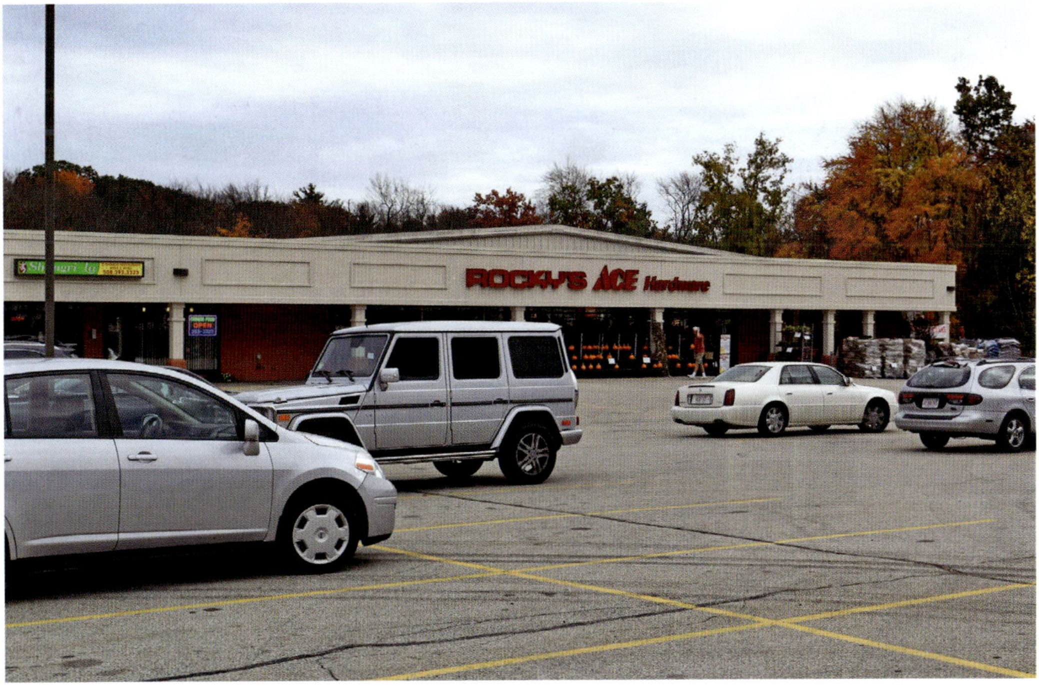

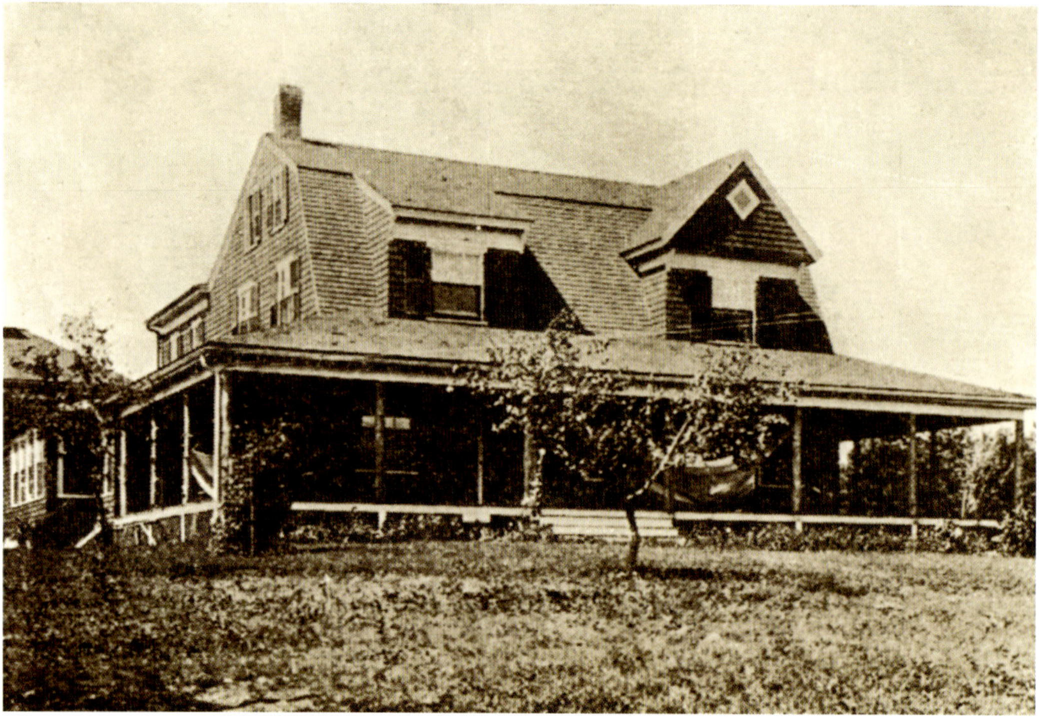

FROM VISITORS TO RESIDENTS: The Elm Tree Inn fed and housed guests traveling through Northborough on stagecoaches in the eighteenth and early nineteenth centuries. In the twenty-first century seniors congregate in nearby Whitney Place, an assisted living residence at 238 West Main Street.

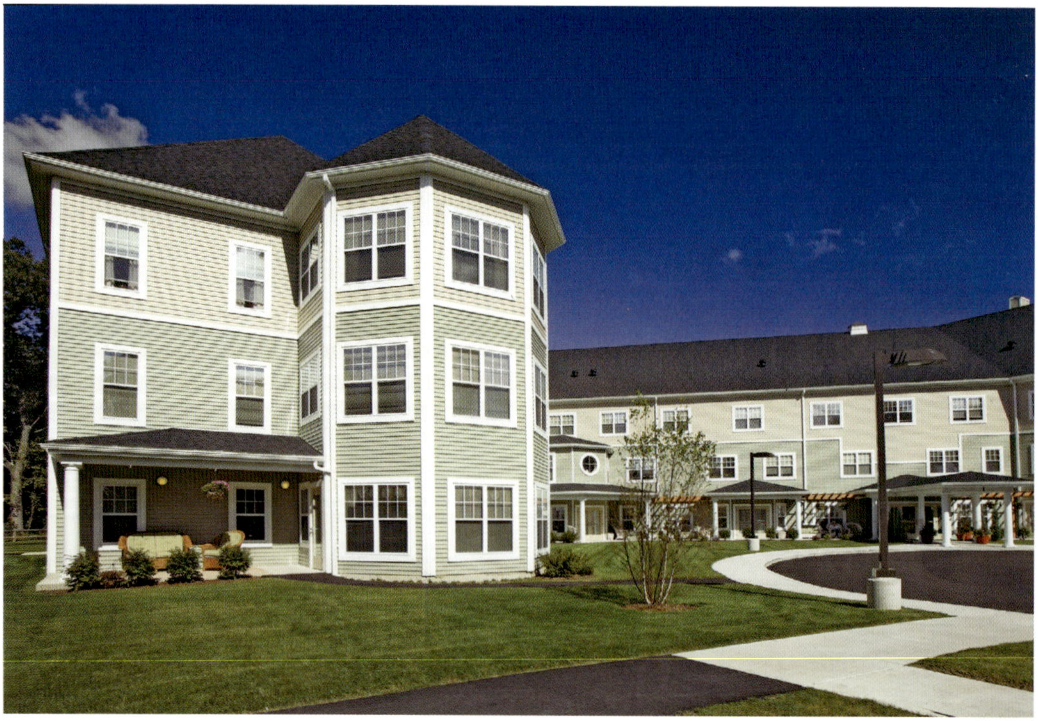

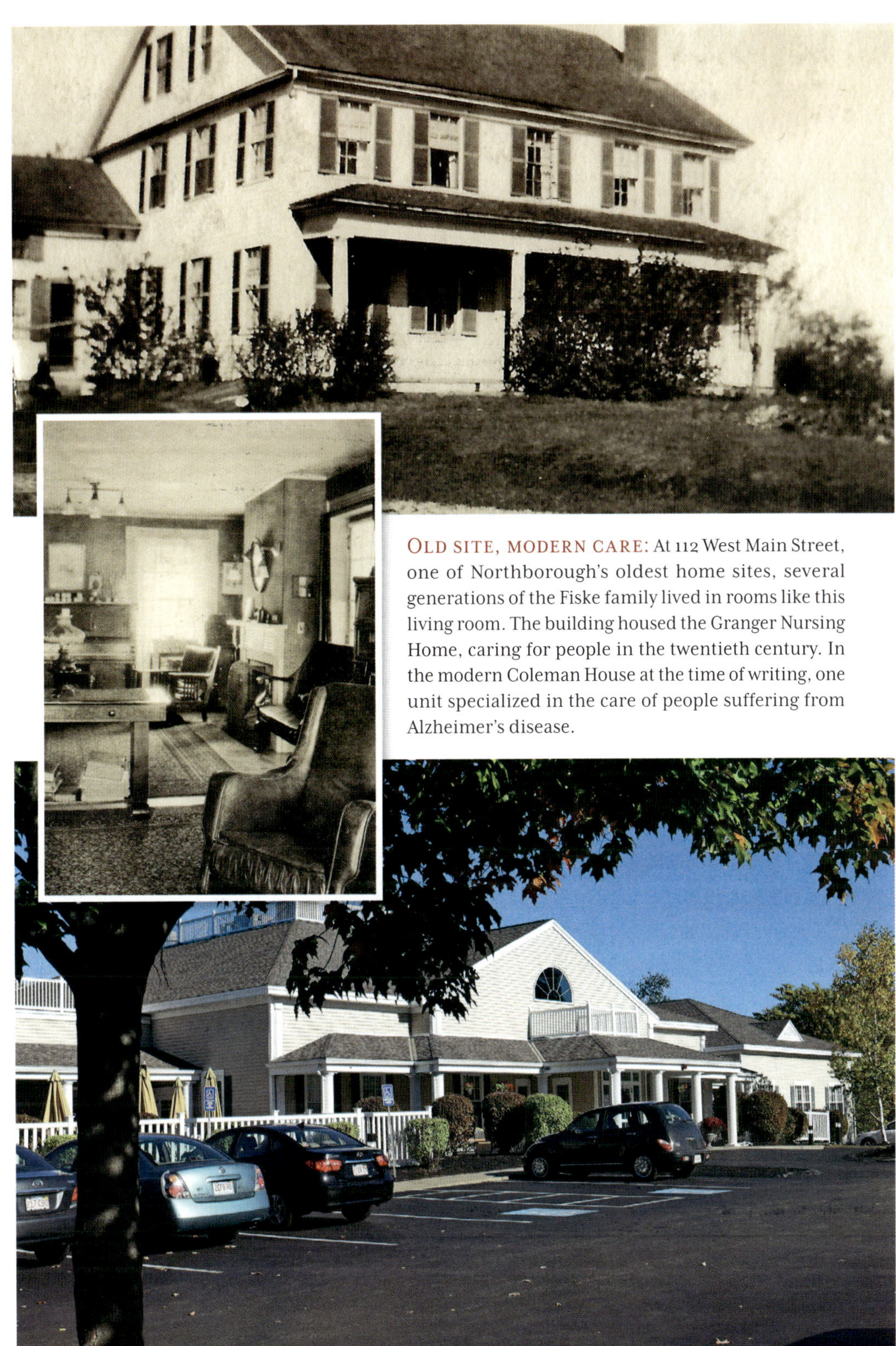

OLD SITE, MODERN CARE: At 112 West Main Street, one of Northborough's oldest home sites, several generations of the Fiske family lived in rooms like this living room. The building housed the Granger Nursing Home, caring for people in the twentieth century. In the modern Coleman House at the time of writing, one unit specialized in the care of people suffering from Alzheimer's disease.

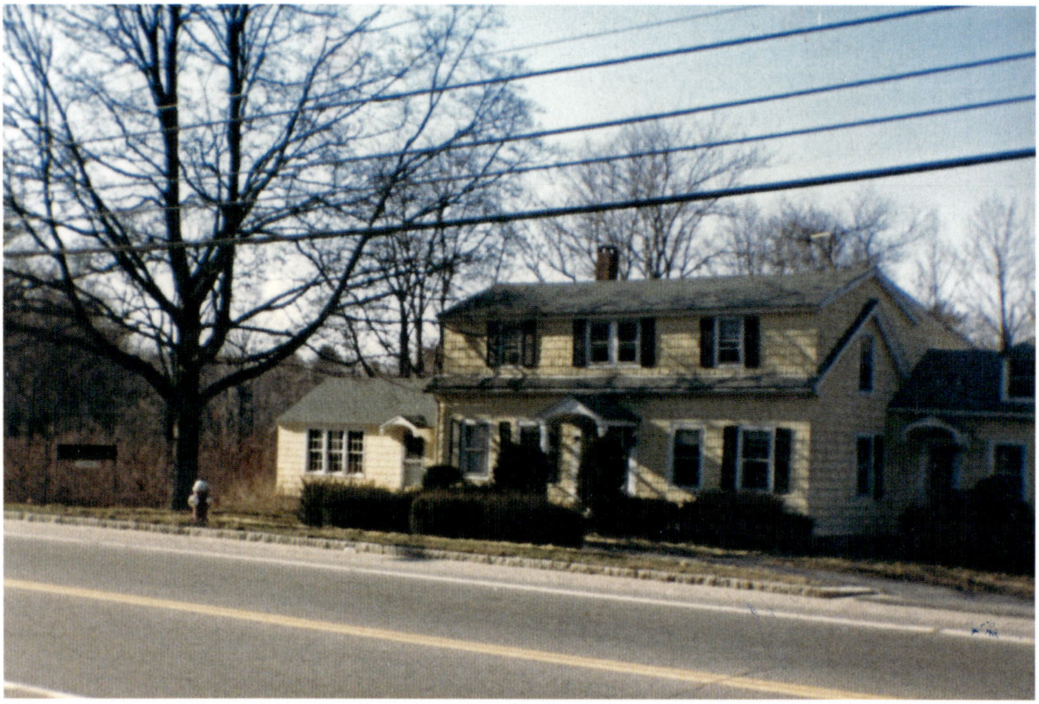

GUISES OF BUSINESS: In 1955, 70 West Main Street was a place of business for an antique dealer and an attractive home for the Tildens. Eventually the long narrow lot along West Main Street looked more like a purely business site – a typical displacement of a home business by a franchise in the later twentieth century.

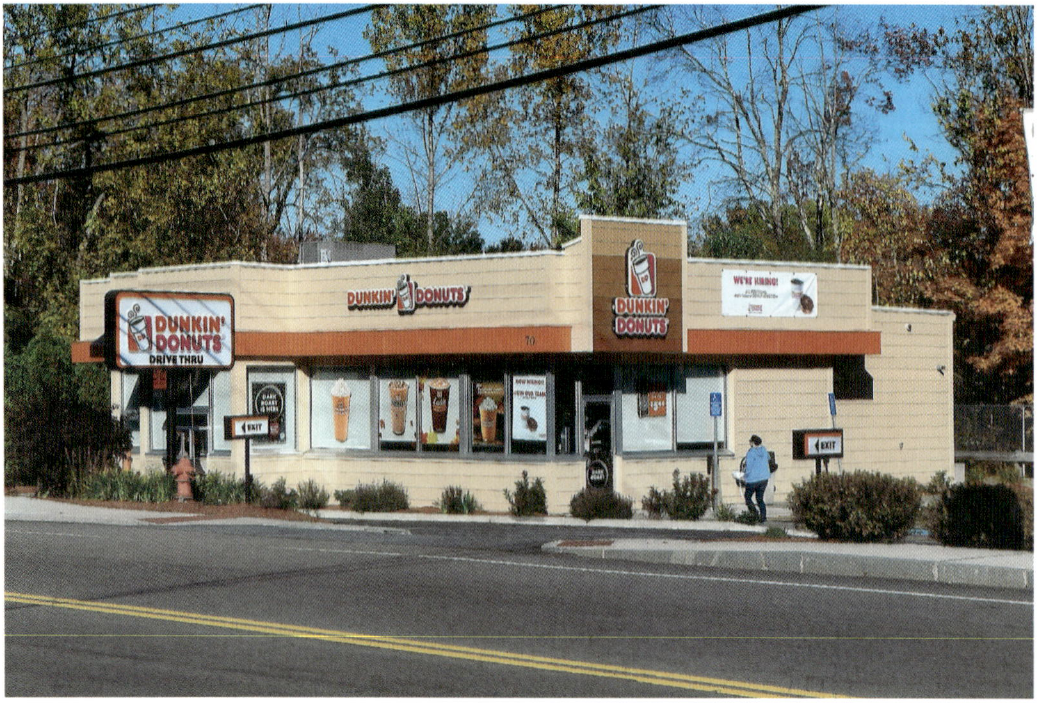

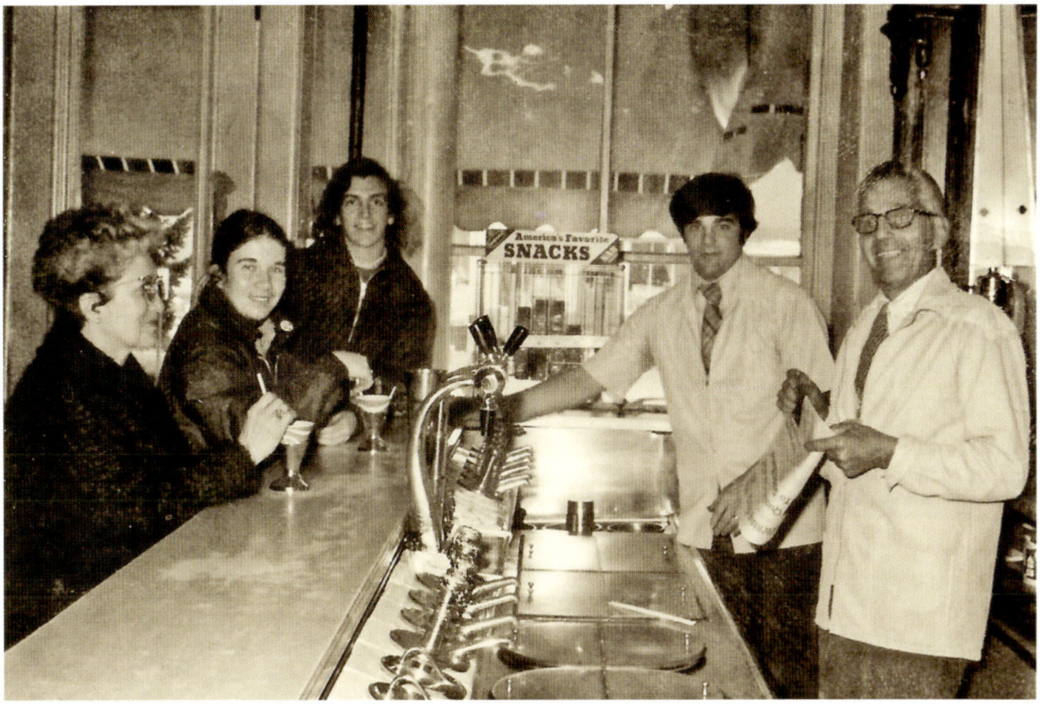

SHATTUCK'S SODA FOUNTAIN: In the 1960s and '70s, Shattuck's Pharmacy, located in the old Town Hall, hosted a popular ice cream counter. In 2015 local townspeople can frequent such places as LaLaJava at 290 W. Main Street for lunch, pastry, coffee and meeting with friends. Ellen Racine, Melanie Magee and Cathy Cairns have done just that.

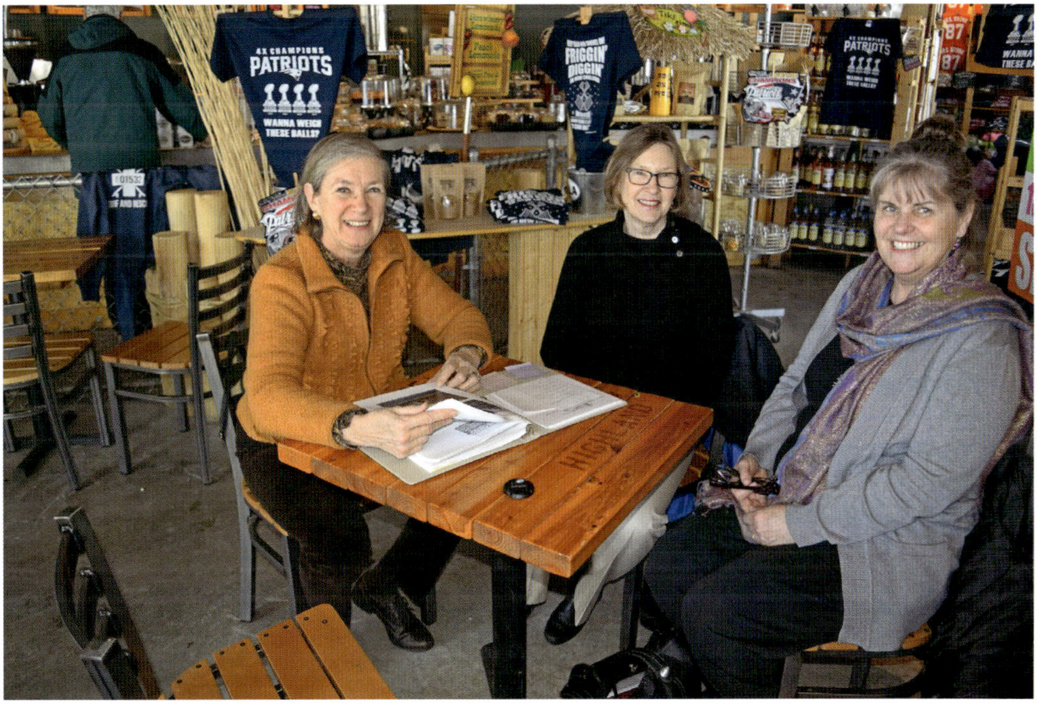

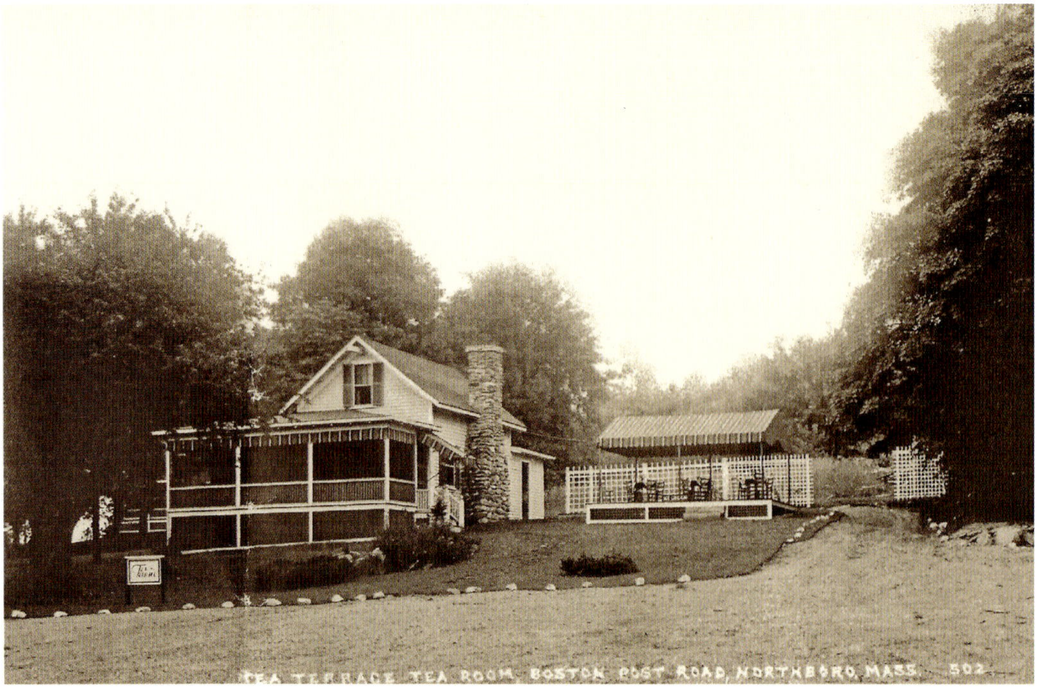

TEA TERRACE TEA ROOM. BOSTON POST ROAD, NORTHBORO, MASS. 502

WHERE DID IT GO? In 2003 a Northborough woman, wondered about the Tea Terrace, seen in a 1900 post card: "I cannot locate where it was on the Boston Post Road." It was still there although described as being on intersecting Monroe Street, while not having moved an inch from the Post Road. It is a residence in the twenty-first century. In 2015 one can enjoy tea, lunch and pastries at Special Teas on Church Street as did Kathy Pierce, Cindy Atwood and Carol McElwee.

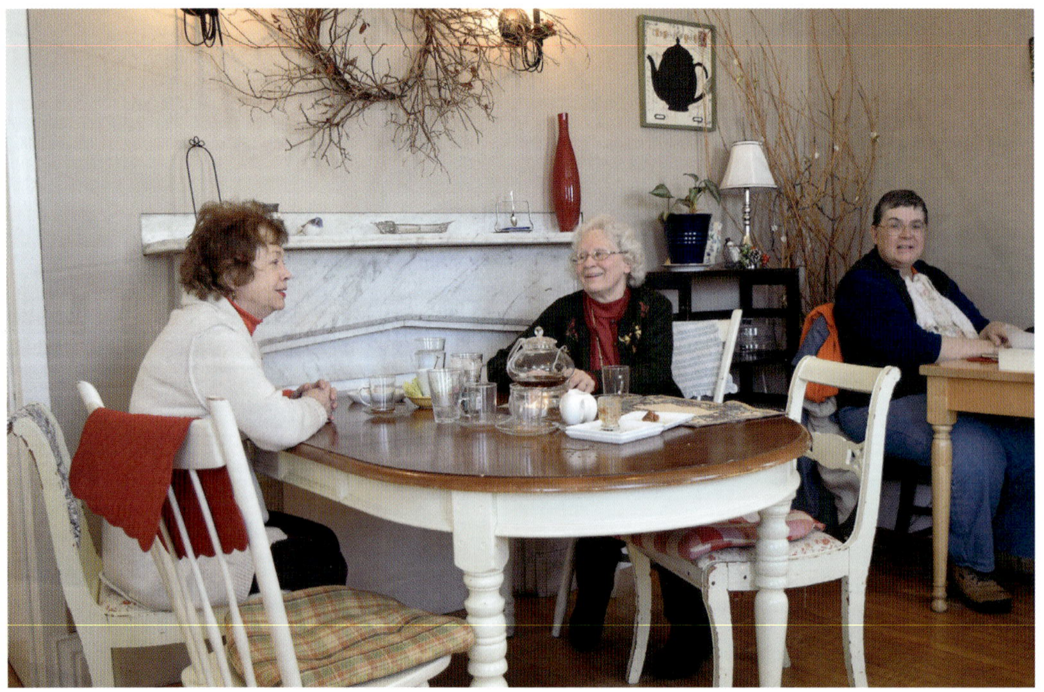

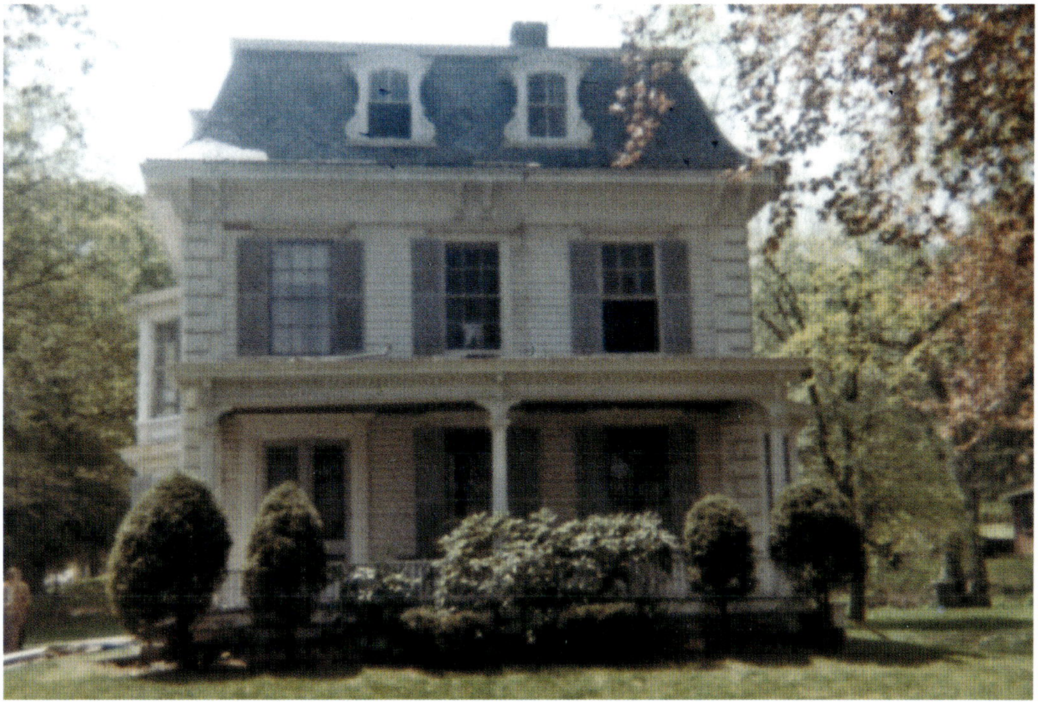

Bank arrives, setting perseveres: At the corner of 56 West Main and Monroe Streets near the site of Northborough's Civil War monument, this house once boasted a formal garden and full-time gardener. After some years of neglect, however, it was razed in 1979. Two years later a bank rose on the site. The setting remains pleasantly tree-lined, but a parking lot has replaced the rear garden.

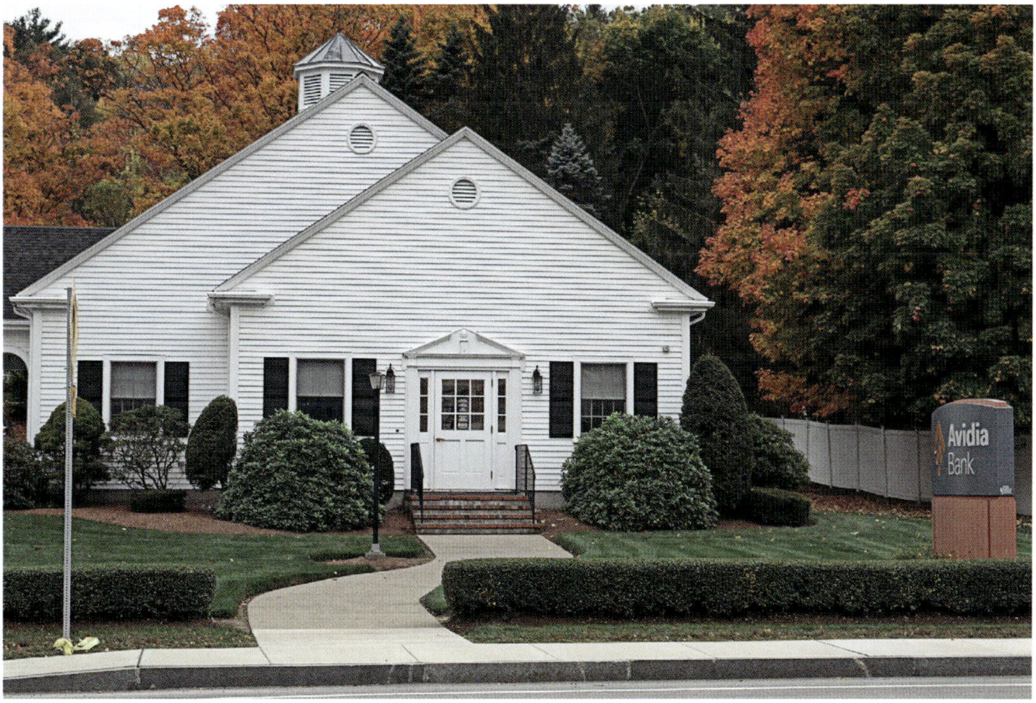

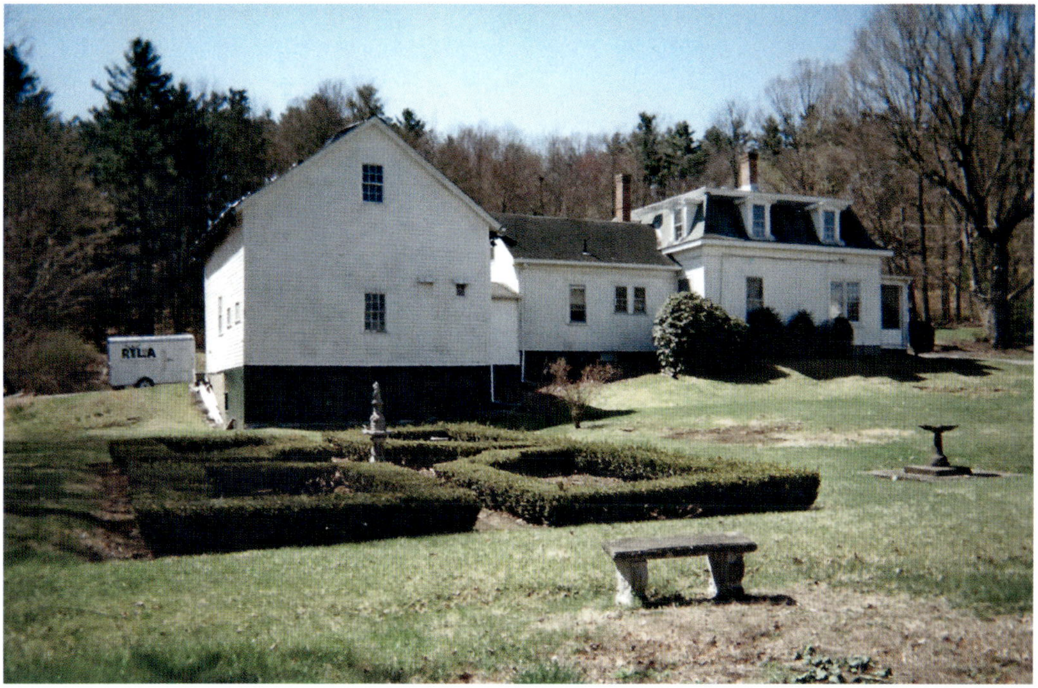

NINETEENTH-CENTURY HOUSE FALLS: Richard Newton, the carpenter who in 1860 constructed the Baptist Church on Main Street that became the quarters of the Northborough Historical Society in 1960, also built this house at 9 Monroe Street. His family lived there for more than fifty years. When the site was purchased for "commercial condominiums" constructed in 2014, anyone who could move this house could have it, but no one did, and it was razed.

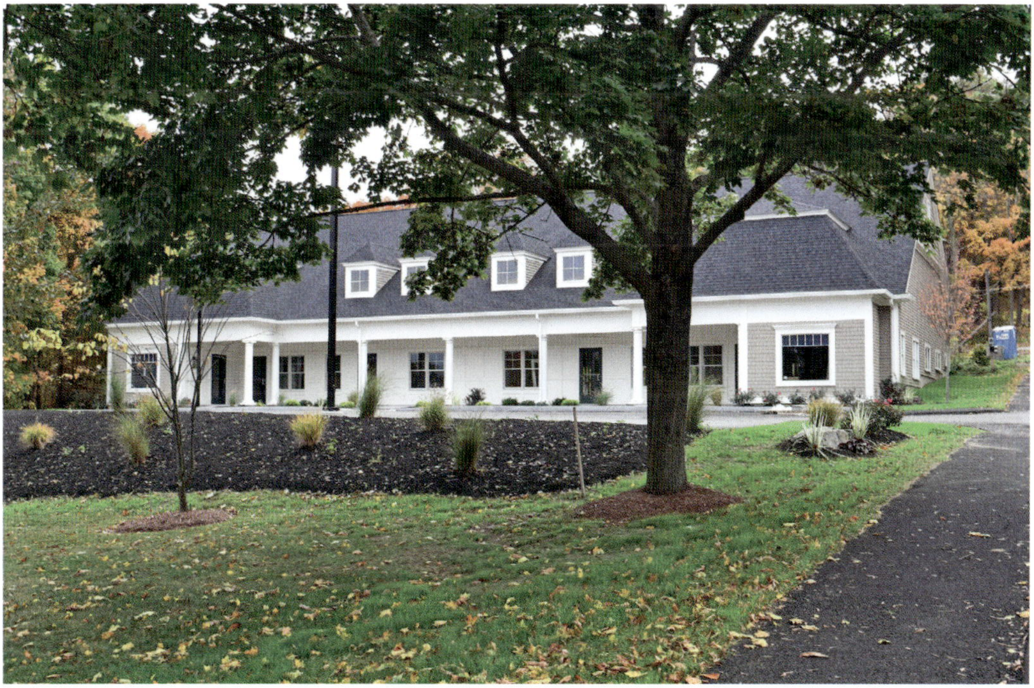

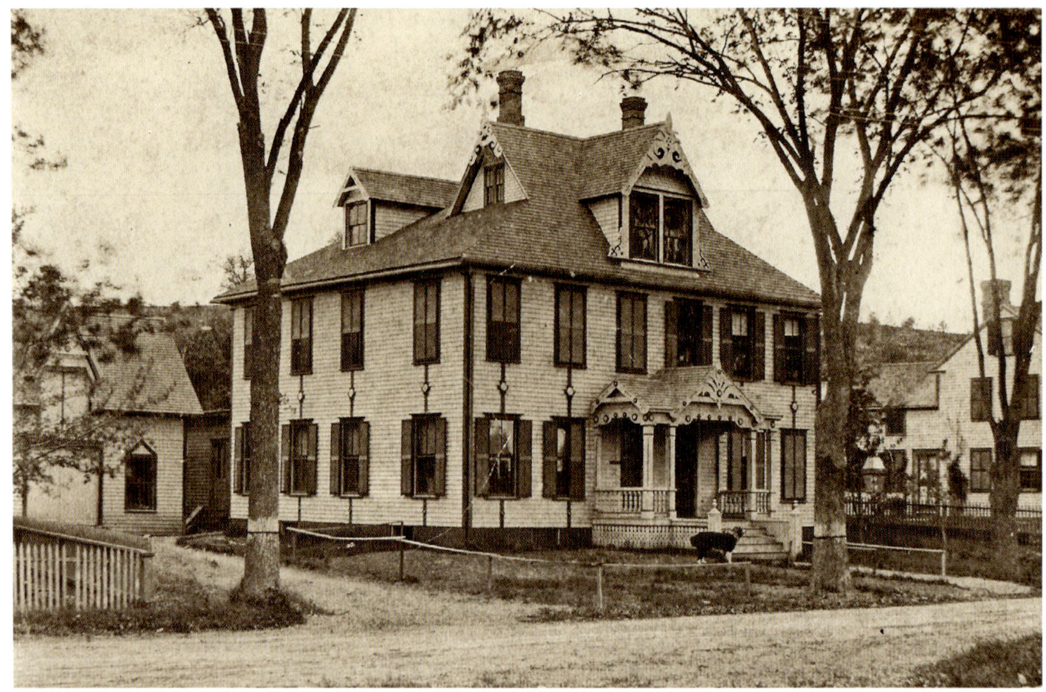

A HOUSE MUCH ALTERED: In 1894 a local newspaper informed its readers that "Dr. Guptill is to greatly improve the house he recently purchased." What he did we don't know. Was the gaudy entranceway new? The alterations made a century later in this house at 39 West Main Street are very visible. Would the good doctor have understood the removal of the front gable windows or the building's transformation to storefront businesses?

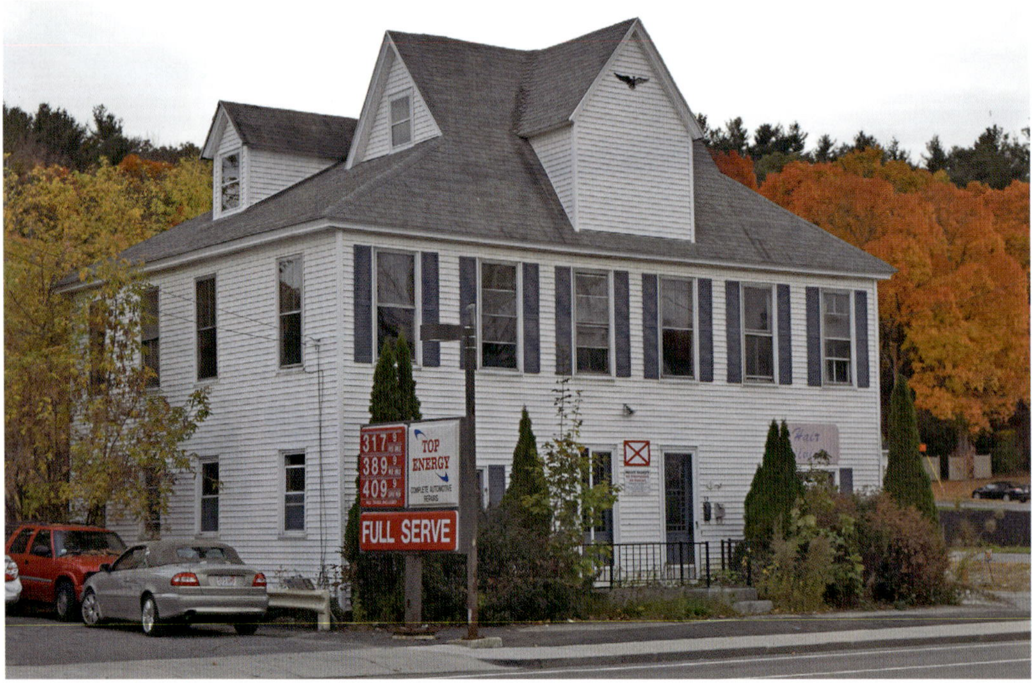

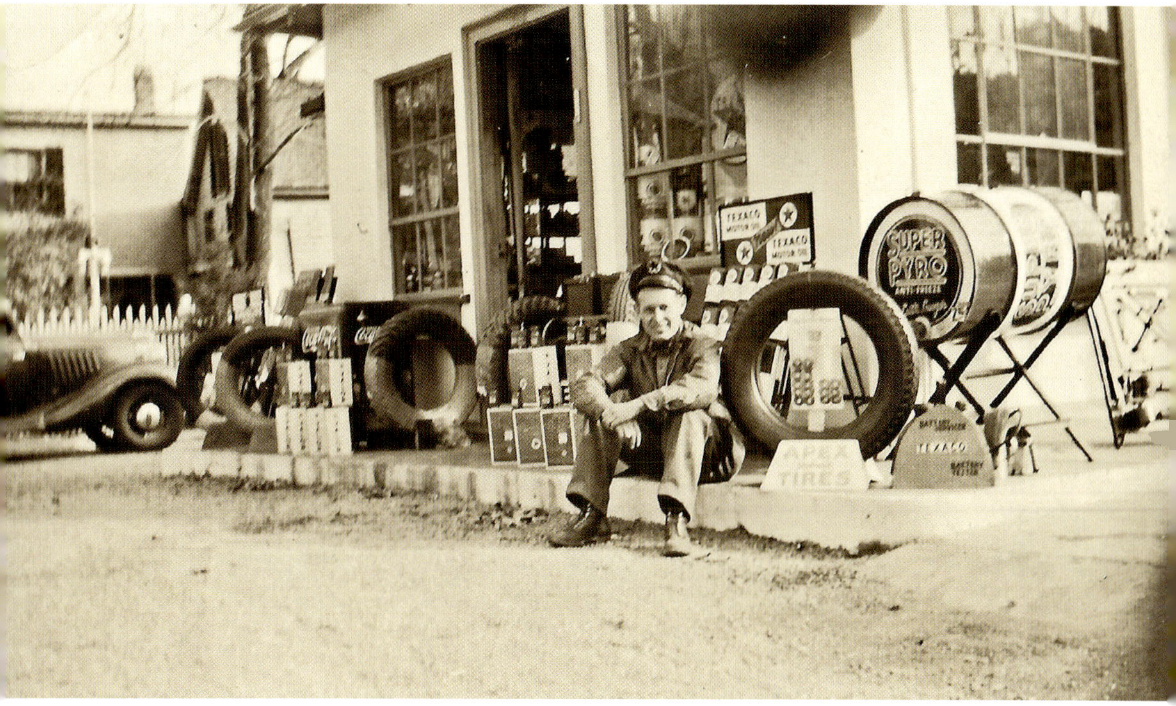

A MAN OF TEXACO: In the 1930s Jack Schleyer takes a break at the Texaco station in the town's center. Some eight decades later a much bigger station, showing a Citgo triangle instead of the Texaco star, appears too busy to allow time for a break, although of course the man near the vehicle at the left may only be chatting. It is independently owned and operated in 2015.

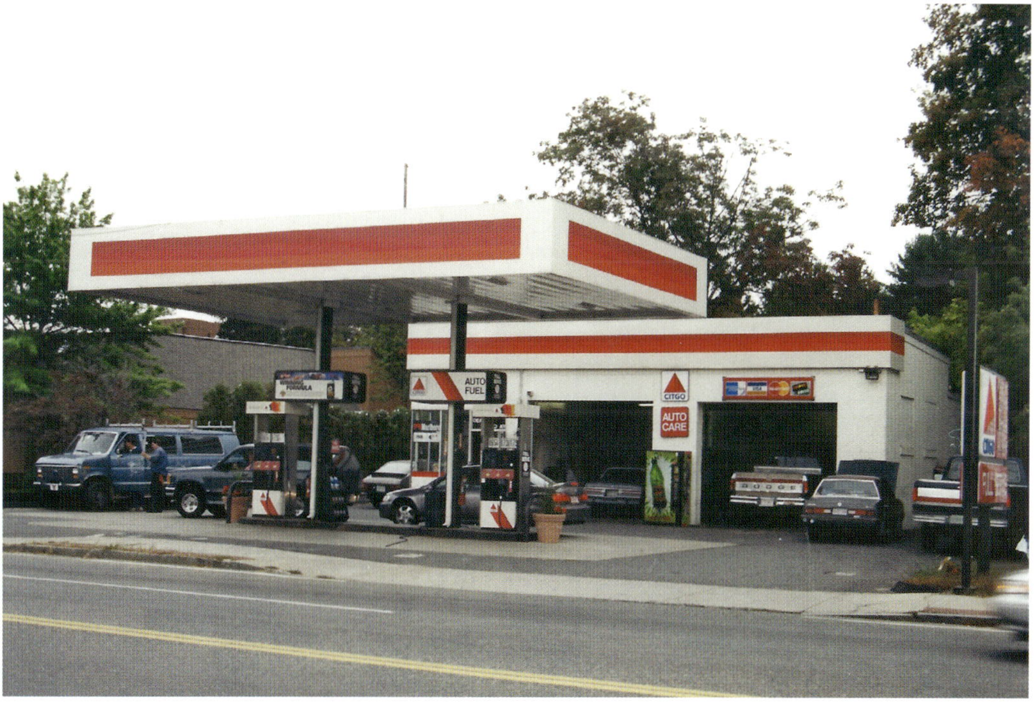

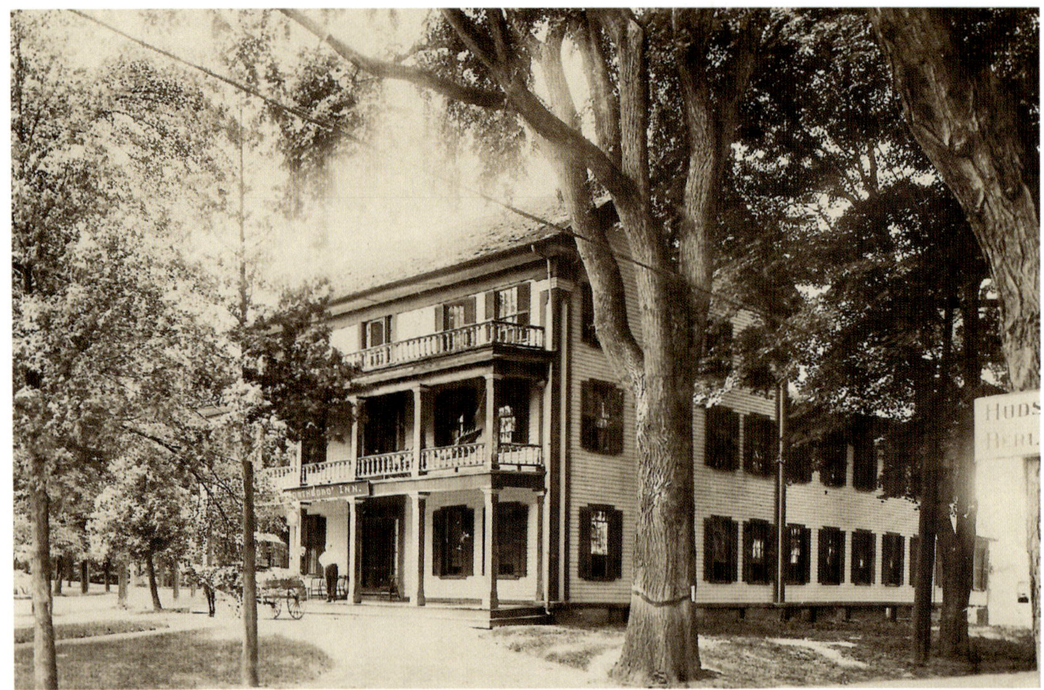

TO REST OR NOT: The Northborough Hotel, built sometime in the 1860s, was a noble structure as was its contemporary, the Town Hall. A place for the weary traveler, or for those with more energy, dances were held on the innovative spring dance floor on the second story. The hotel burned in 1926. To the west of the hotel was the carriage shed, later Walker's Market, run by Elizabeth Walker from 1936-1945, and most recently R & T Furniture, shown in 1966. It is vacant at the time of this writing.

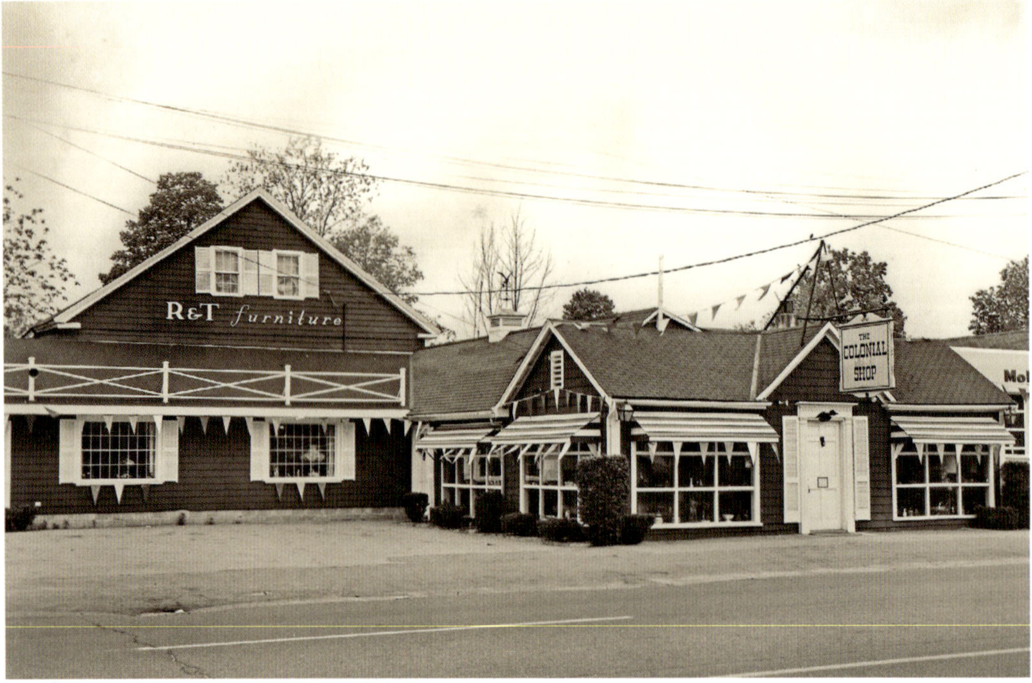

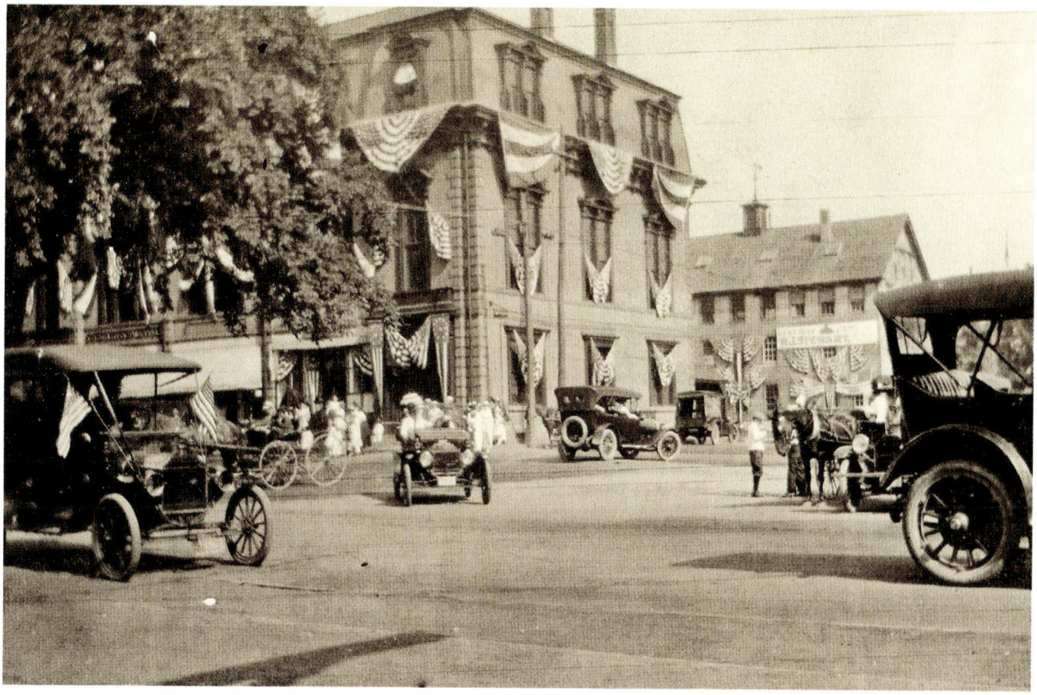

TOWN HALL, TOWN TRAFFIC: We see the nineteenth-century town hall in a festive state, the town's 150th birthday, in 1916. After the building burned seven decades later, a replica (no longer a town hall) was constructed, different in some details. The contrast of automobiles over practically a complete century stands out sharply. The building to the right on Blake Street is still there, though being reduced to two stories.

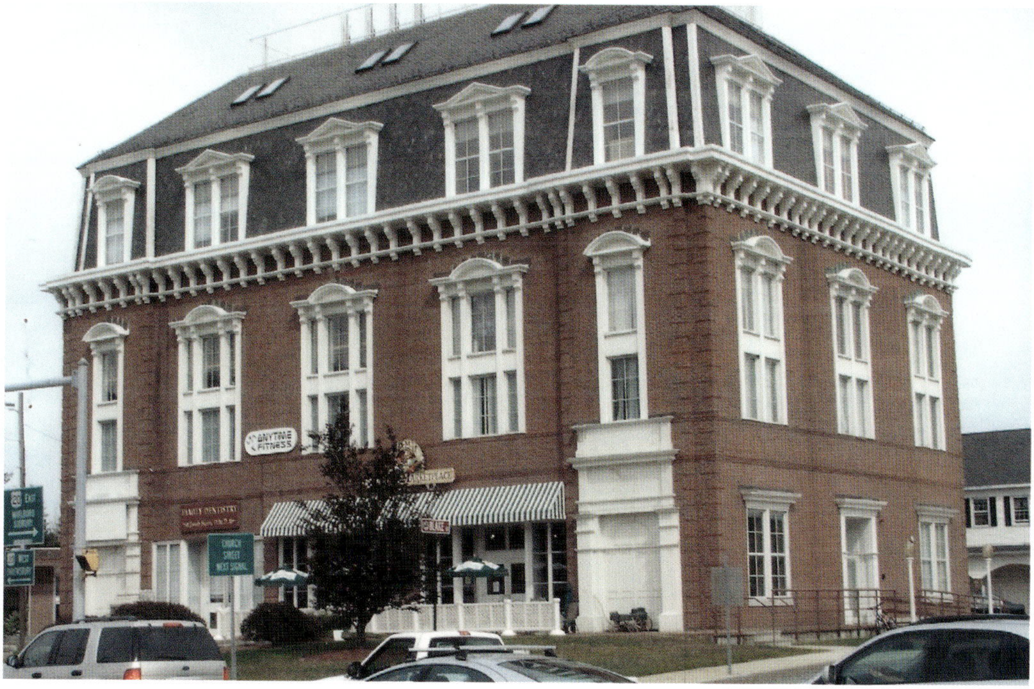

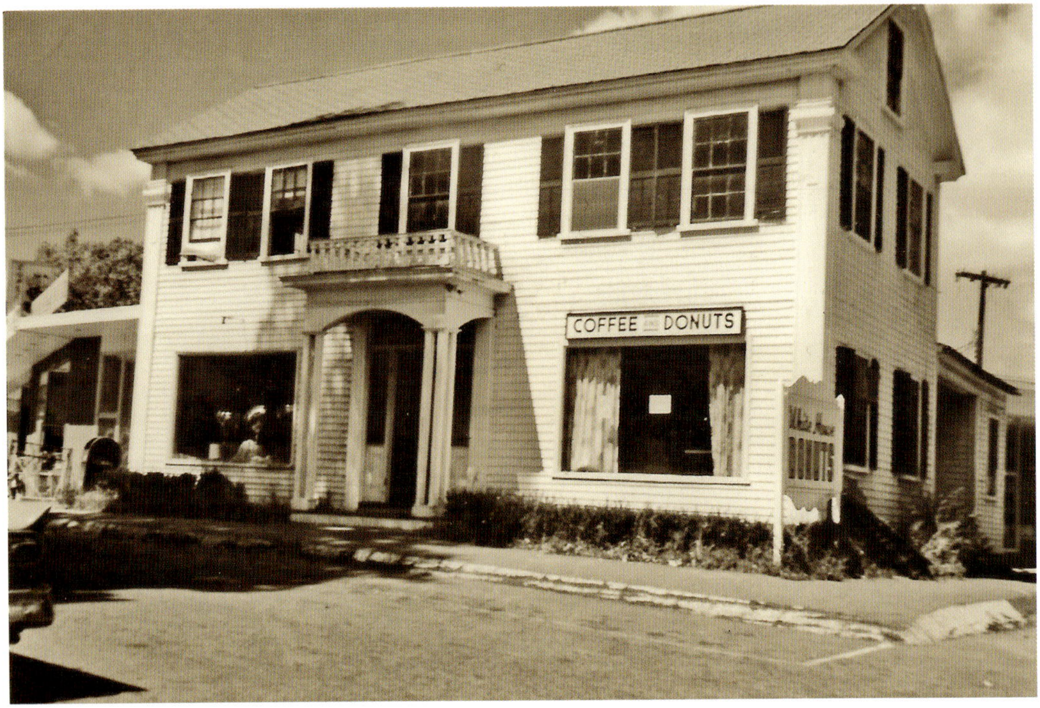

New setting for doughnuts: In September of 1963 a mall, at left, has emerged in the town center behind the Crossley house, converted to the service of coffee and doughnuts. A few years later coffee and doughnuts remain, not in the house of 24 W. Main Street, but in an extension of the mall which has replaced it.

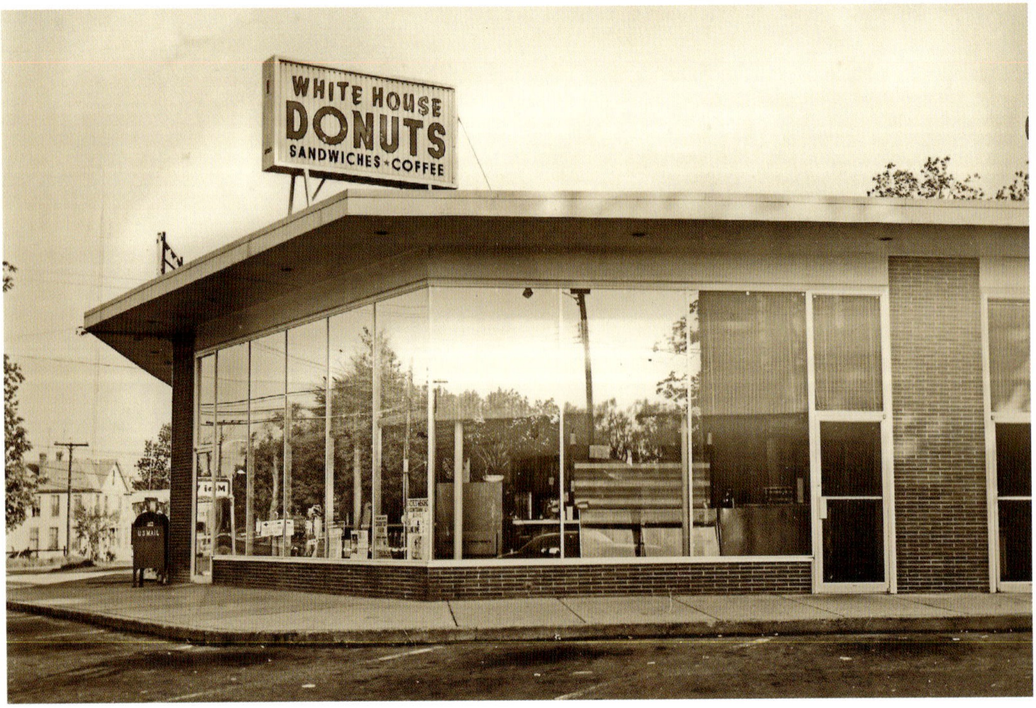

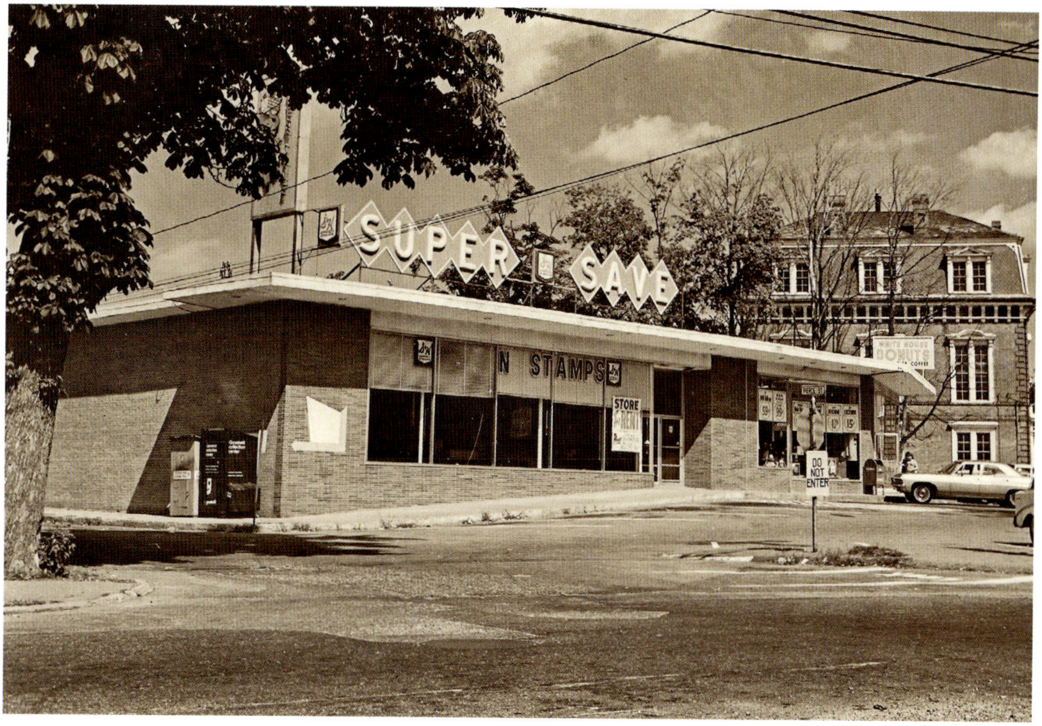

TRANSITION IN TOWN CENTER: In 1966 a relatively short-lived supermarket at 24 W. Main Street has closed in the downtown mall, not spacious enough for changes in merchandising. Nearly a half-century later a new building on the same site replaces one pharmacy with another, CVS.

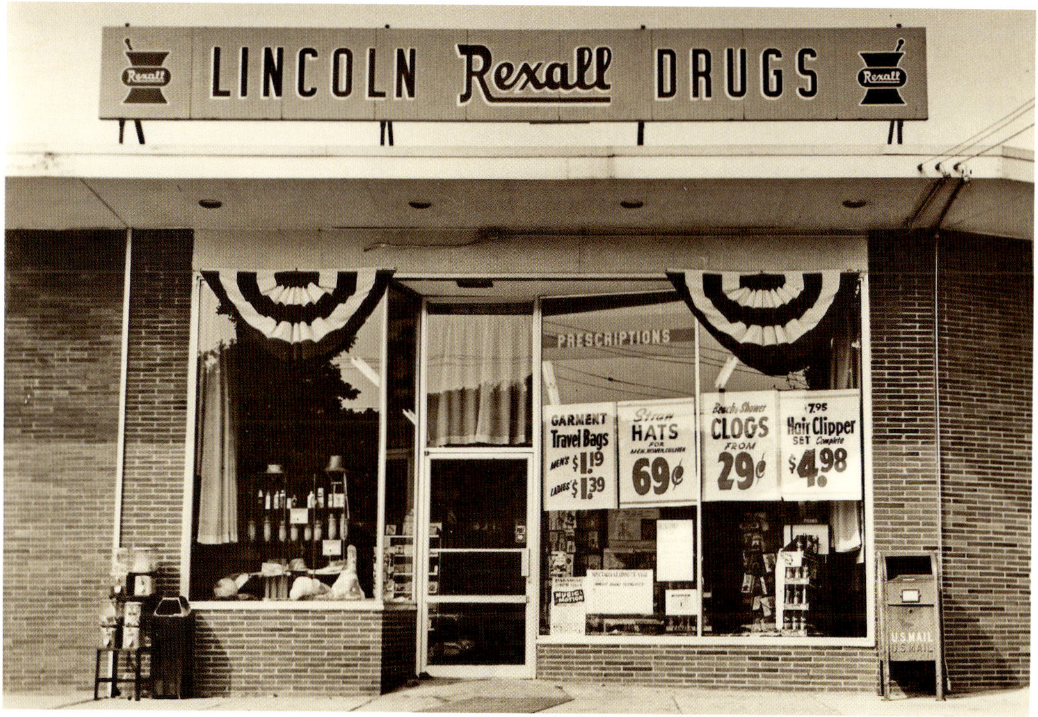

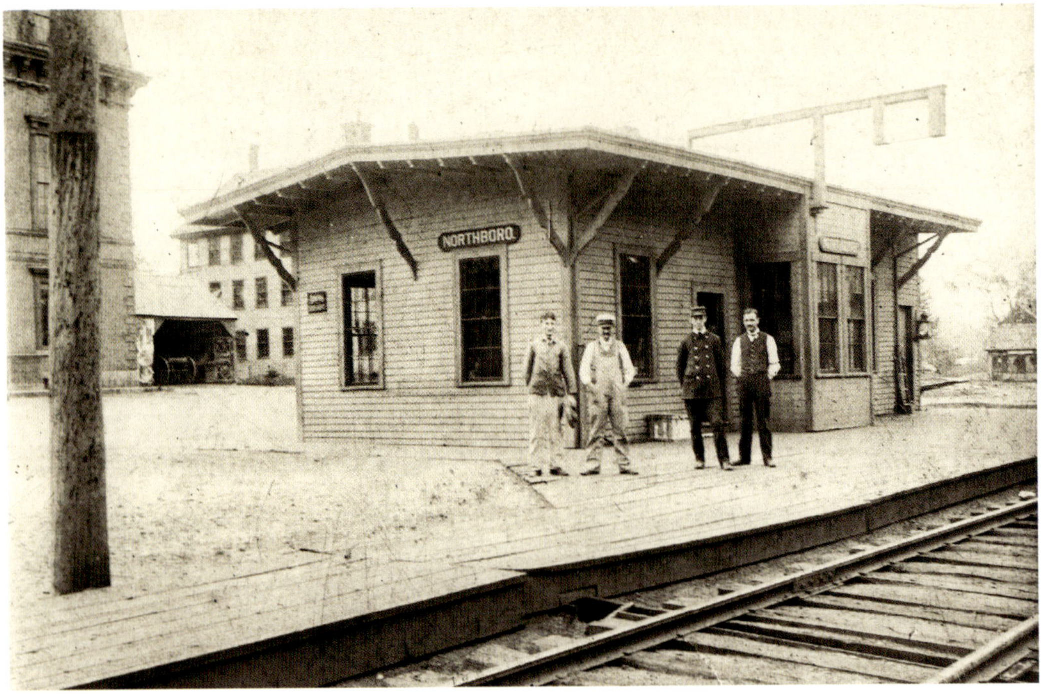

DOWNTOWN STATION: Northborough had two railroad stations in the late nineteenth century up to the midpoint of the twentieth century, one serving the nearby Westborough State Hospital. This one, providing for the downtown area, disappeared after passenger traffic had ceased. Freight continued and around 2000 the stanchion suggests the mode of regulating Main Street traffic. Automobile travel stands as the main reason for the decline of passenger service.

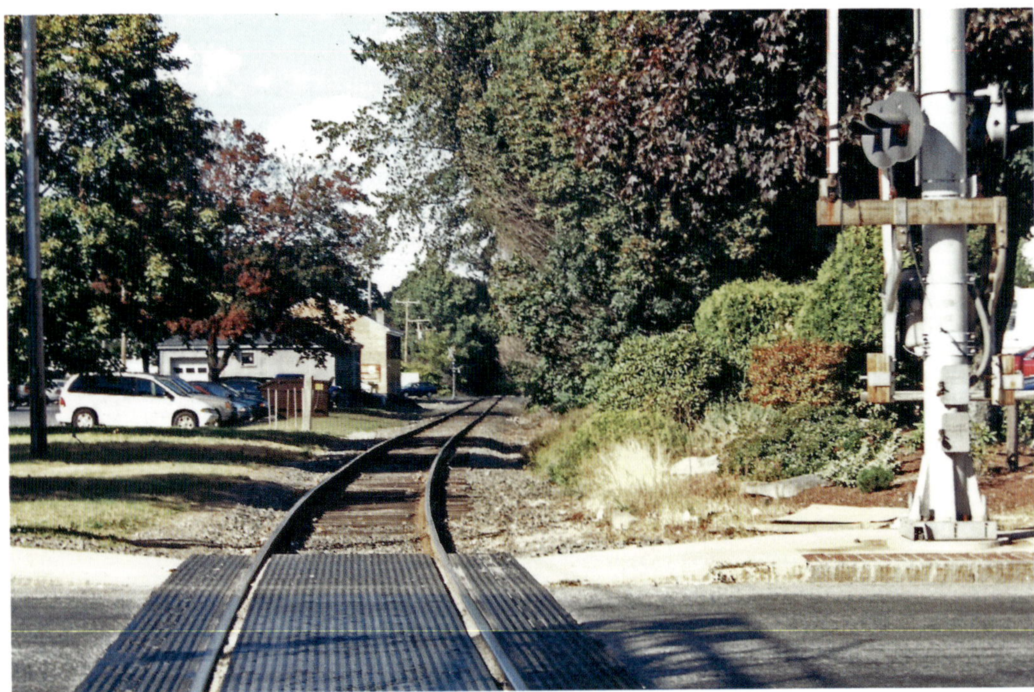

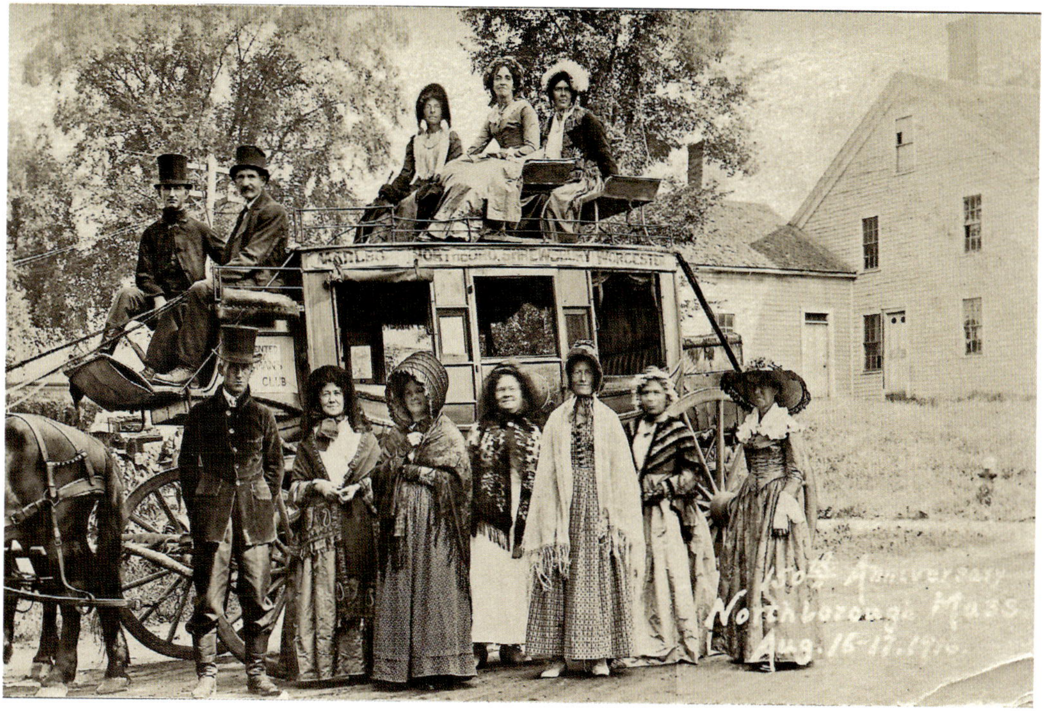

A STAGE COACH, 1916 AND 1966: At the town's 150th anniversary this coach, bearing near its top its appointed stops in the days of stage travel, "Marlboro, Northborough, Shrewsbury, Worcester," is facing west on Main Street near River Street. In the 1966 bicentennial it is moving east on Main Street. In its seat of honor, dressed in colonial black, is Edwin Proctor.

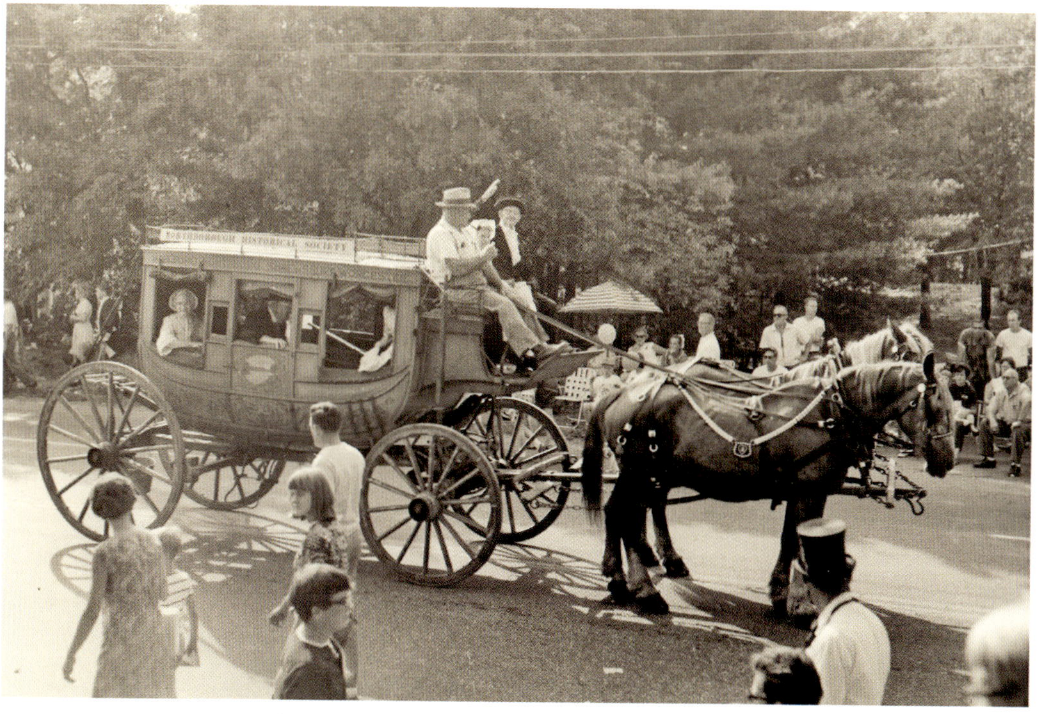

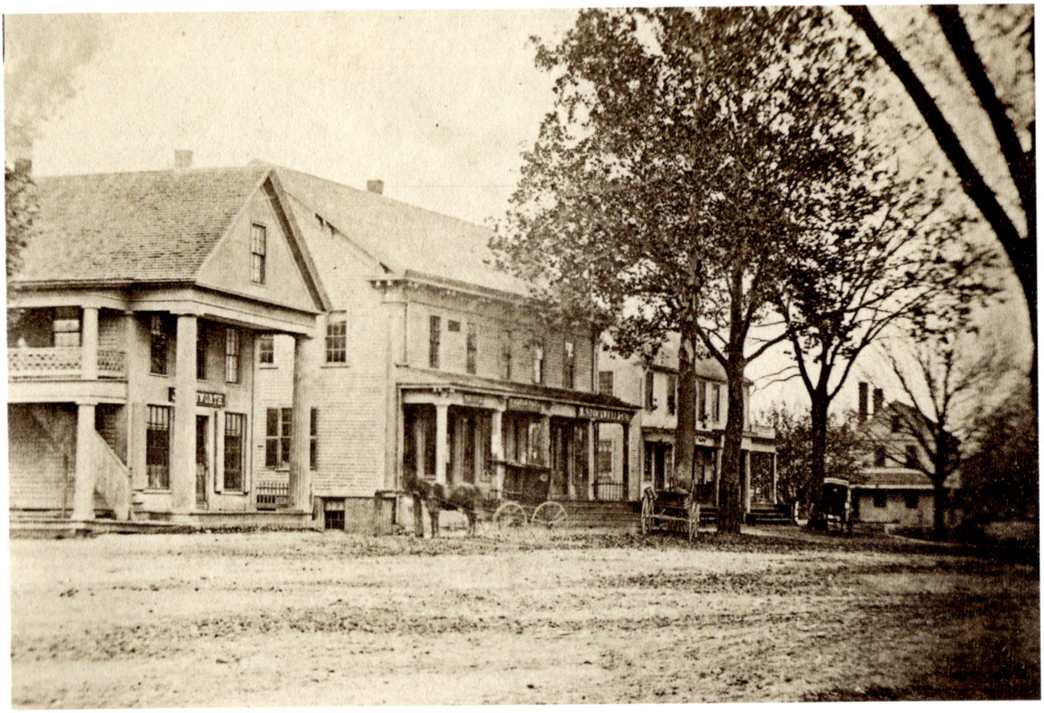

MAIN STREET IN THE 1800S: Many of the buildings in this row on West Main Street were destroyed by fire on July 22, 1871. The central building in the 1890s view below, at the western corner of South and Main, replaced the building at the left in the earlier view. A general store like its predecessor in 1979, it too burned. The street looks nearly vacant; horses and wagons are the only form of transportation.

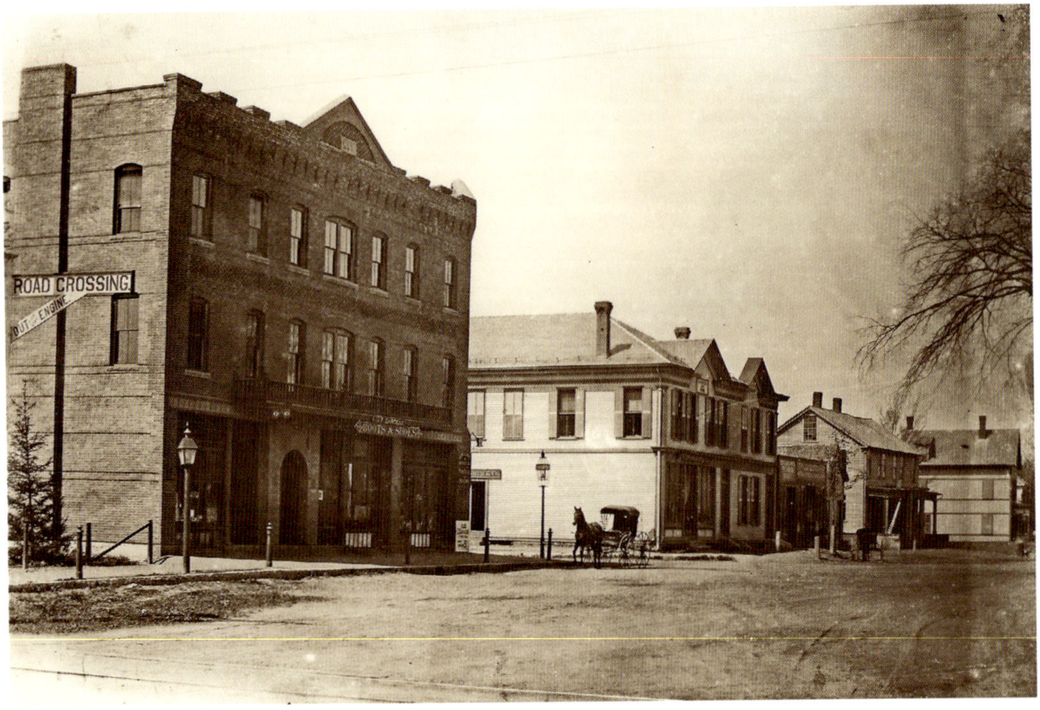

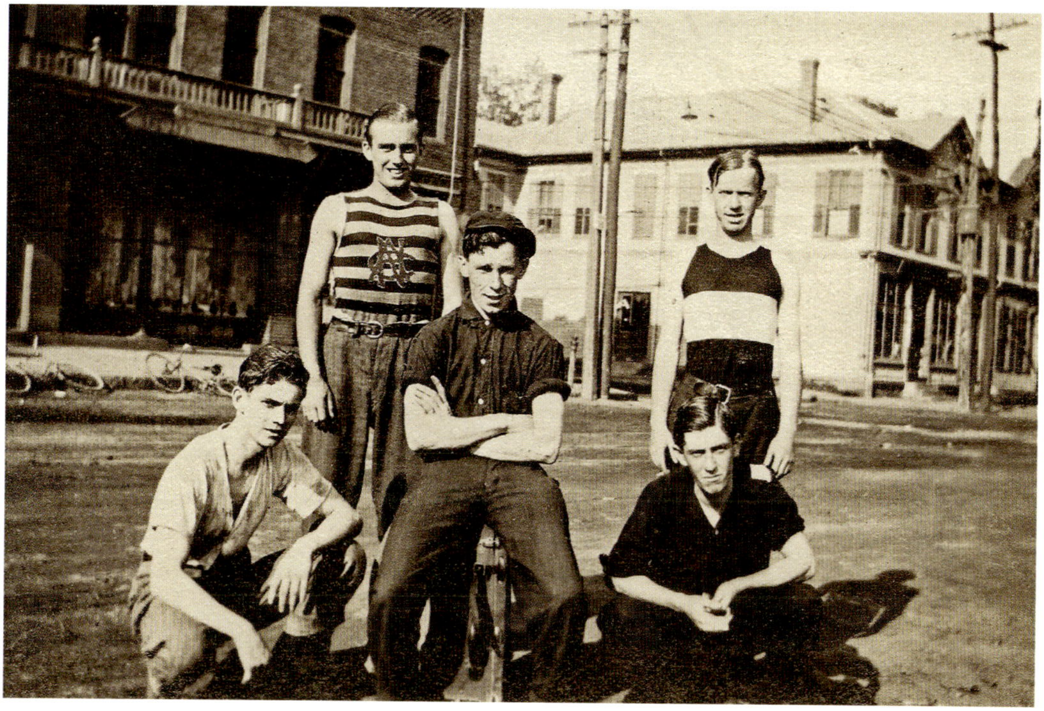

Occupiers of Main Street: On July 4, 1911 these youths could gather in the middle of Main Street on a holiday. Their counterparts would hardly dare such a setting when in an early-evening photograph by Geoff Wilson of a busy Main Street, now showing a convenience store on the twice-burned corner, and revealing not a single pedestrian, only automobiles.

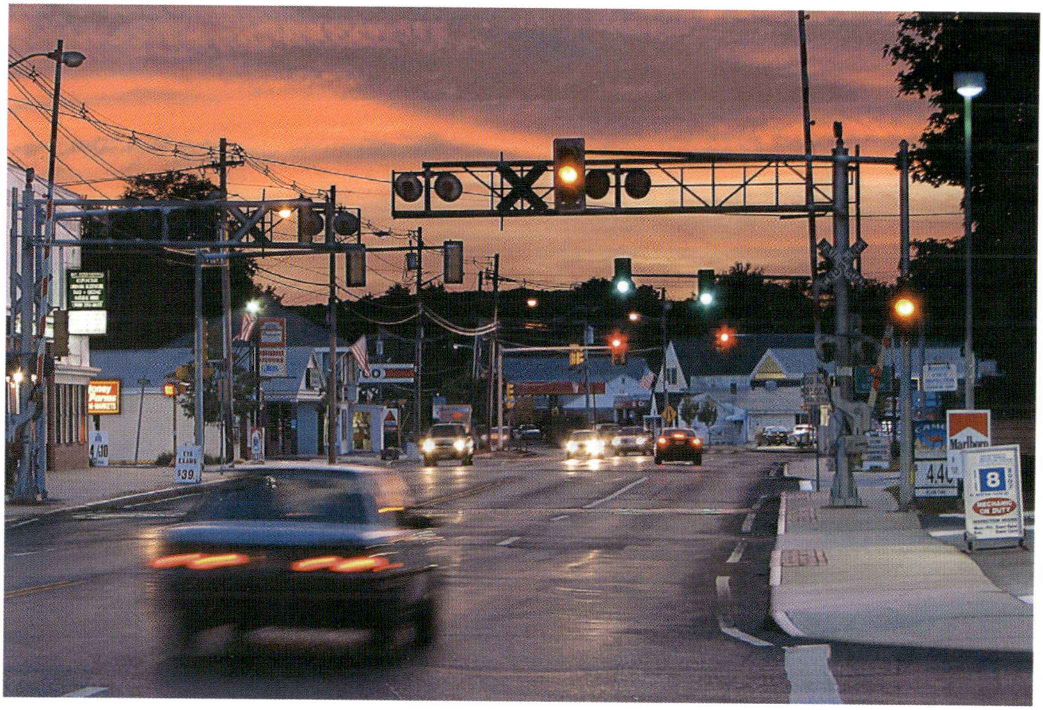

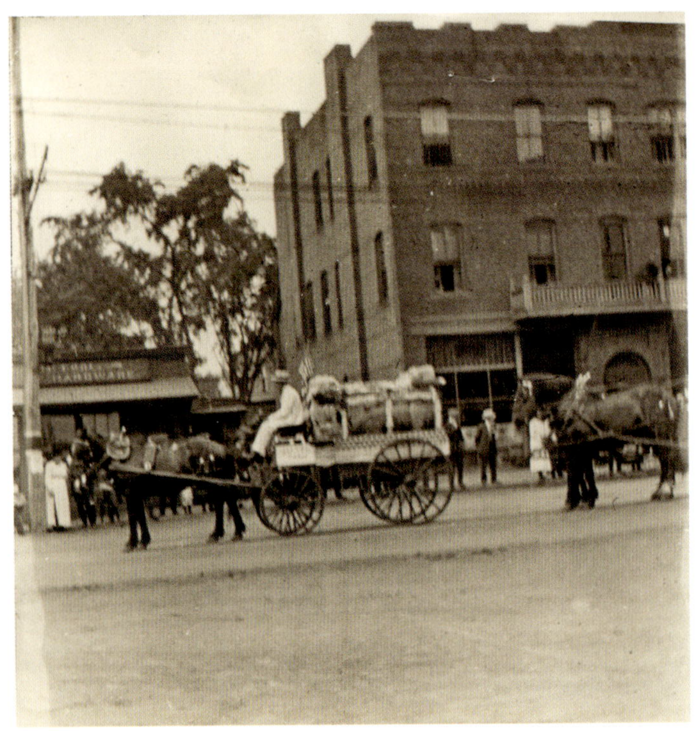

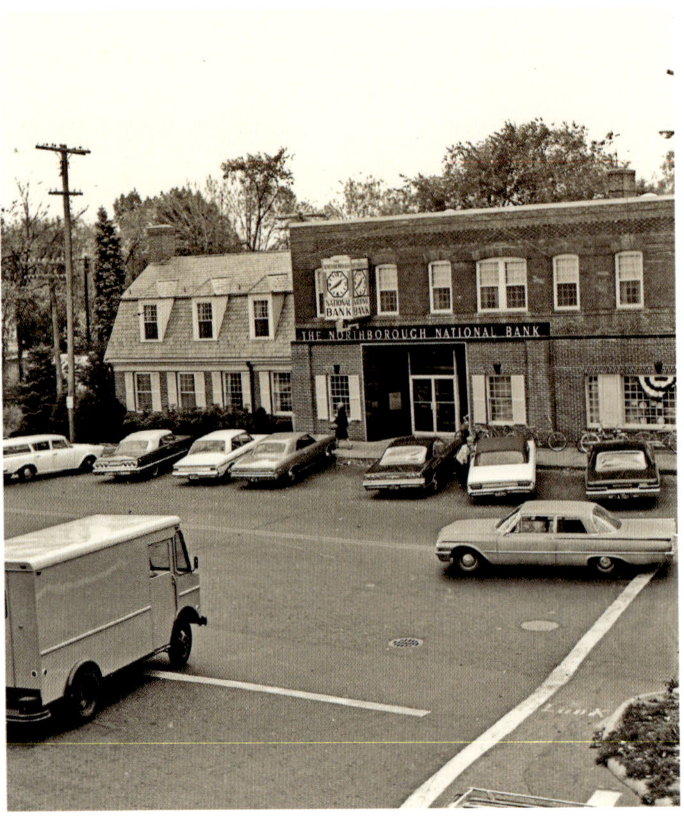

10 Main Street:

Three stories high, the 1882 Winn-Whitaker building seemed to tower over Main Street in its earlier days before poles and wires intervened. A little after 1898, when the trolley arrived in Northborough, a wagon from Valley Farm (see panel below the driver) was apparently running along the trolley tracks. After the brick building had become the Northborough National Bank decades later, few people recognized it, minus its third floor and balcony as the old Winn-Whitaker building.

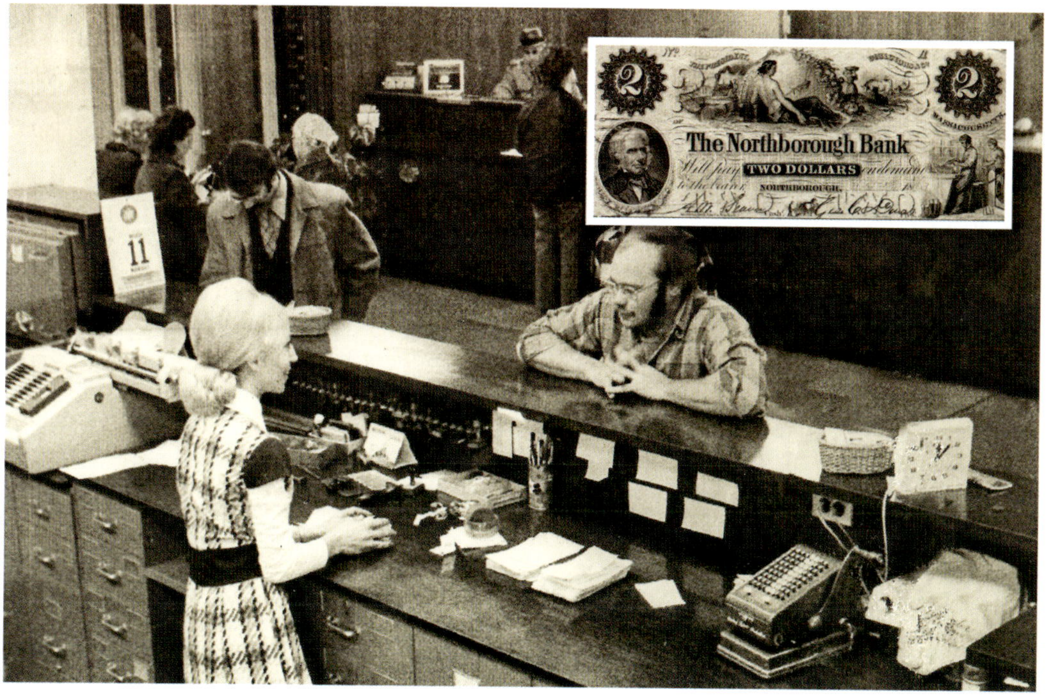

TAKING CARE OF BUSINESS: The Northborough National Bank, founded in 1854 met the needs of the surrounding towns, being the first of its kind in the area. It could print its own money – with the $1, $2, $3 and $5 bills displaying a portrait of Gov. John Davis (see inset). In 2015, with newer technology, the Marlborough Bank is ready to serve the community – complete with a drive-up window, though Arlene Marshall preferred to come inside for a visit with Susan Looney.

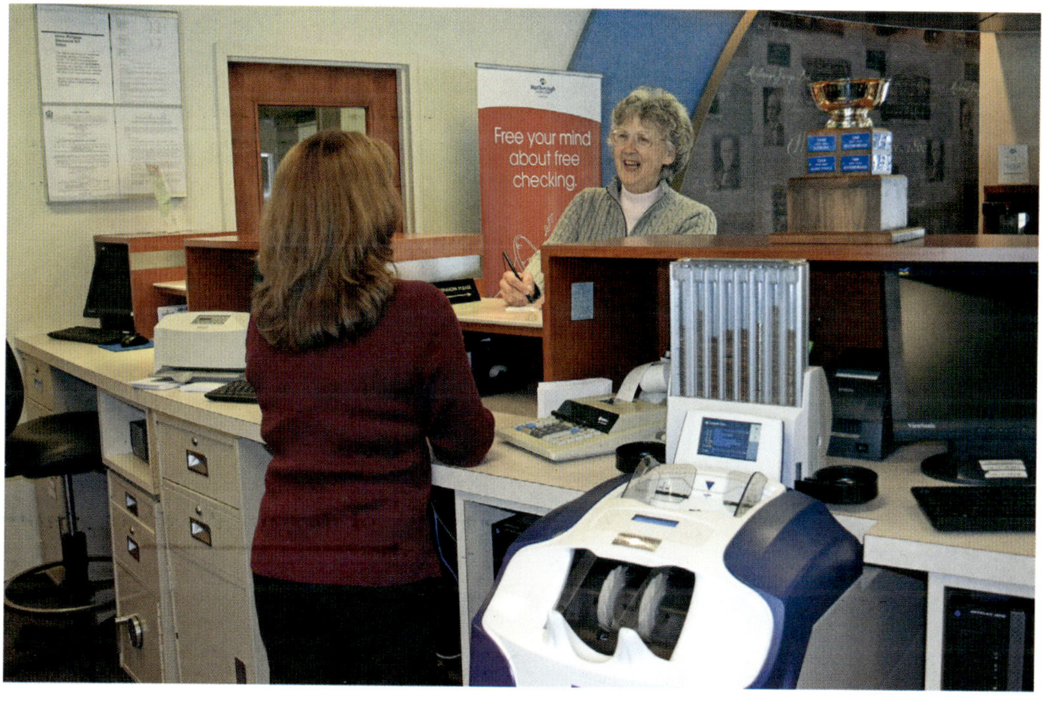

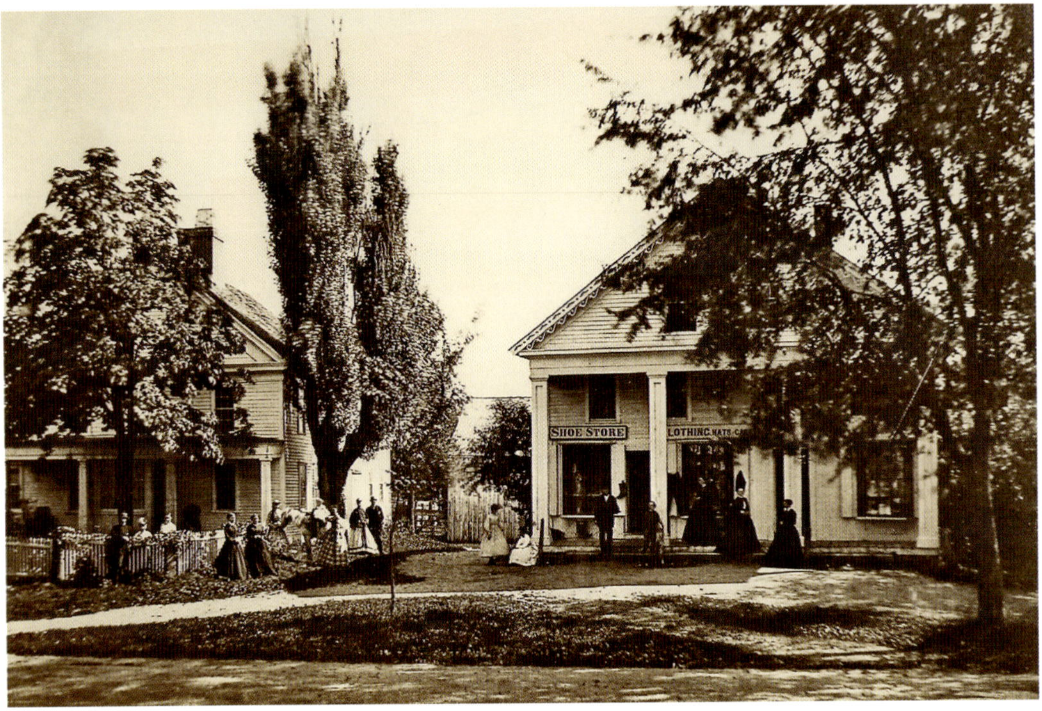

DOCTOR'S RESIDENCE, STORE, LIBRARY: Dr. Stephen Ball and Dr. Stephen Ball II lived and practiced in the house at the left, 34 Main Street, dating from 1730. The younger Ball maintained an apothecary in the building at the right. Later one could buy shoes and clothing, very possibly made in town. From 1895 one could borrow books. At the time of writing it remained, considerably augmented, as the public library.

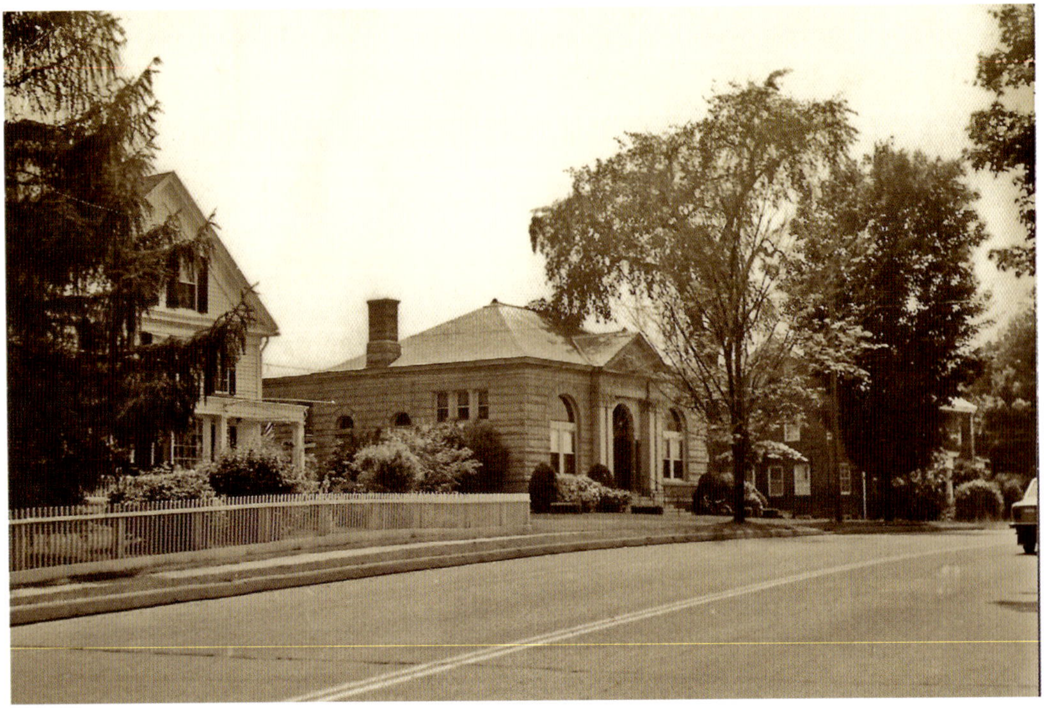

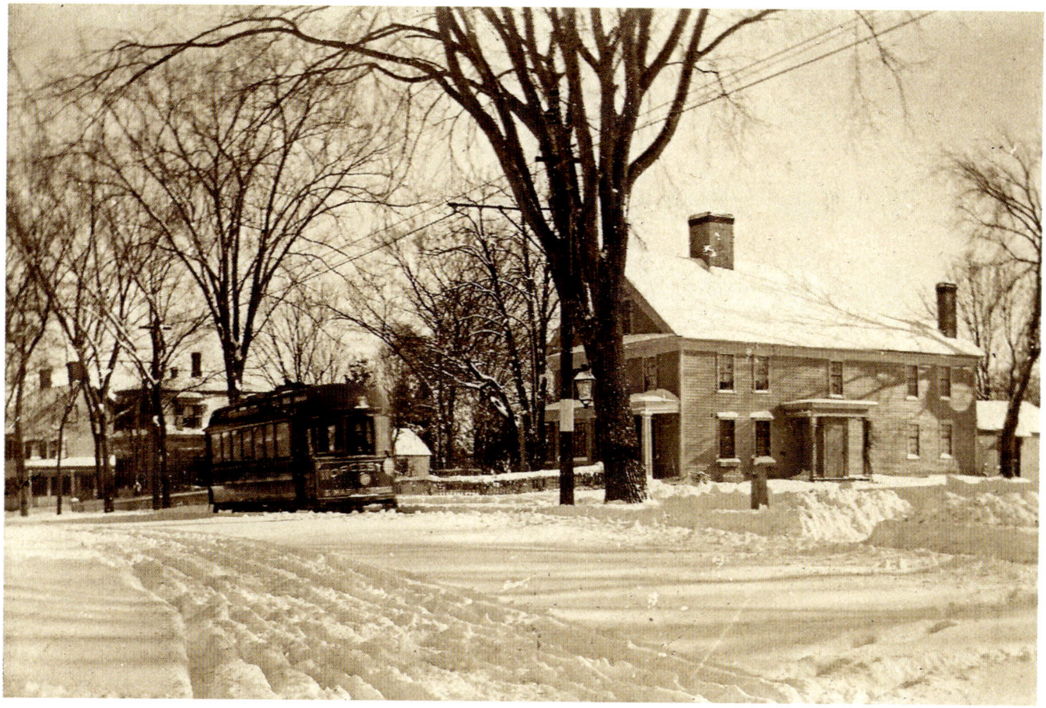

Incoming from Marlborough: From 1898 to around 1925 a trolley might often be spotted traveling westward in front of this same Main Street residence dating from 1730. In the present century the trip is made more frequently and privately. Below, the house to the left of the 1895 library building (just out of sight to the right in the top picture) remains a fixture early in the present century.

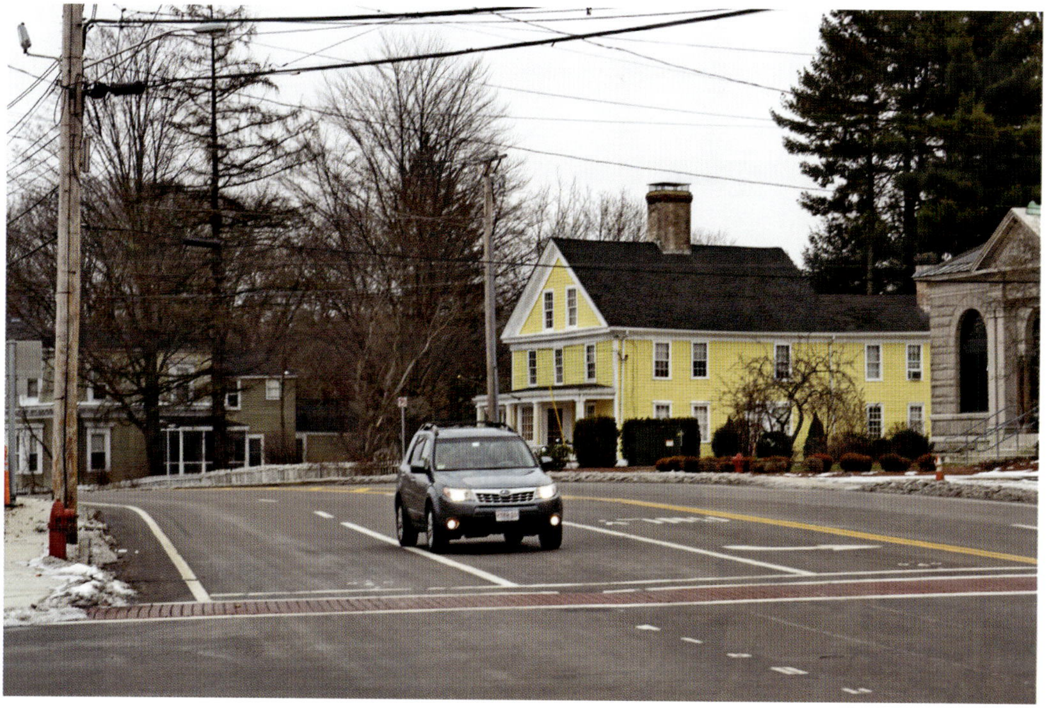

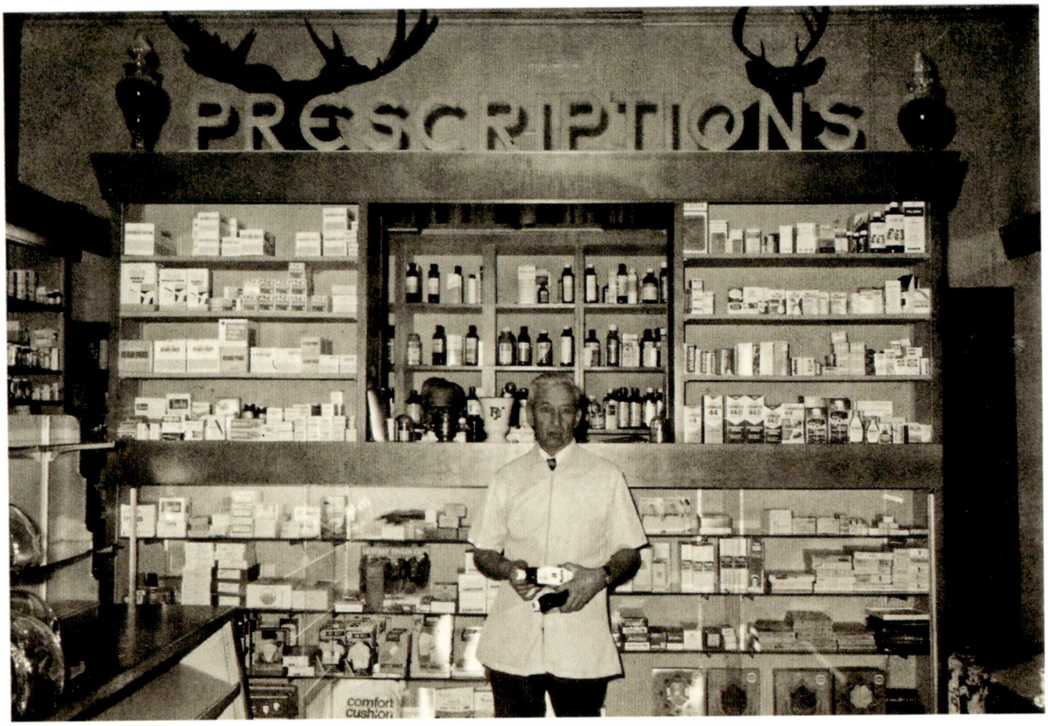

BE WELL: Claude T. Shattuck bought E. W. Wood's drug store in 1898, then housed in the Town Hall building. It passed to Howard Shattuck, pictured above, and now to third generation owner, Paul Shattuck. In 1974 they moved into a new building across the street.

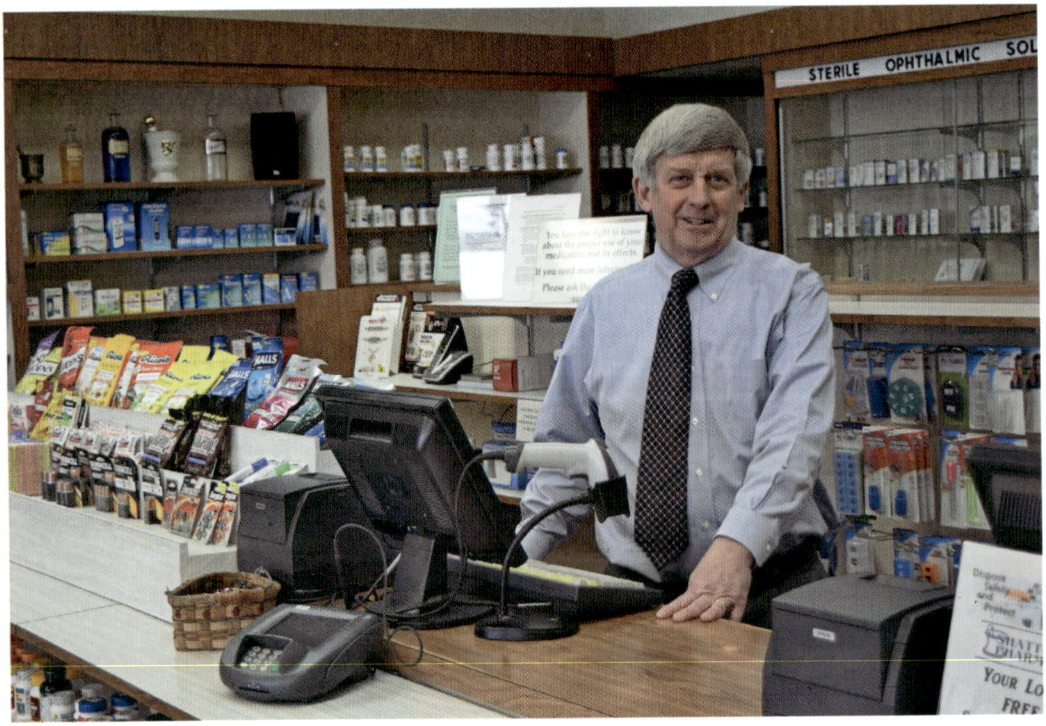

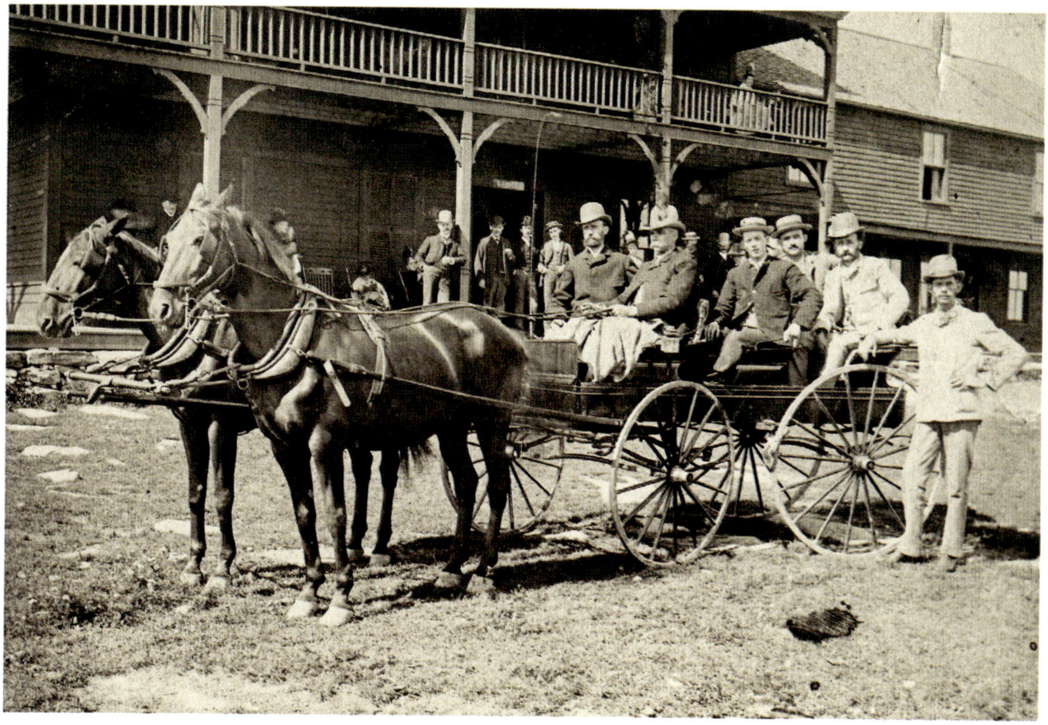

GETTING AROUND: C. J. Mack, livery owner and driver, enjoyed the view from atop Mt. Wachusett with Northborough friends around 1885. Transportation styles progressed rapidly over the next thirty years as evidenced by this Studebaker car meet held in 2002 at the Northborough Historical Society.

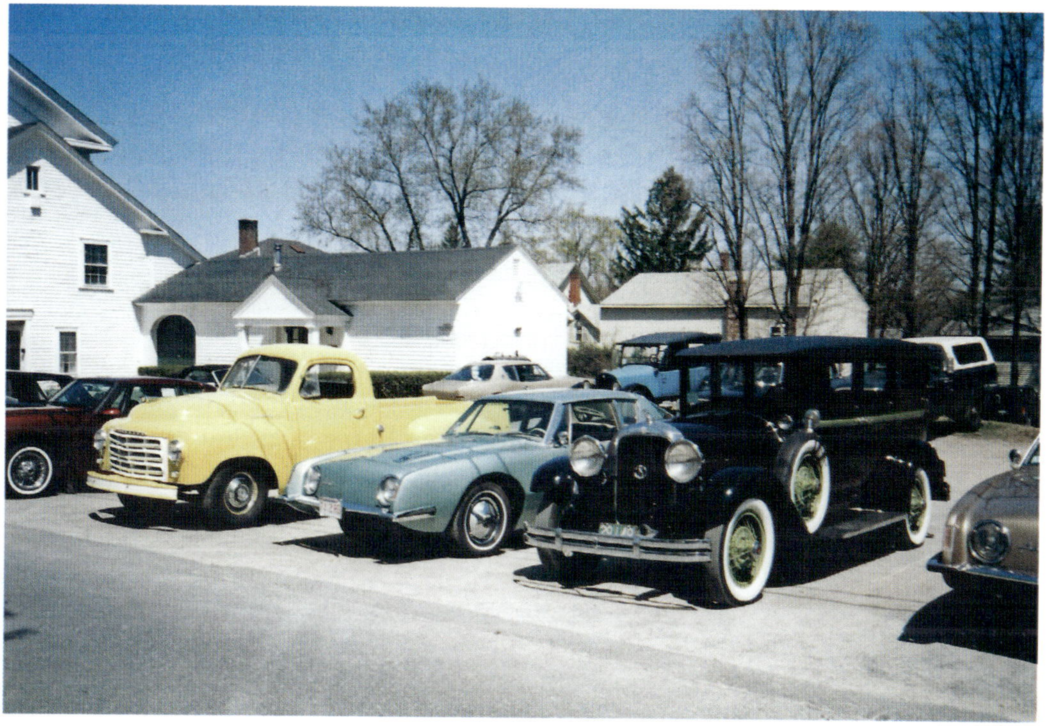

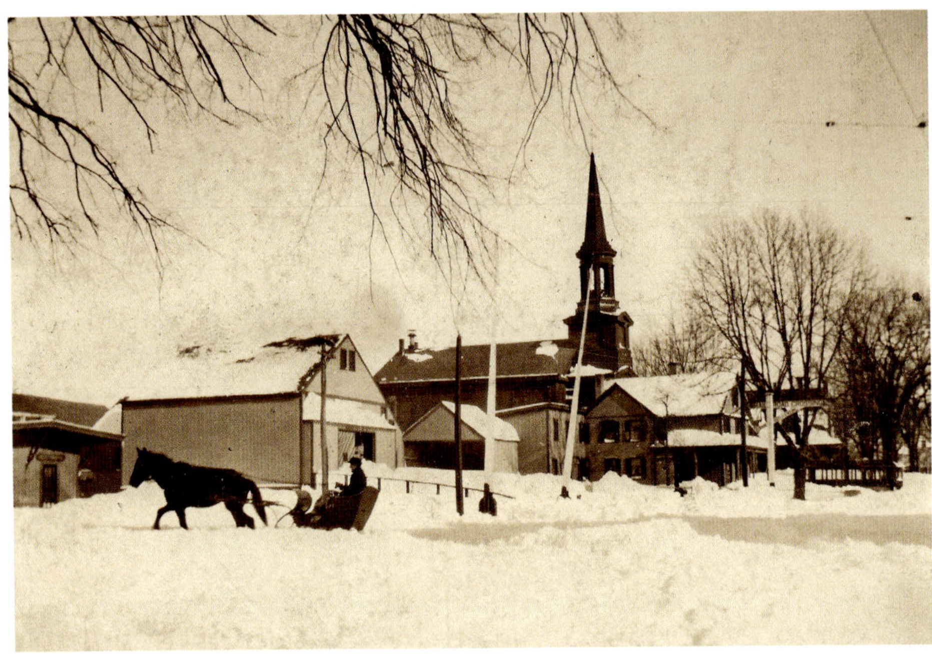

BY HORSE OR BY CAR: Everything in these photographs except for the church steeple, speaks of transportation. Like most merchants of his day, Anson Rice lived close to his work on the corner of 15 Main and Hudson Streets, his stable next door. In the mid-twentieth century a gas station and a Chevrolet dealer occupied the site. By the early twenty-first century the site had proved inadequate for an automobile dealer but serviceable as a combination convenience store and gas station.

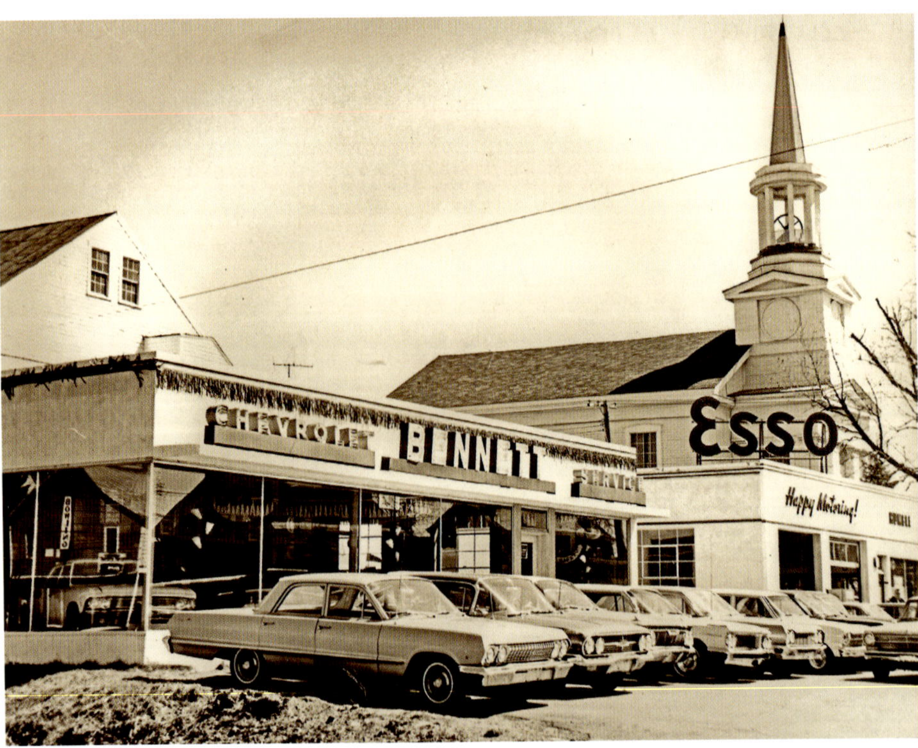

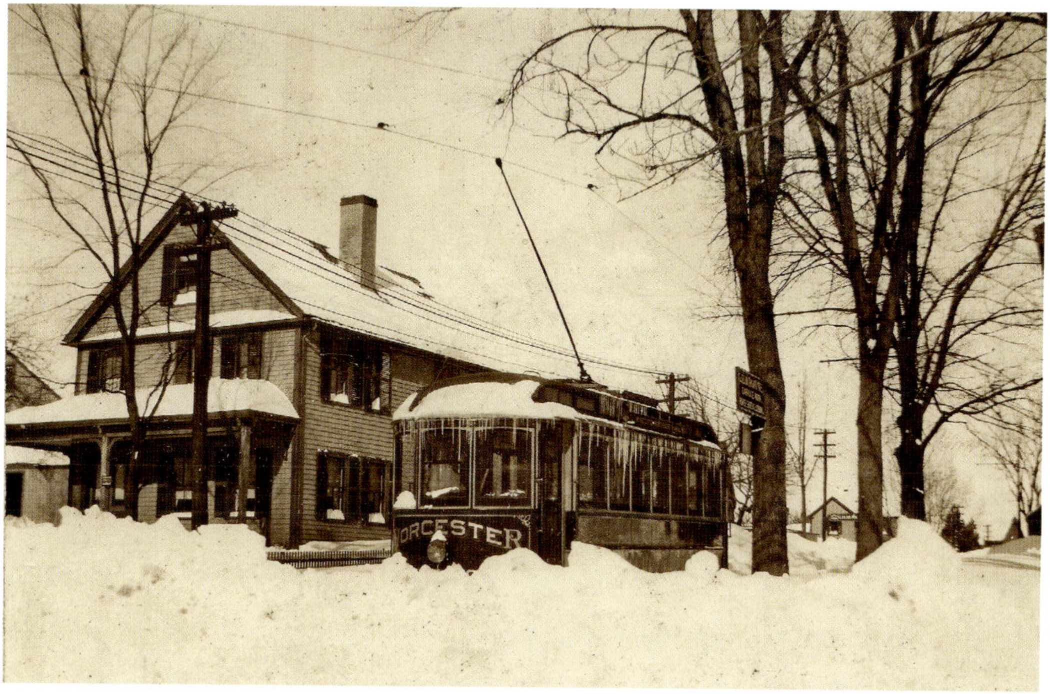

A HOUSE DISPLACED: Around 1955, for the sake of a gas station, Anson Rice's Greek Revival home was turned ninety degrees and pushed back from downtown Main Street to 9 Hudson Street, where it stands at the time of writing. Here, a half century earlier, Mr. Rice could view two challenges, one might call them, to his stable business: the town's railroad, just out of sight but bounding his property on the left, and the frequently passing Worcester and Marlborough trolley.

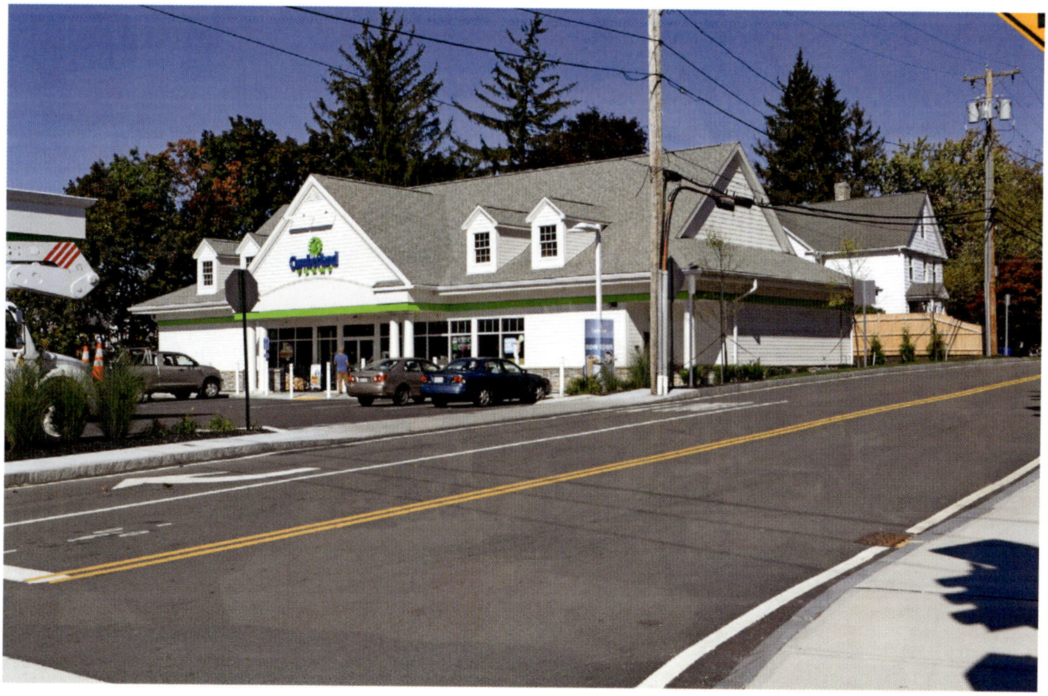

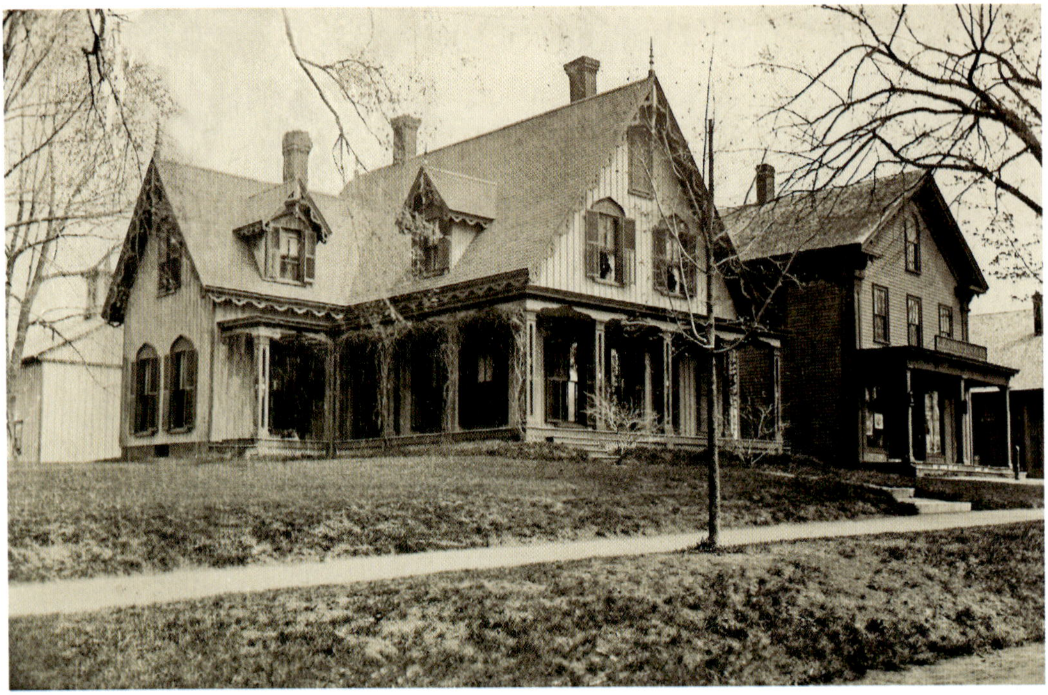

THREE CENTURIES OF USE: In the early 1800s James Maynard lived in a house which probably dated from the eighteenth century. It was moved from its site in 1867. Its successor, the much more elegant Noah Wadsworth home, shown in both photos, persisted well into the twentieth. Dr. J. M. Stanley, the last occupant, slides by the same location. By 1960 the house yielded to a parking lot for Trinity Church next door.

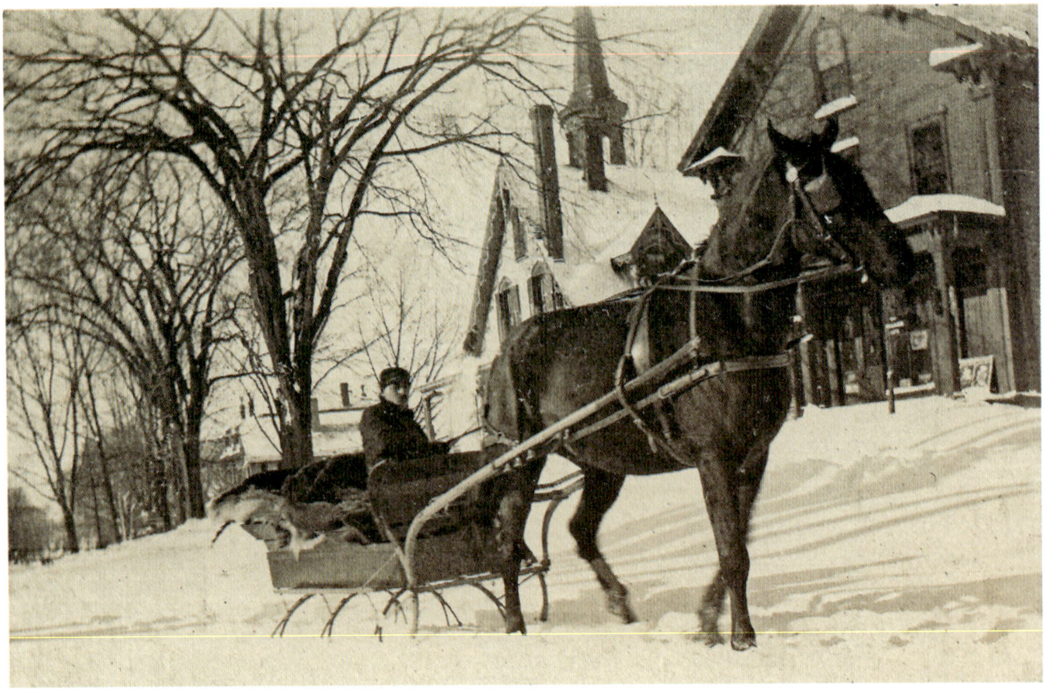

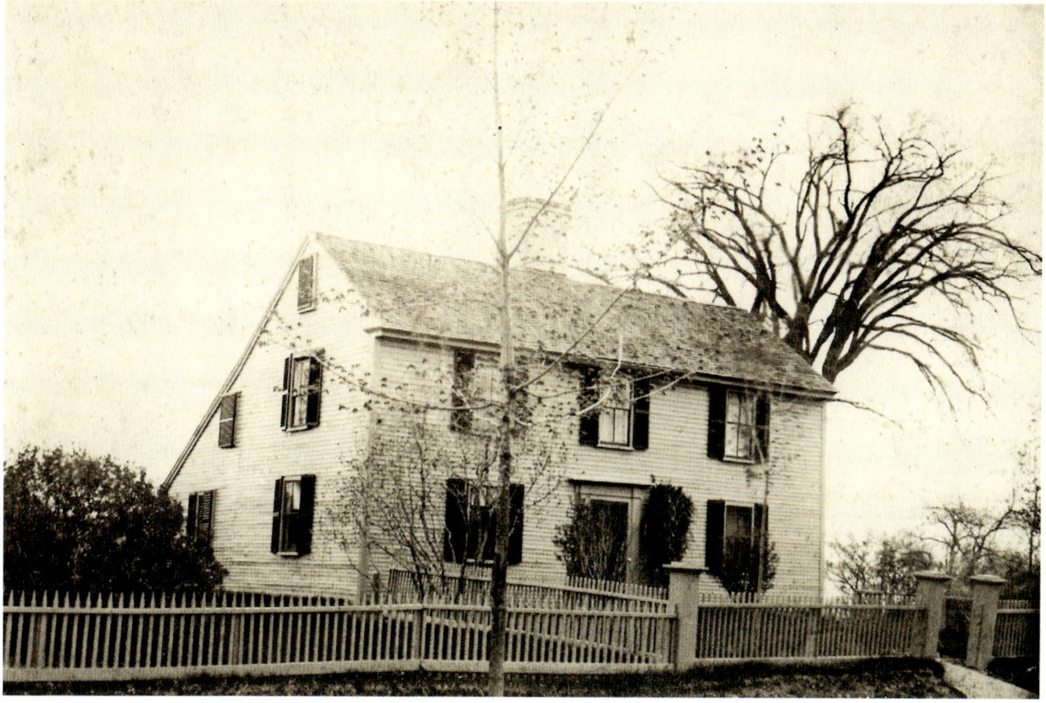

63 Main Street: Henry Gassett recalled that as a small boy his house, one night in November 1777, held British soldiers of General Burgoyne captive under an American escort. In much of the nineteenth century Samuel Clark, Northborough's only attorney, lived here. The brick building that replaced it served as Northborough High School from 1938 to 1959 and from 1978 as the Northborough Town Office building.

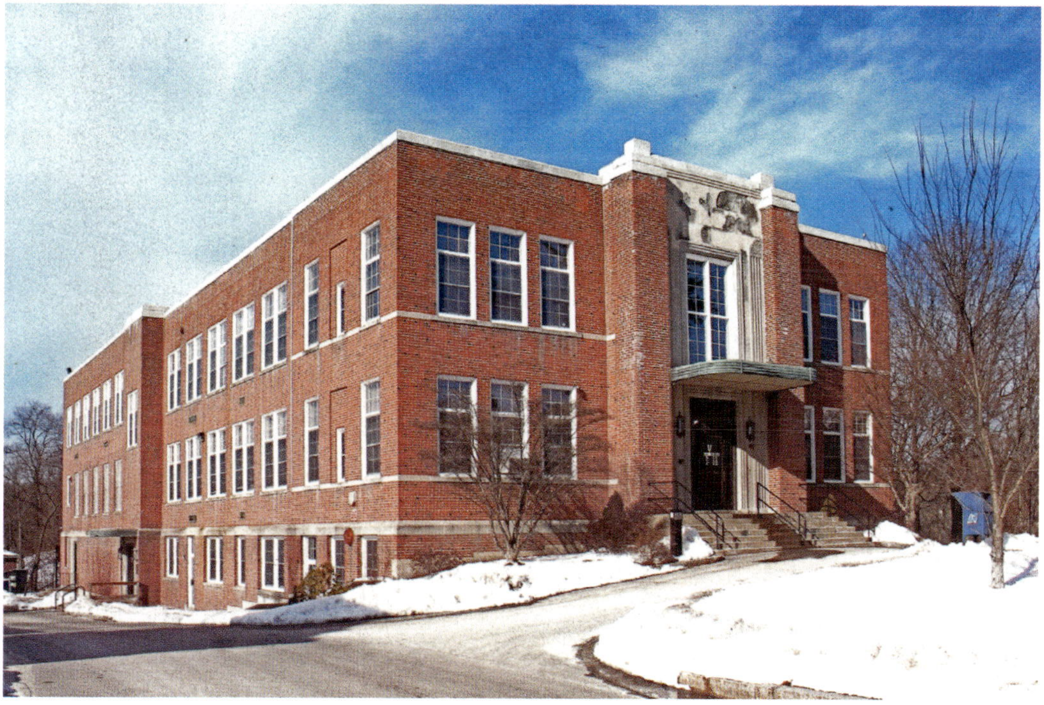

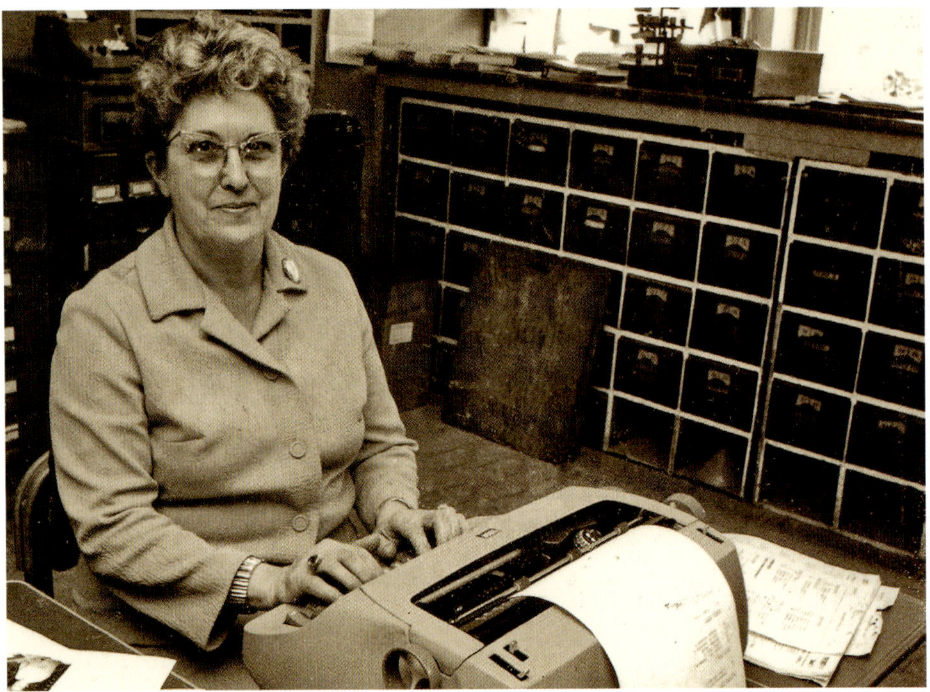

TAP, TAP, TAP: Janice Bigelow Parmenter conducts her Town Clerk duties on her IBM Selectric in the former Town Hall. Janice was an avid historian and wrote a history of Northborough for the 1966 bicentennial. A computer and a new office location at 63 Main Street is where Andrew Dowd, our current Town Clerk, works. He assists residents with licenses, permits, voter registration, election procedures, official record keeping, and an occasional wedding ceremony – all part of the job.

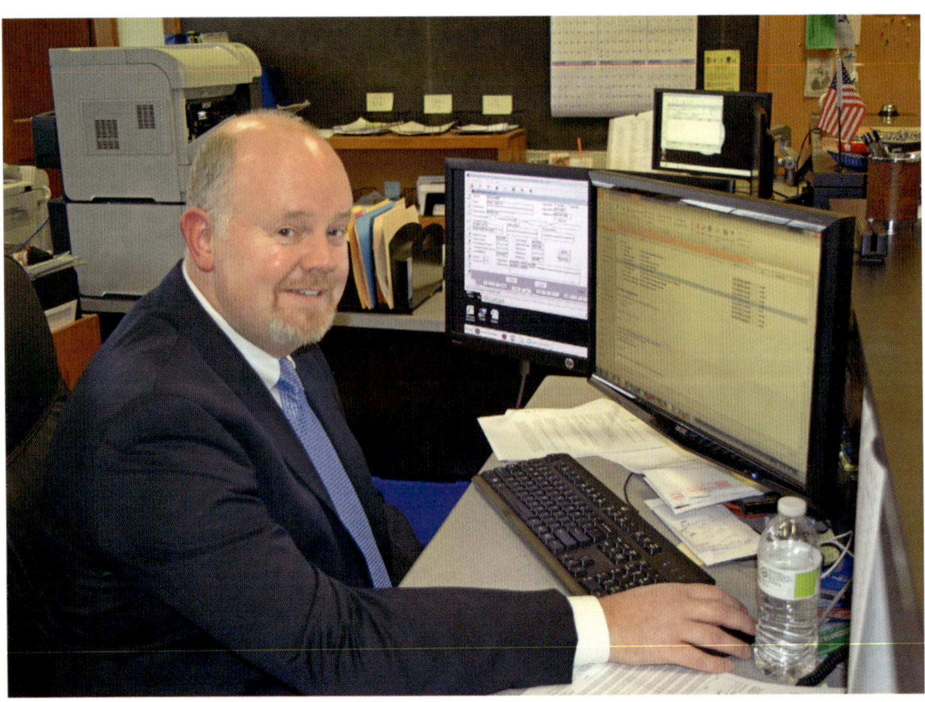

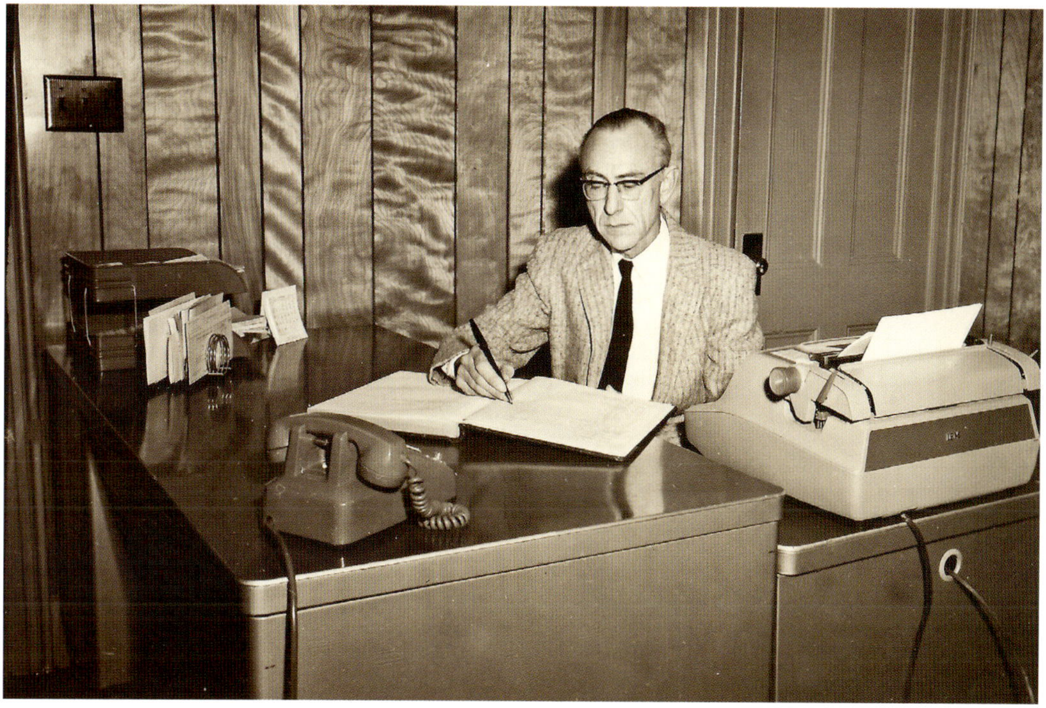

TOWN ACCOUNTANTS: Allyn M. Phelps served as Town Accountant from 1958 to 1983; Jason Little holds the post at the time of this printing. Perhaps the biggest difference between them is their equipment, from the chairs they sit in to their basic machines: typewriter and computer. It is difficult to say which man had the more demanding job.

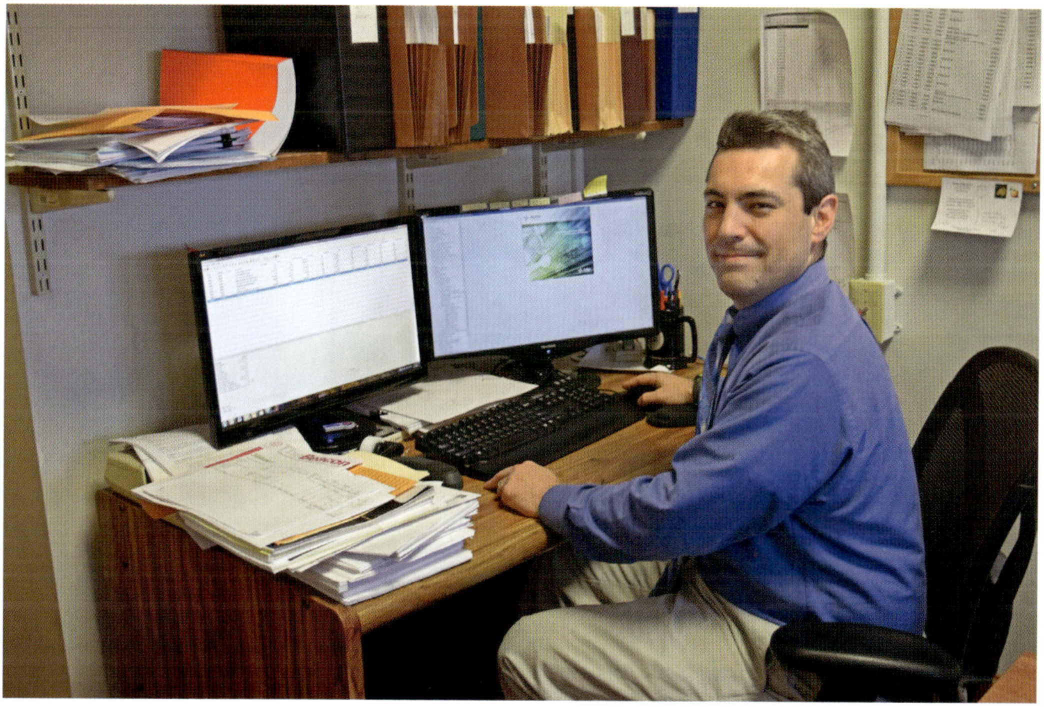

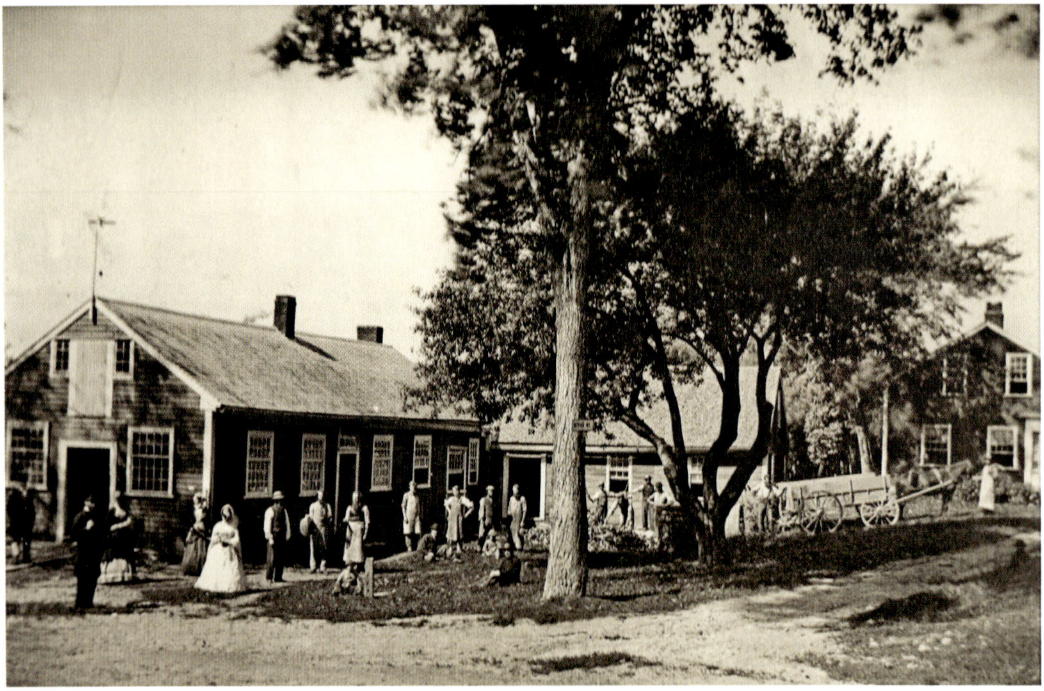

WATER POWER IN USE: Since the mid-1700s the Assabet River at Main and River Streets has powered industries. A clothier's mill, bone mill, iron works, nail and wood shops and the Wesson rifle factory prospered here. Thomas Lyon used this building from 1823-36 for repairing looms and building mill machinery. Later Milo Hildreth built a larger structure for comb making, followed by Thomas Blair's factory in the early 1900s. Stone's Cycle Shop now occupies this site on busy Main Street.

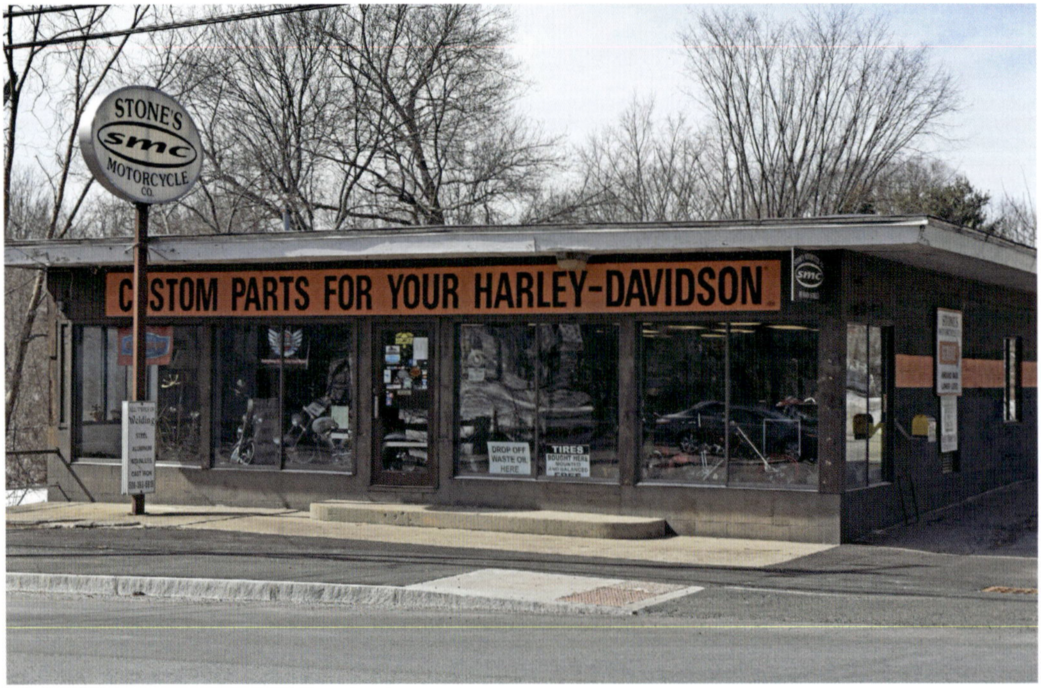

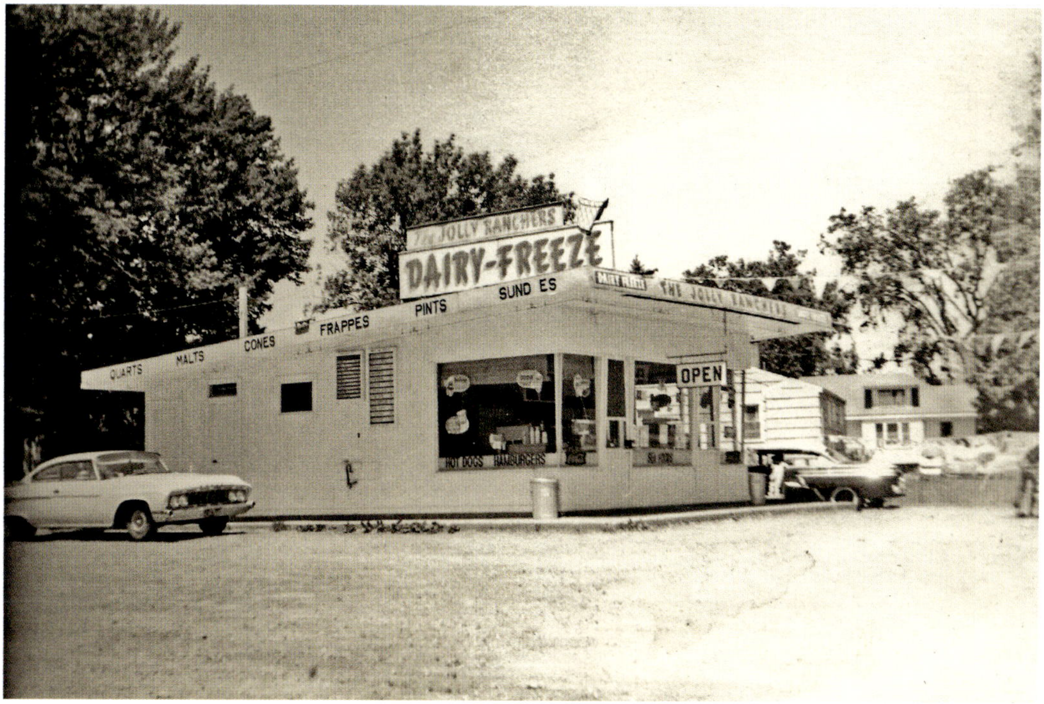

WHICH WILL YOU HAVE? In 1960 you went to the Dairy-Freeze for ice cream; a more recent shop supplies pizza or ice cream at the same Main Street building, with picnic tables that invited you to partake on site. Oddly, it announces its address as East Main Street, which is behind the building, while it continues to face Main Street.

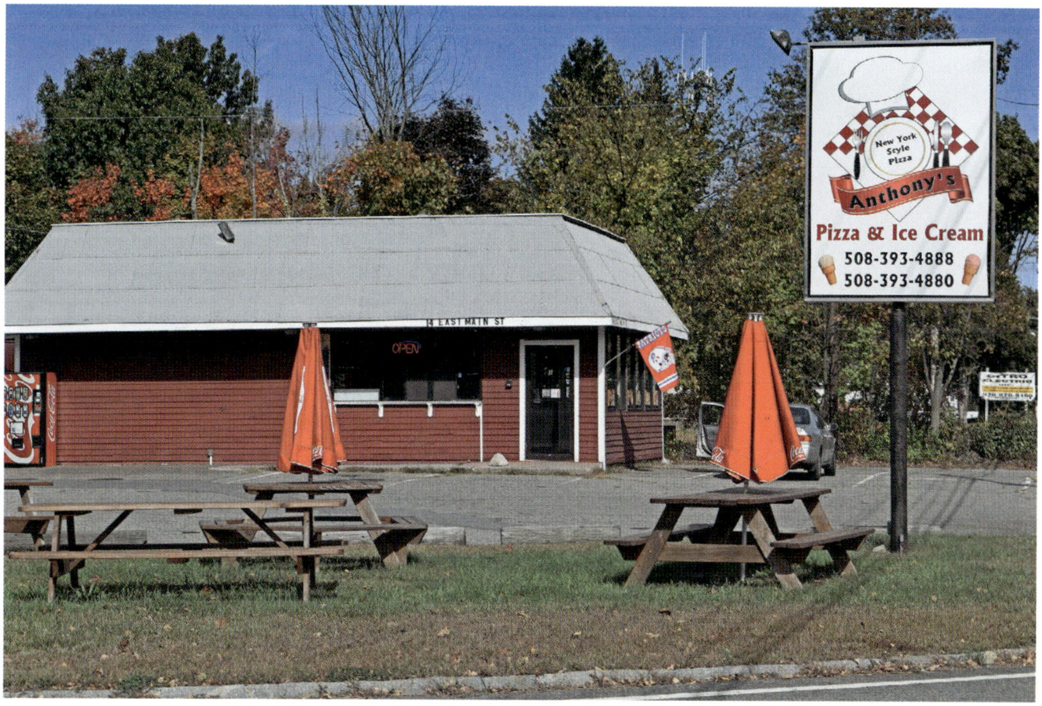

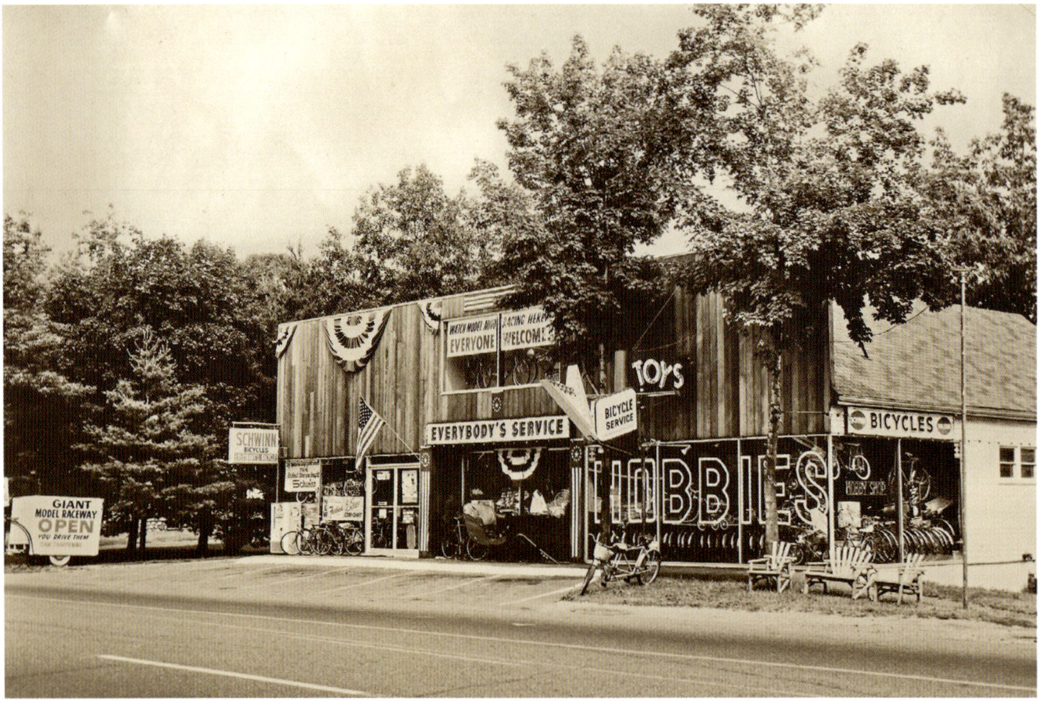

THE PLACE FOR BIKES: In the 1960s Everybody's Bike Shop was a popular Main Street location. Owner Bob Trimble maintained a "raceway" and a traveling bicycle museum; a simulated rocket (out of sight) also decorated the site. After he retired, the building turned into a more subdued business on behalf of better kitchens and bathrooms.

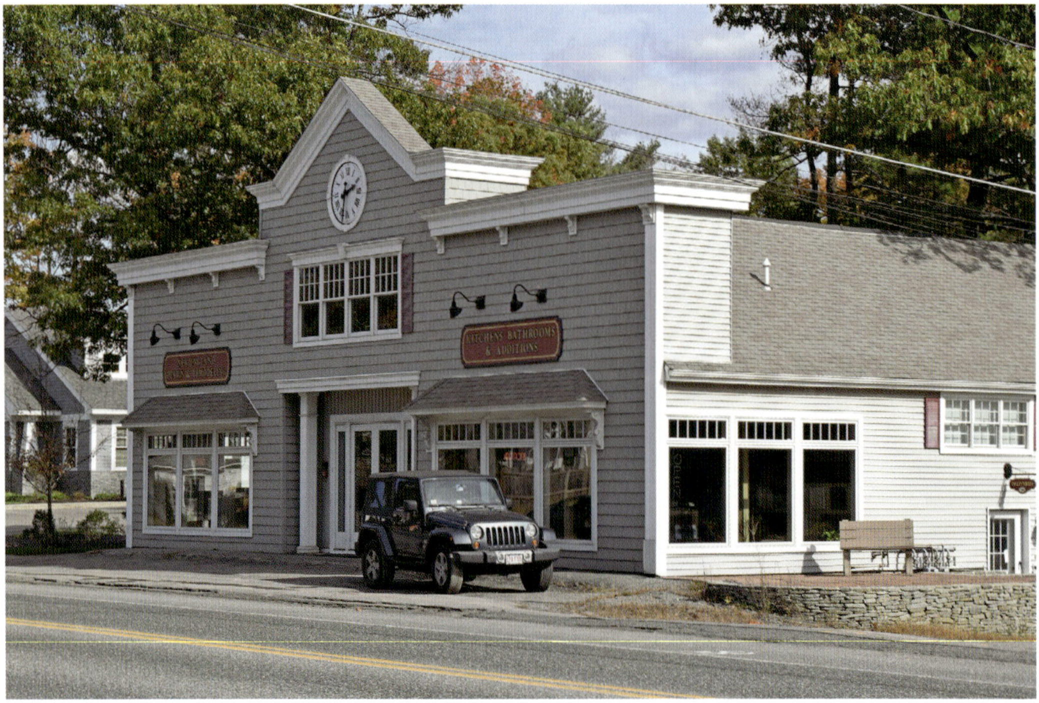

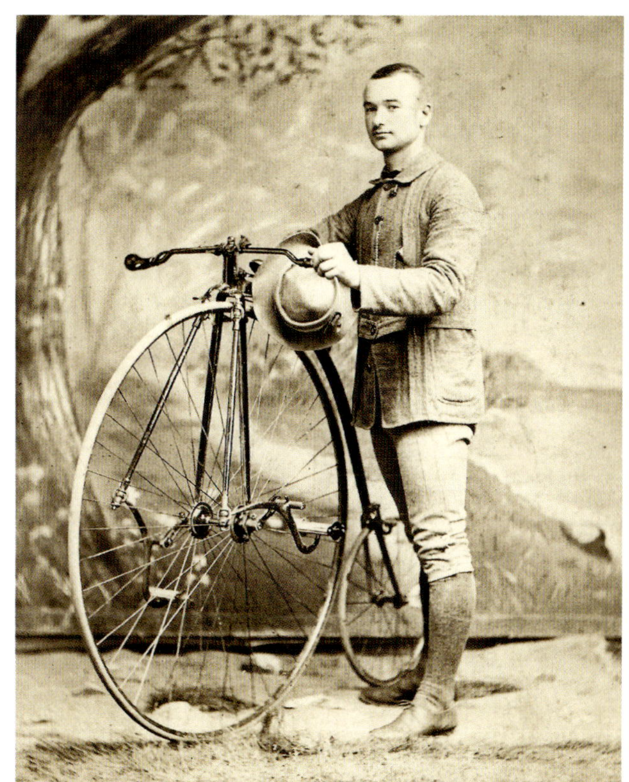

WHEELS KEEP TURNING: Harry Wilcox is proud to be photographed with his hi-wheeler in 1886. A current photo shows Lisa Ludwig of Northborough with fellow cyclists Mark Petrozzino, Acton, and Barry Greenberg, Westford, as serious competitors in the racing world. Lisa's triumph was competing at the world-class level in Italy in a 60 kilometer race, including two mountain climbs, in her age group.

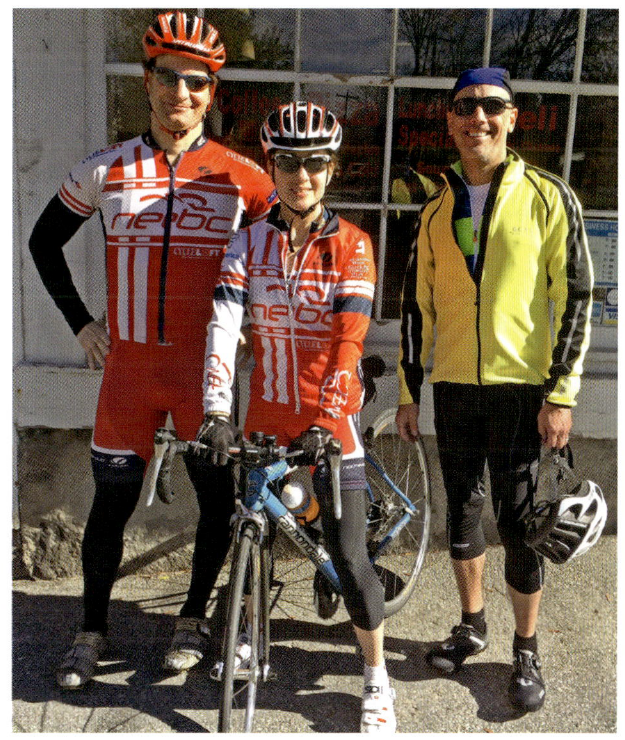

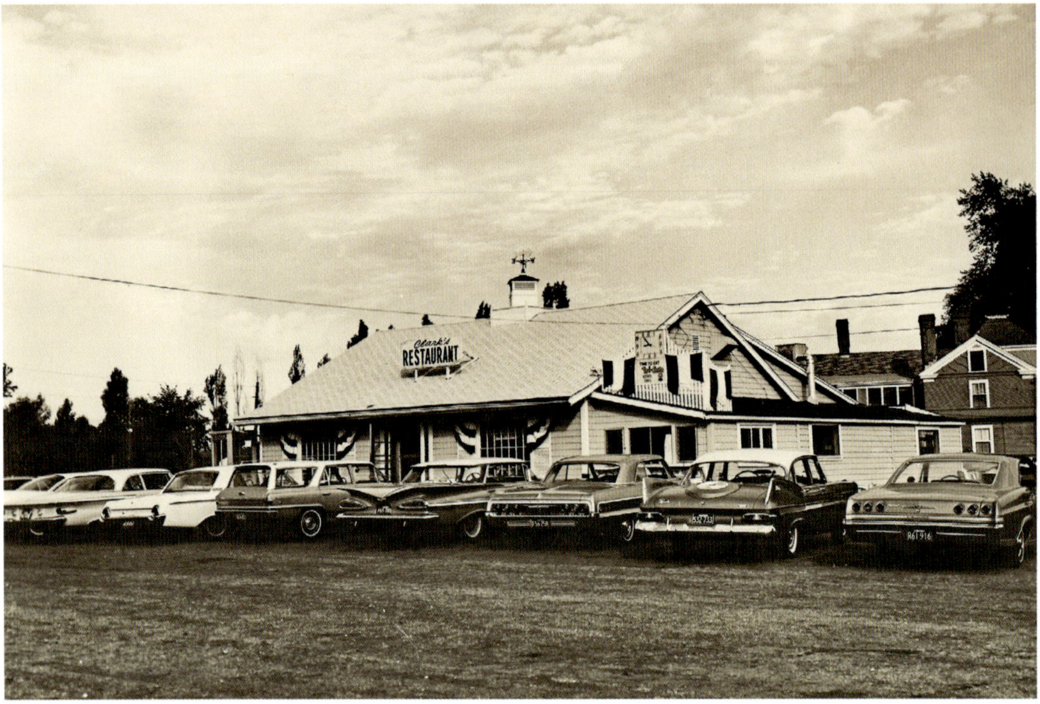

A FAVORITE RESTAURANT: Of several restaurants on the former site of Daniel Wesson's greenhouse the corner of Main and Maple Streets, Clark's was by far the most popular. The styling of the cars illustrates one aspect of the 1960s. A fire destroyed a later version of the restaurant. A vehicle parked in front of the bank on the same corner exemplifies a style often seen in the twenty-first century.

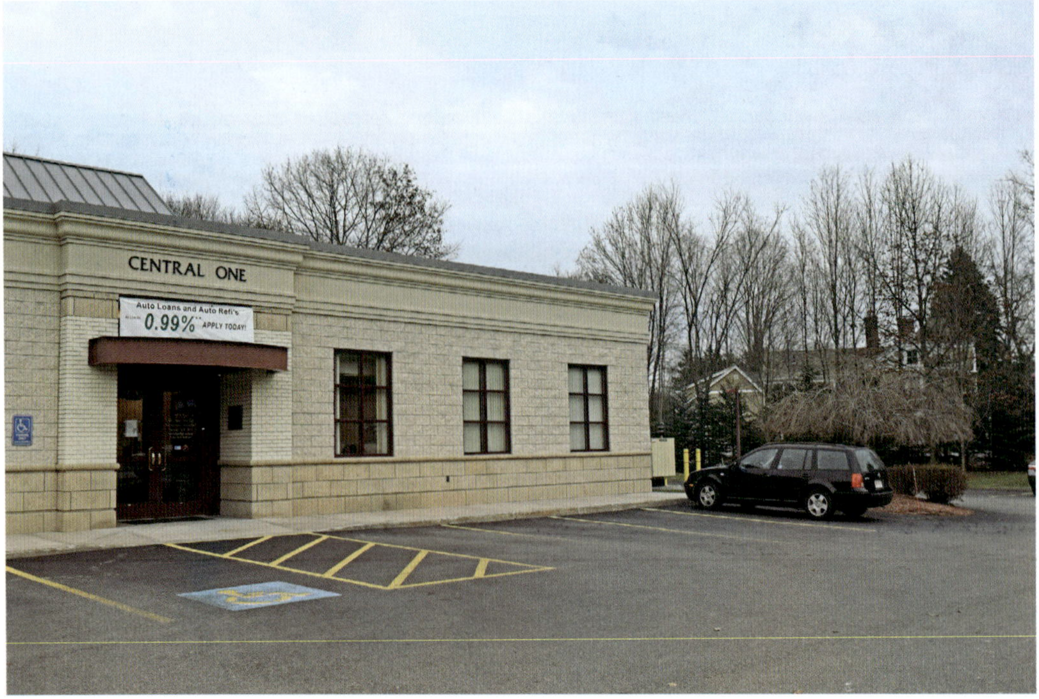

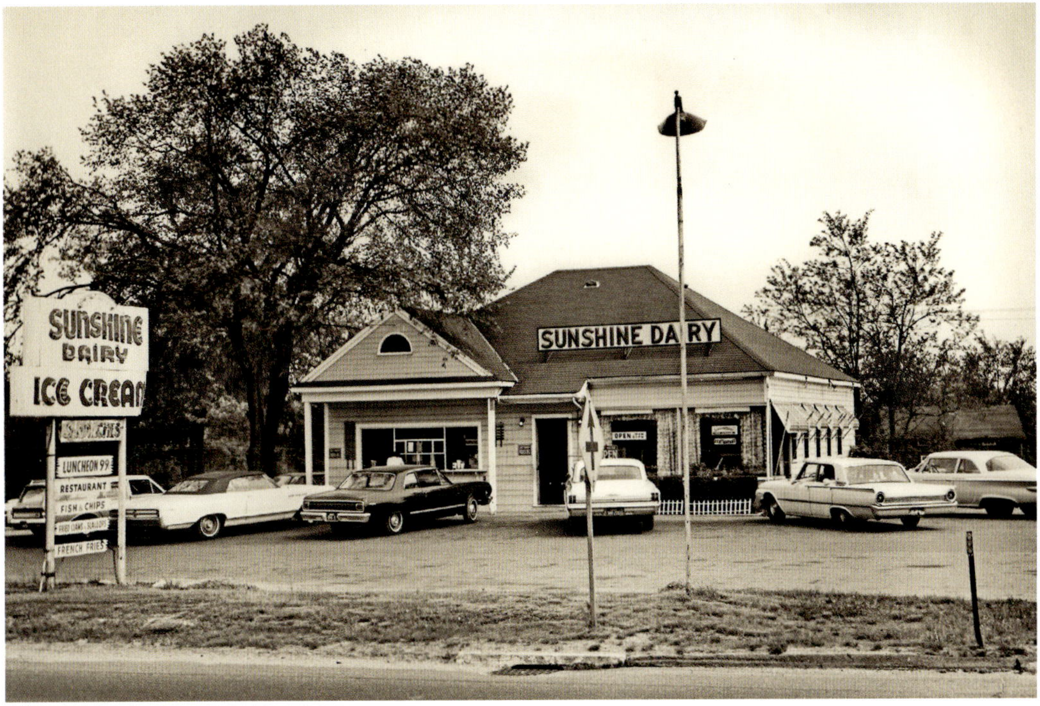

IMAGES OF DINING OUT: In the 1960s among Northborough's few restaurants, the Sunshine Dairy, where a luncheon could cost less than a dollar, was a popular dining place. As the number of restaurants increased, so did their ethnic variety. Few external changes were necessary for Thai restaurant, surrounded, it appears, about a half-century later by the same trees.

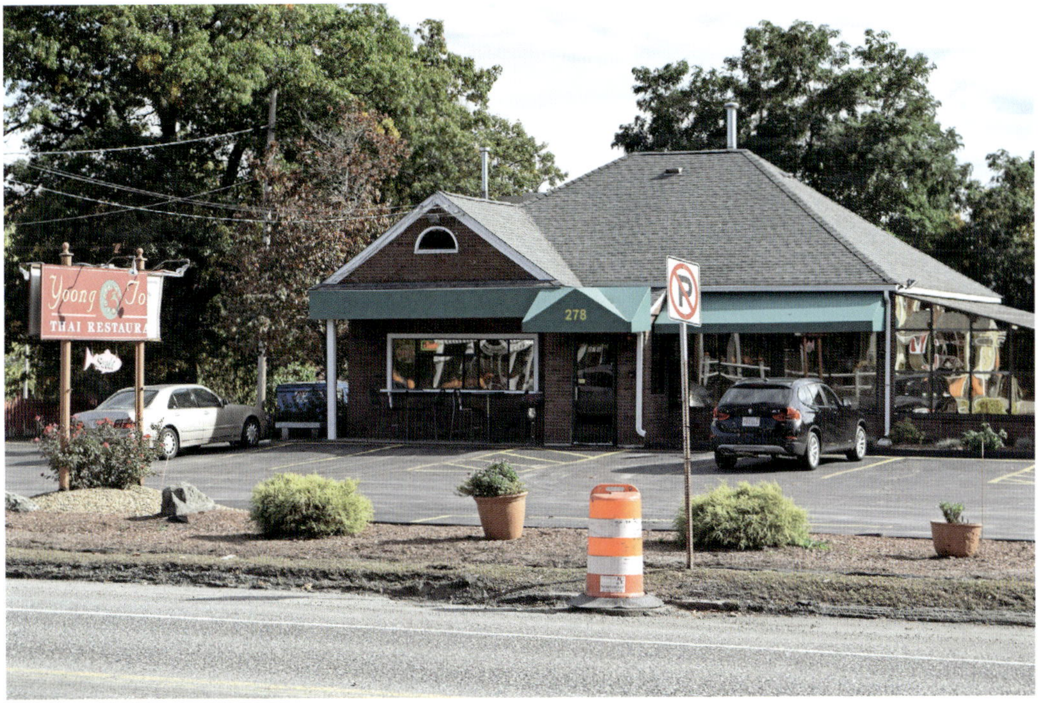

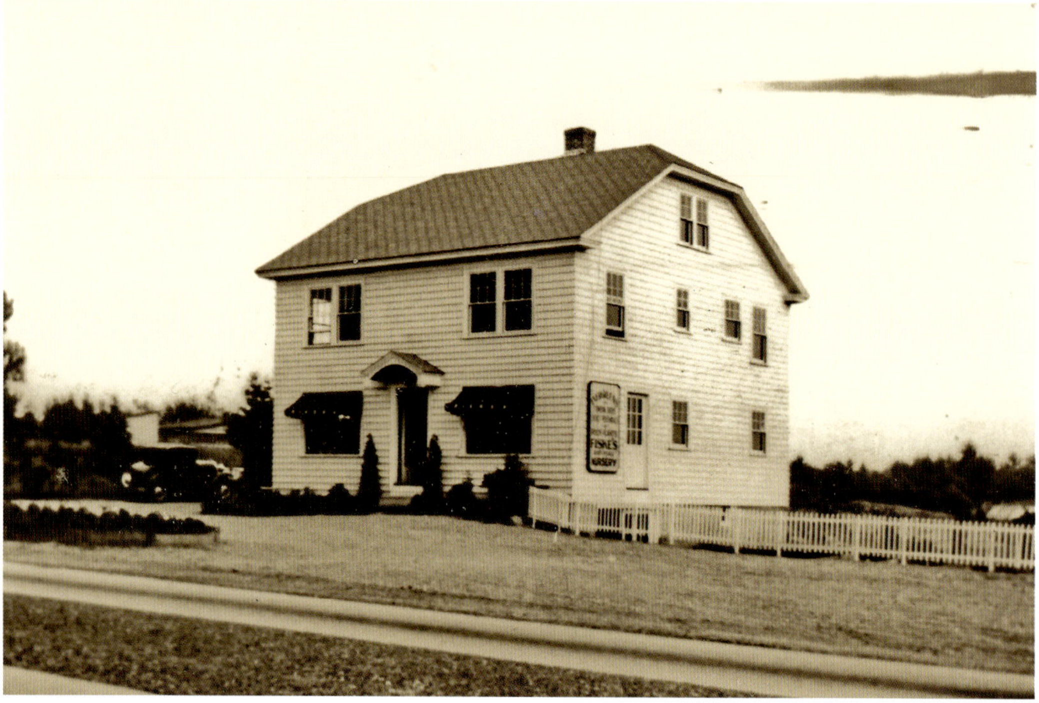

A TRANSPLANTING: Fiske's Nursery grew from this house in the early decades of the 1900s to an extensive business with greenhouses and a vast supply of outdoor needs. To walk along its paths and among its trees, shrubs, flowers, and vegetables was a gardener's treat. After it closed in 2004, this mall completely changed the character of 300 Main Street.

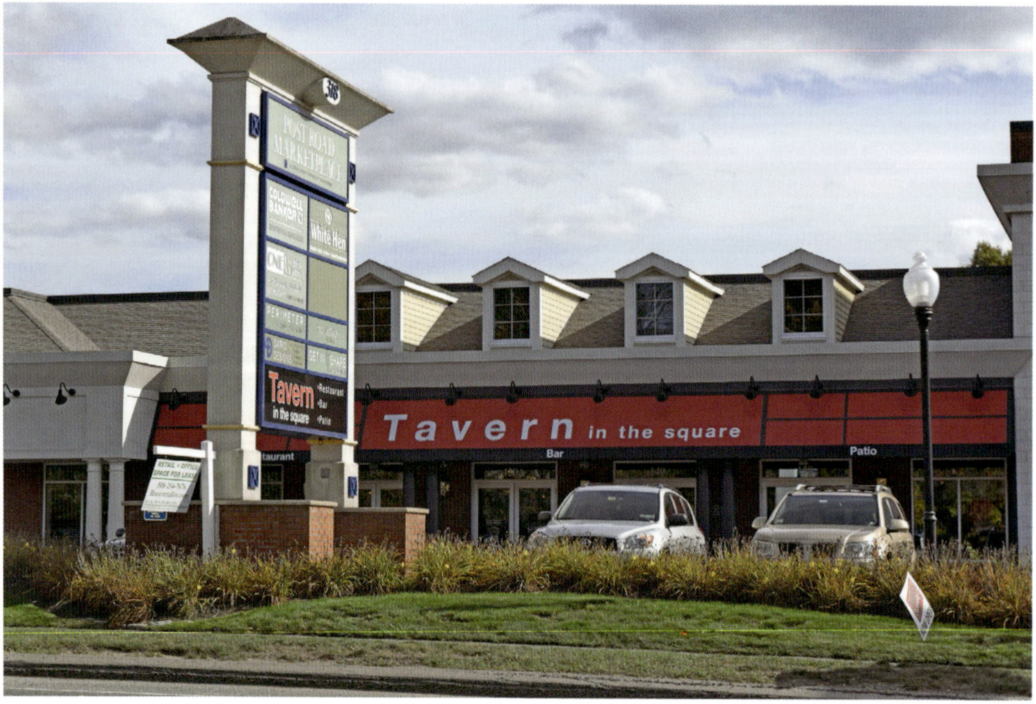

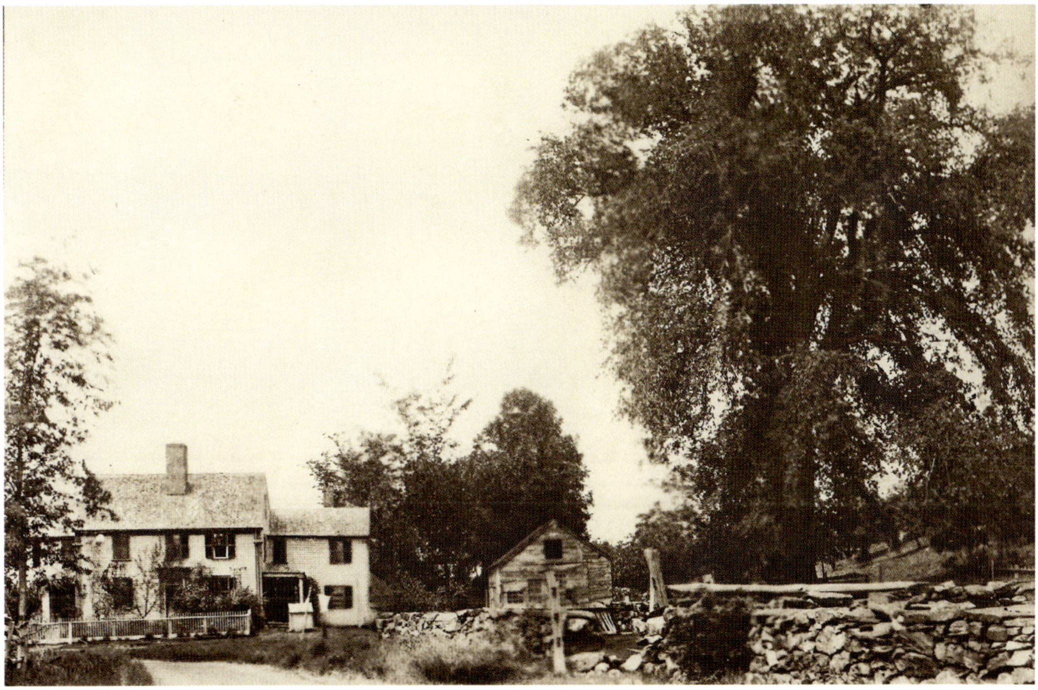

A MAJOR PROJECT: In the 1880s firearms manufacturer Daniel Wesson moved this house to build an elegant mansion. Forty years earlier, the property had belonged to the Hawes family, whose daughter Wesson had married. He spent the equivalent of many million modern dollars to give this summer home to his wife for their elderly years. At the time of writing, the mansion, more recently a function place – thus the numerous and sometimes unhappy alterations – was for sale.

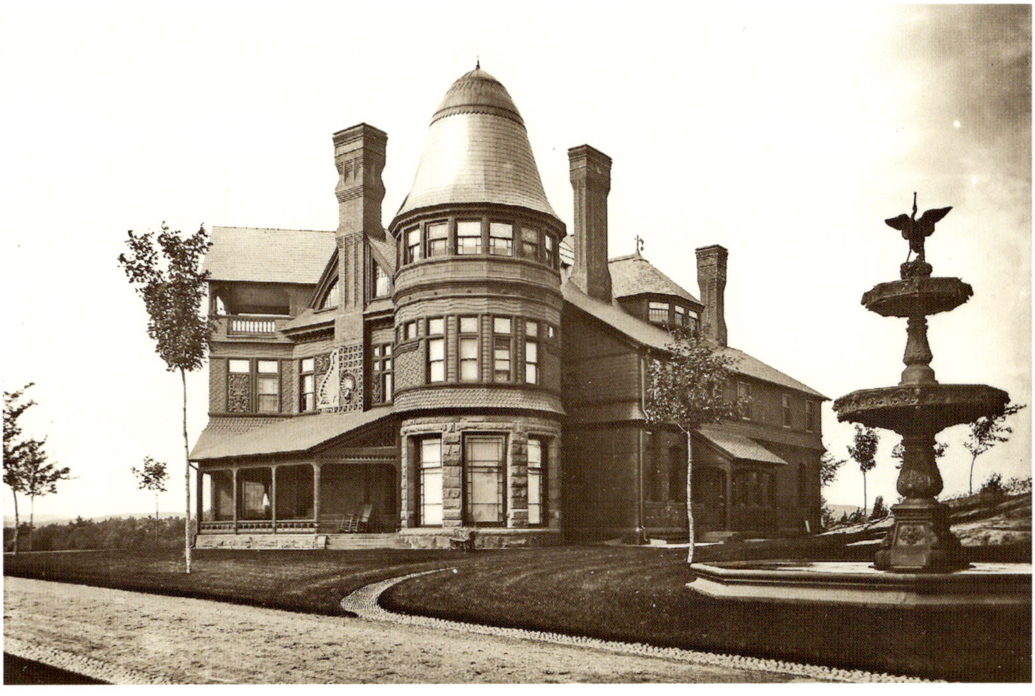

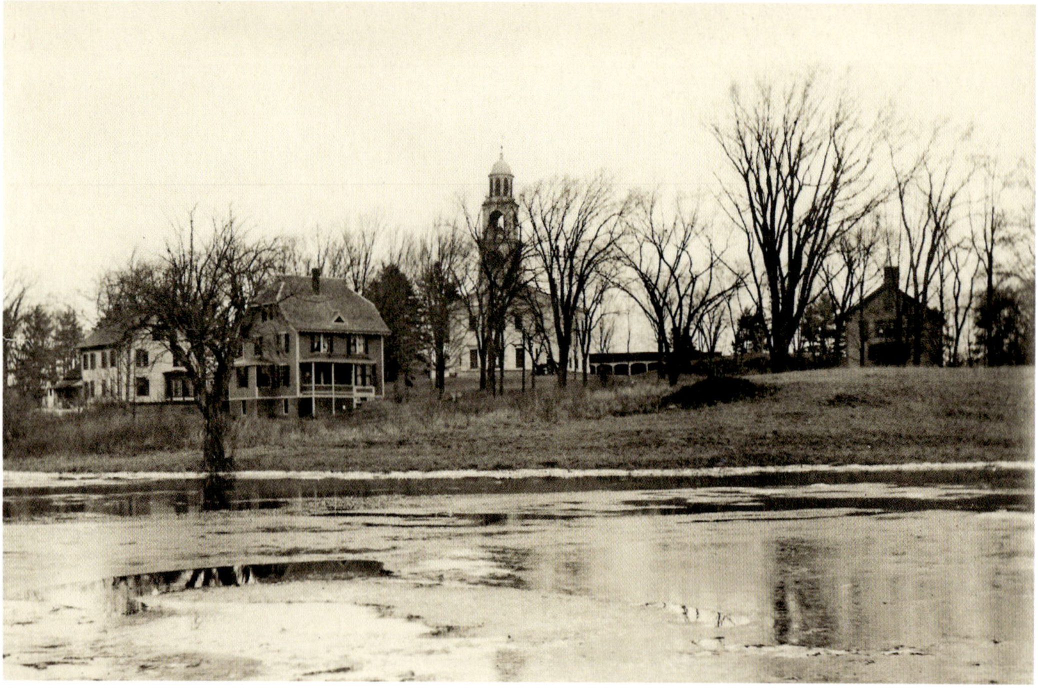

VIEW OVER THE BROOK: Depicted no later than the 1920s (probably earlier) and again in 2014, a glance north of Cold Harbor Brook near Northborough's center revealed the Unitarian parsonage to the left, another dwelling, and the church itself with many similar details. They are two different church buildings, however, the latter a replica made after the former burned in 1945. The building to the extreme right in the older photo was the town's high school until 1924.

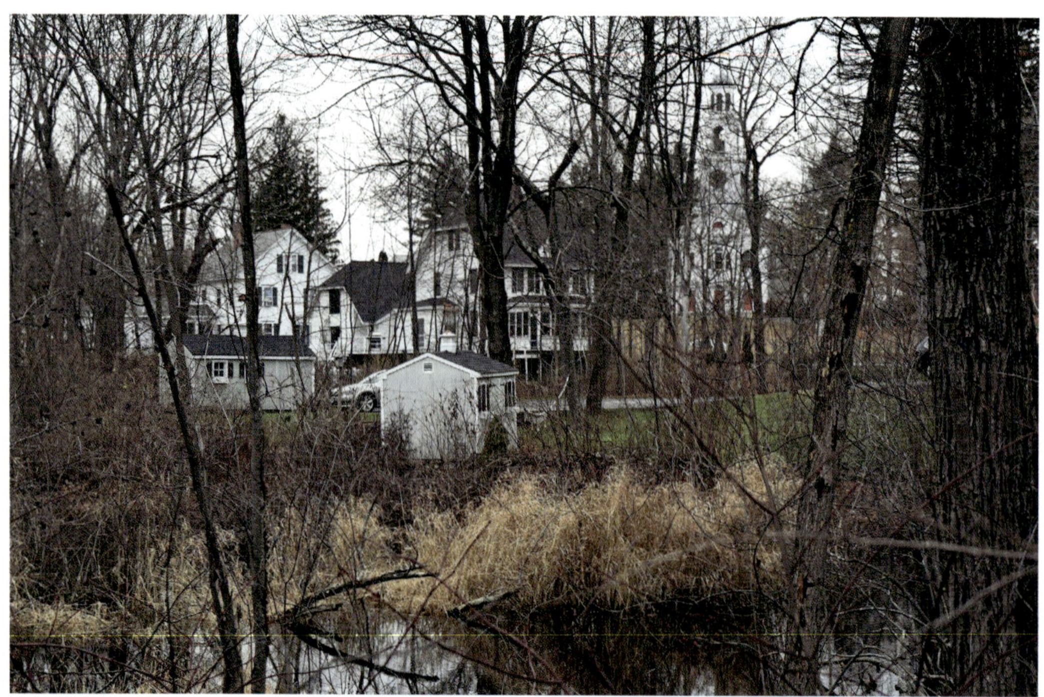

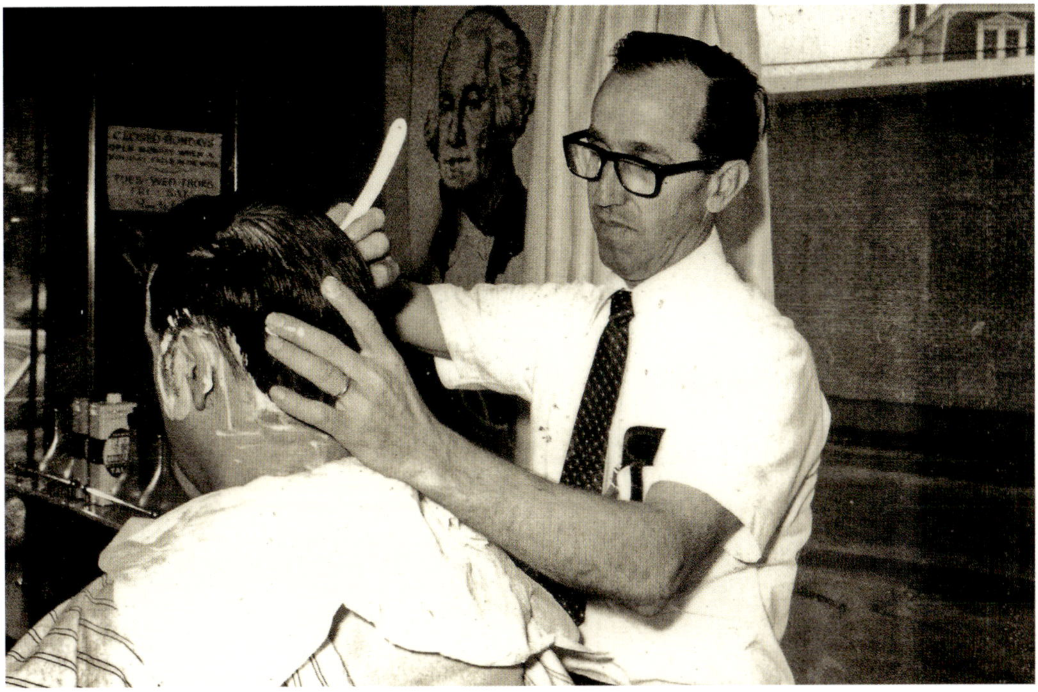

JUST A LIGHT TRIM: In the 1800s a barber was a tonsorial artist performing haircuts, shaves, tooth removal, bloodletting and surgery. Thankfully, those days are gone. Frank Consiglio ran his shop on Pierce Street where one could keep current with town politics, sports, etc. as well as a good look. A former selectman, Frank focused on curbing government spending. In 2015 Bill Buturlia's shop at 94 Main Street meets those needs and has for past forty-one years. Mark Walz is his customer.

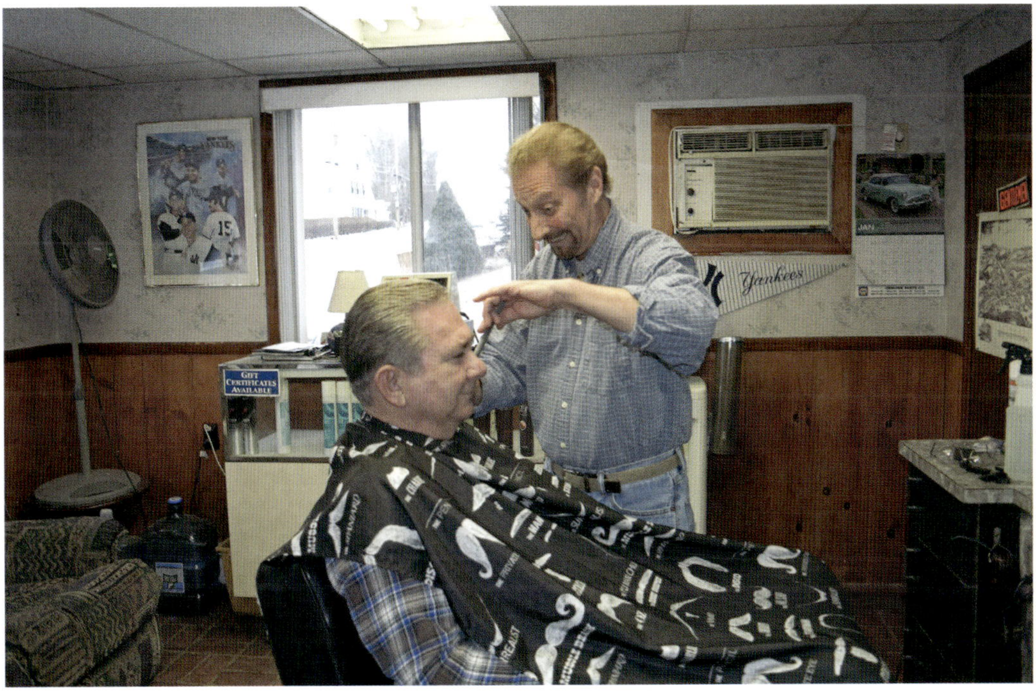

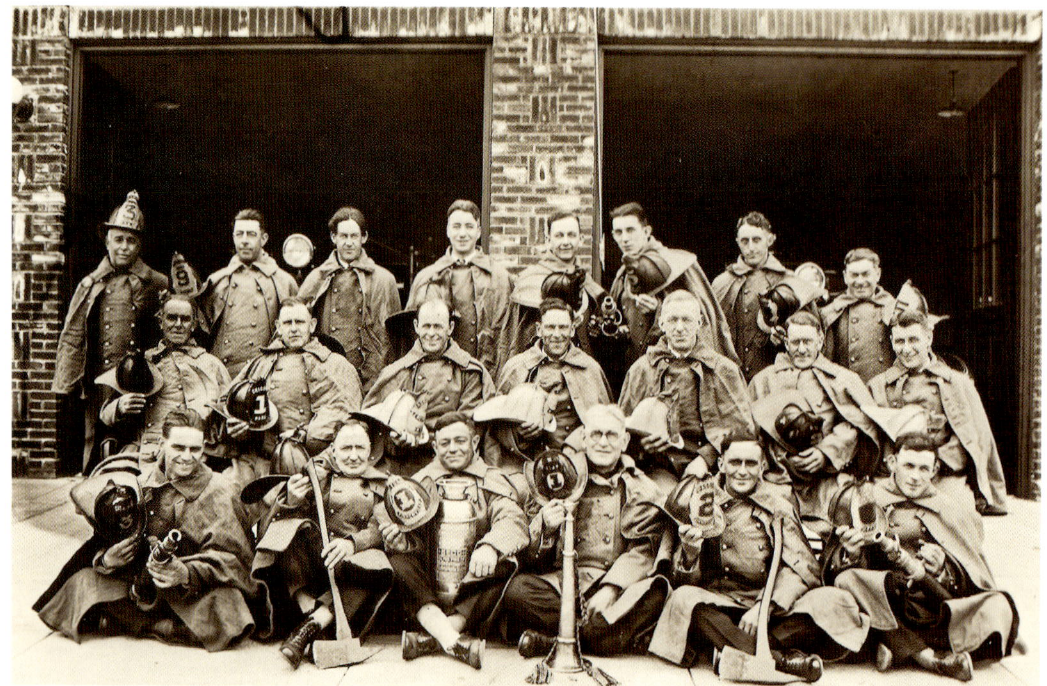

BACK HOME AGAIN: Northborough's volunteer firemen pose in front of the 1926 building on Church Street that housed their 1923 Maxim truck. The town's fire apparatus was already 100 years old when purchased in 1860 for $171.75. After much research and effort, Paul Desautels, center, and wife Libby tracked down "The Volunteer" fire pumper and recently brought it back to Northborough. Former Fire Capt. David Hunt is on the left.

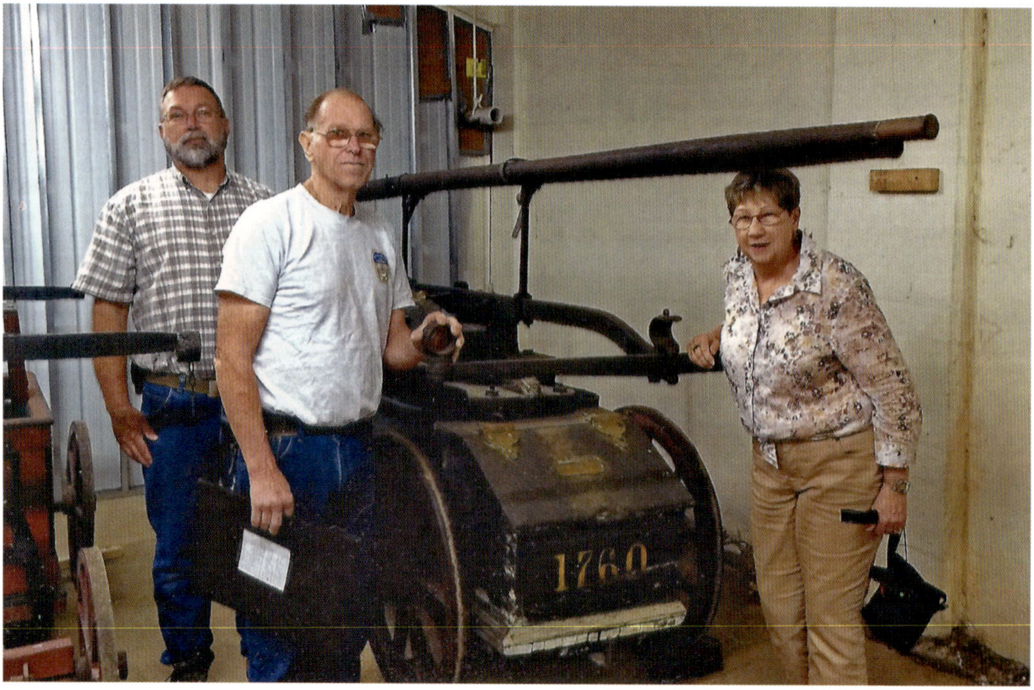

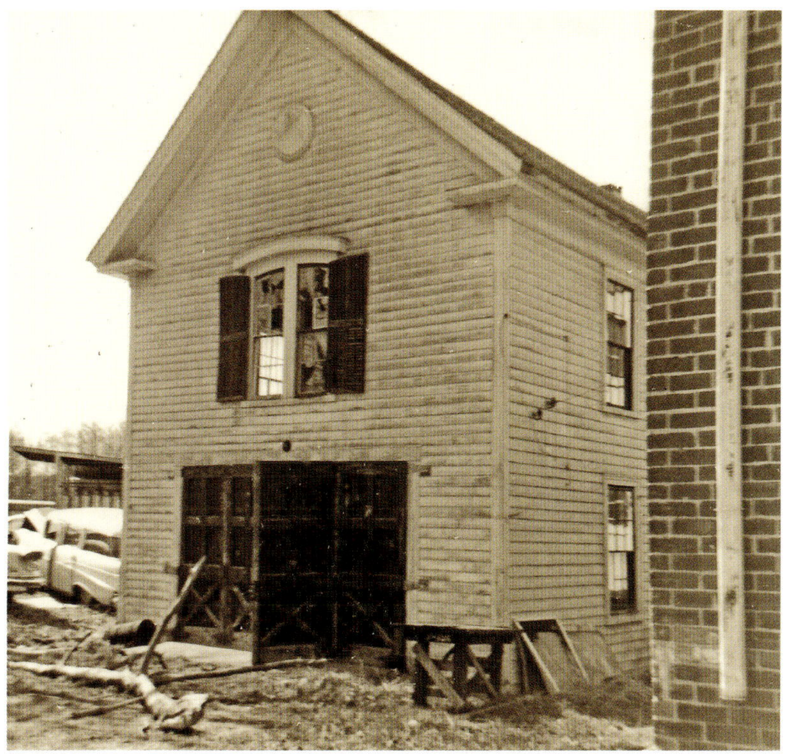

PROTECTION OVER THE DECADES: Northborough, boasting new fire and police stations, finally tore down the wood fire house next door to the 1926 fire house on Church Street. By 1976, however, both stations had proven inadequate. Firefighters lodged in a new building on Pierce Street; the police, after a temporary shift, finally received their new Main Street headquarters in 1989.

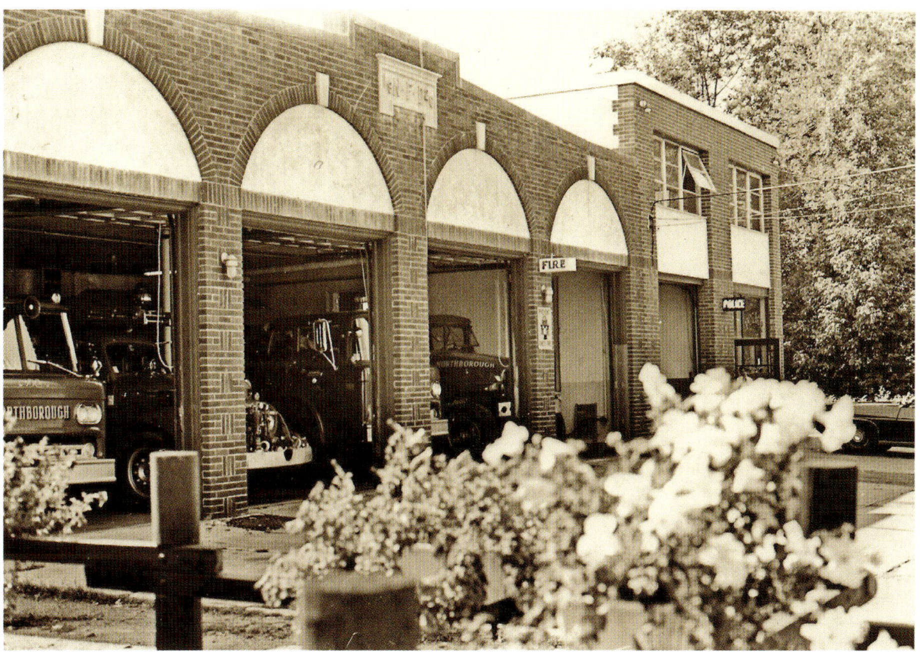

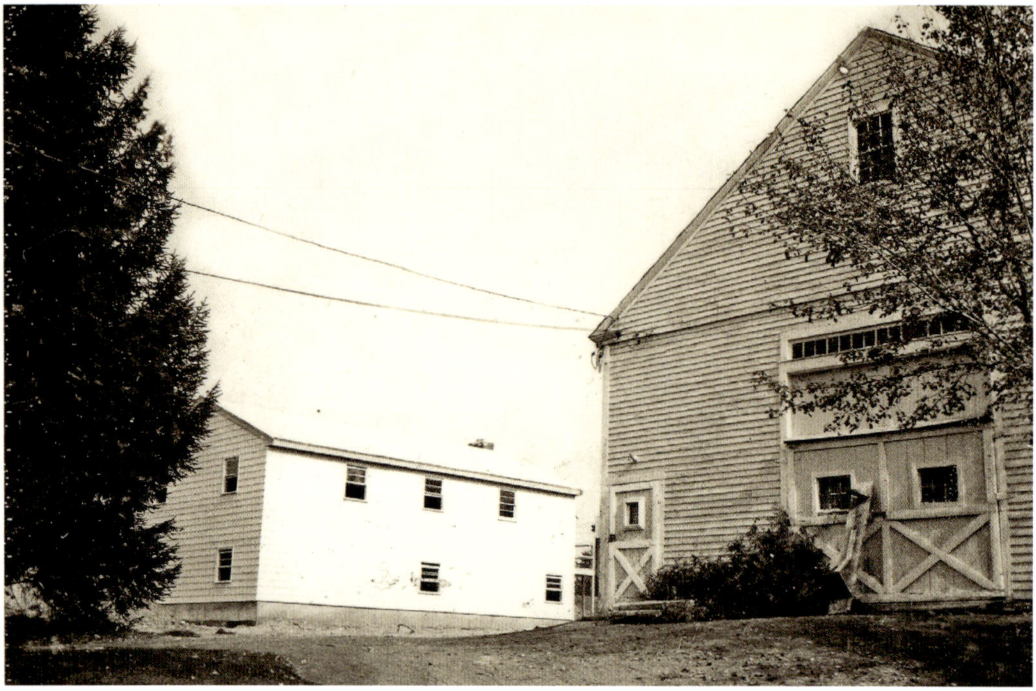

HAIL THE YELLOW BARN: Referring to the time of World War II, one resident put it this way: "The Wrights' 'Yellow Barn' was the magnificent combination of a colonial home surrounded by lush meadows, covered picnic areas plus a huge restored yellow barn ... the most popular spot for dances, weddings, and local hoedowns. The whole town turned out for the famous 'clambakes' in support of the war recruits' Watch Fund." A neighborhood has replaced the lush meadows on Fay Lane.

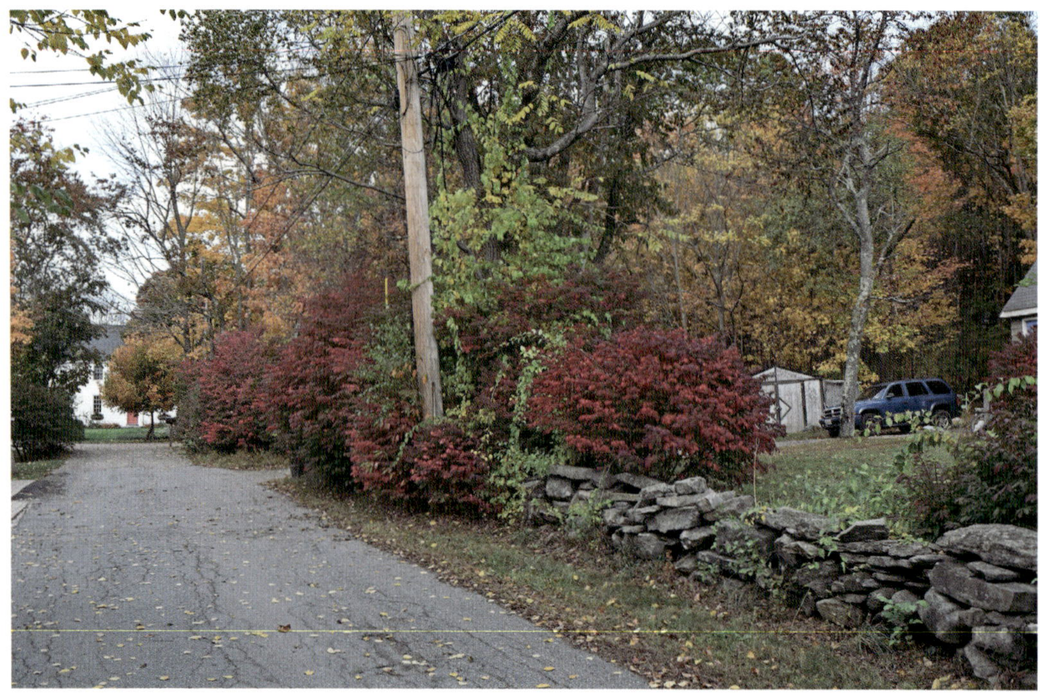

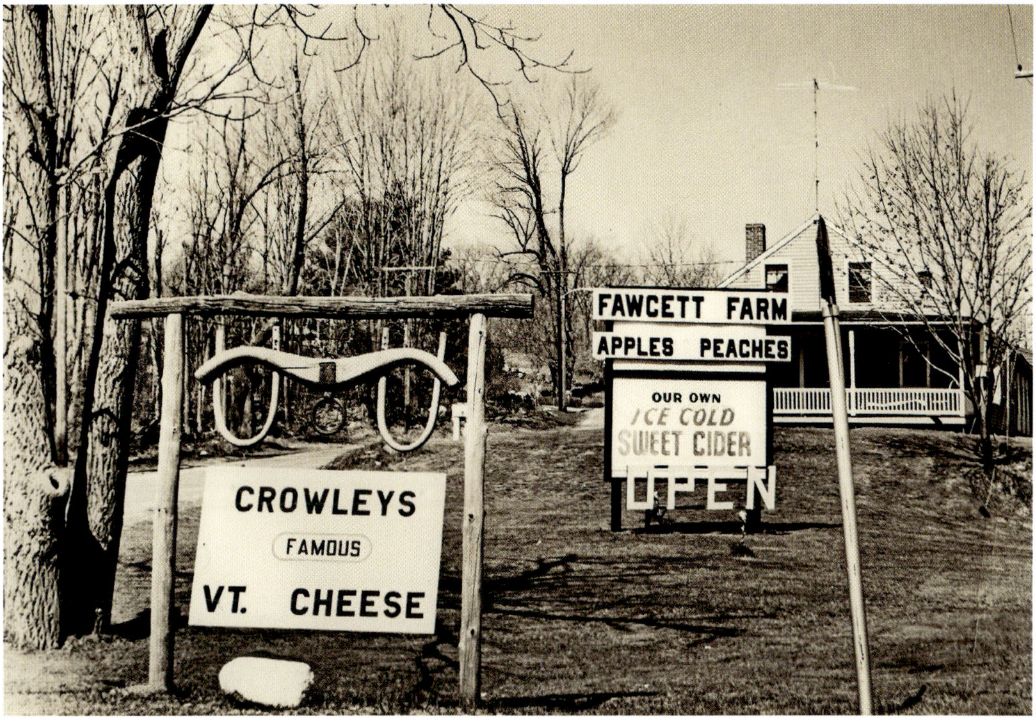

FROM ORCHARD TO INTERCHANGE: After a lengthy orchard business at 6 Reservoir Street, Paul Fawcett moved his center of operations up Ball Street when Rt. I-290 and its Church Street interchange enveloped this popular destination for apple lovers. The familiar property remains as a home site only.

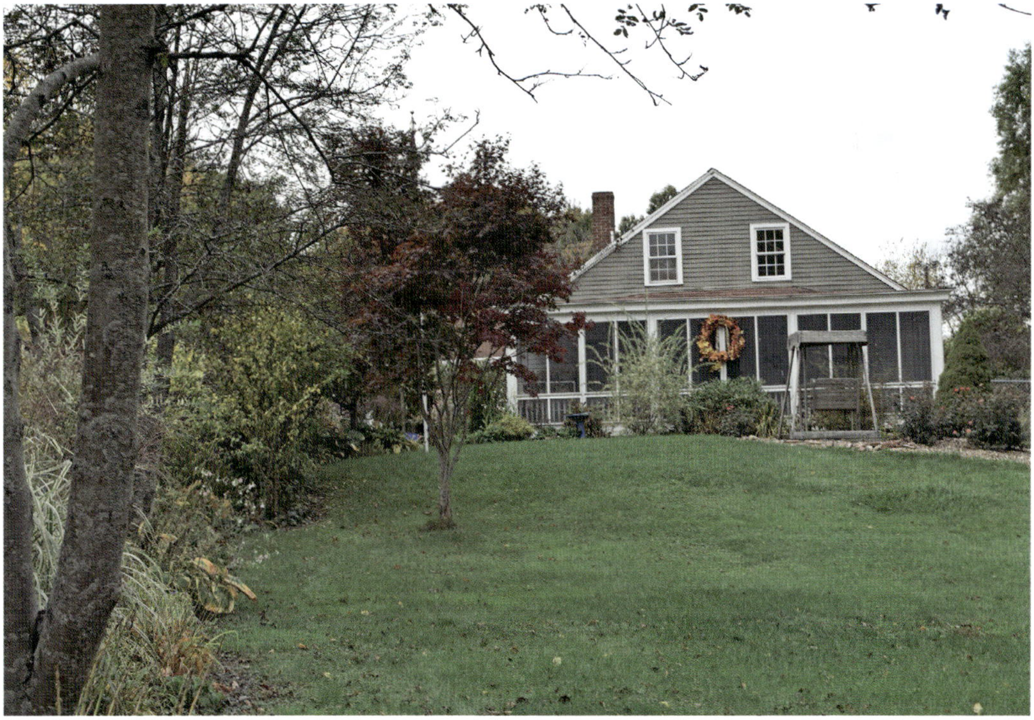

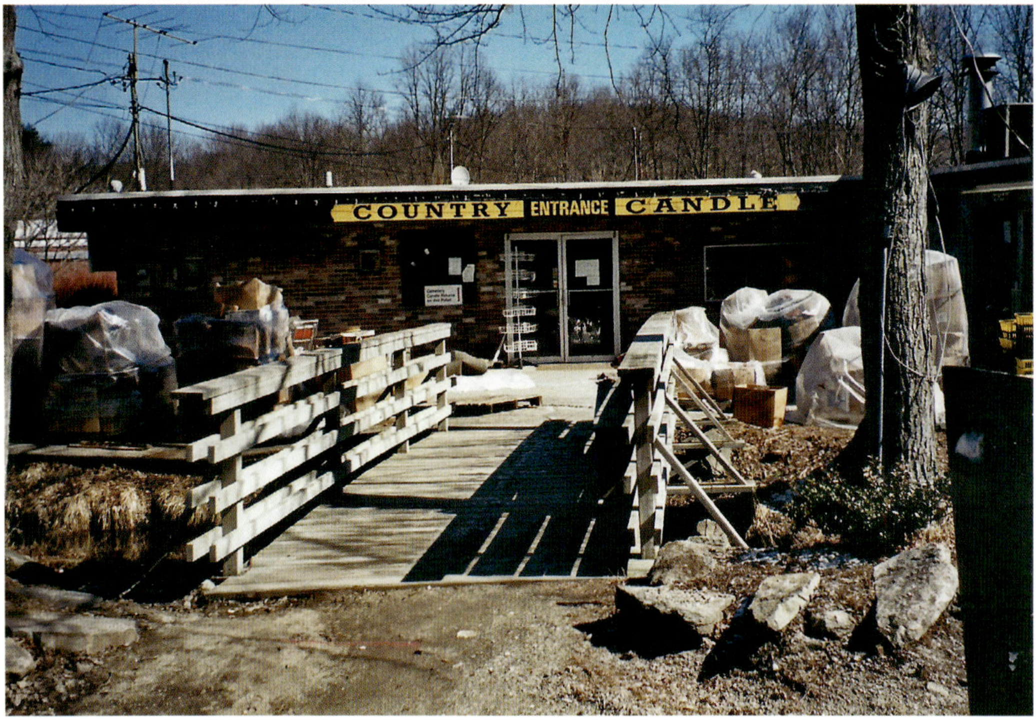

THE CANDLE WENT OUT: On an old and variously used industrial site, the only one on Whitney Street, near the juncture of Howard Brook and Cold Harbor Brook, Country Candle remained a flourishing business for many years in the twentieth century. Early in the following century this site too became residential.

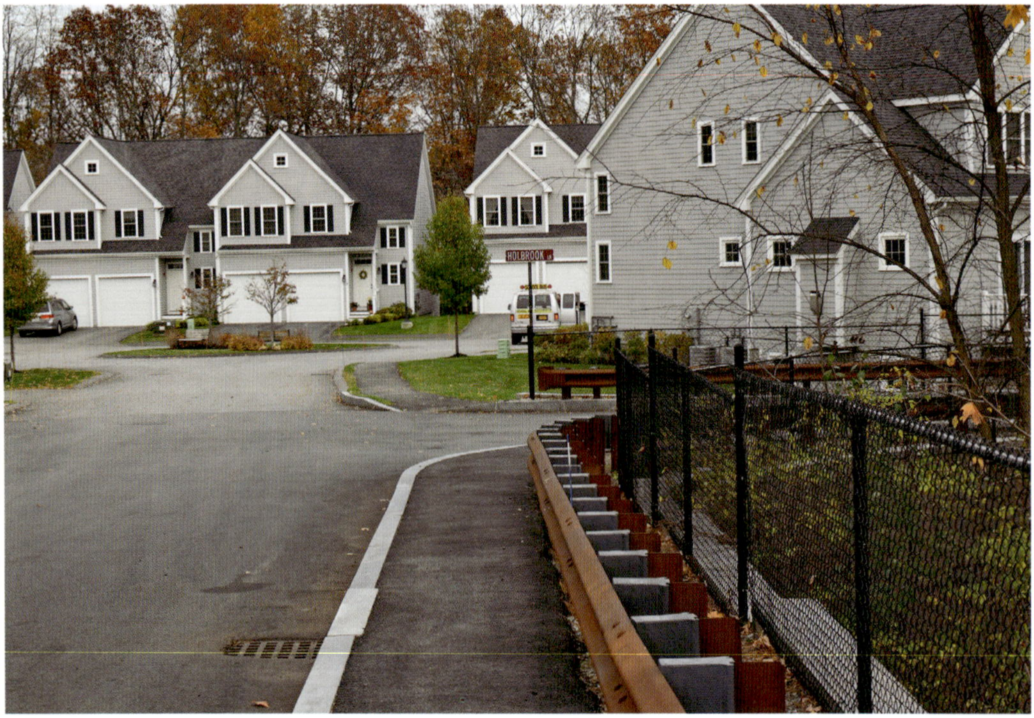

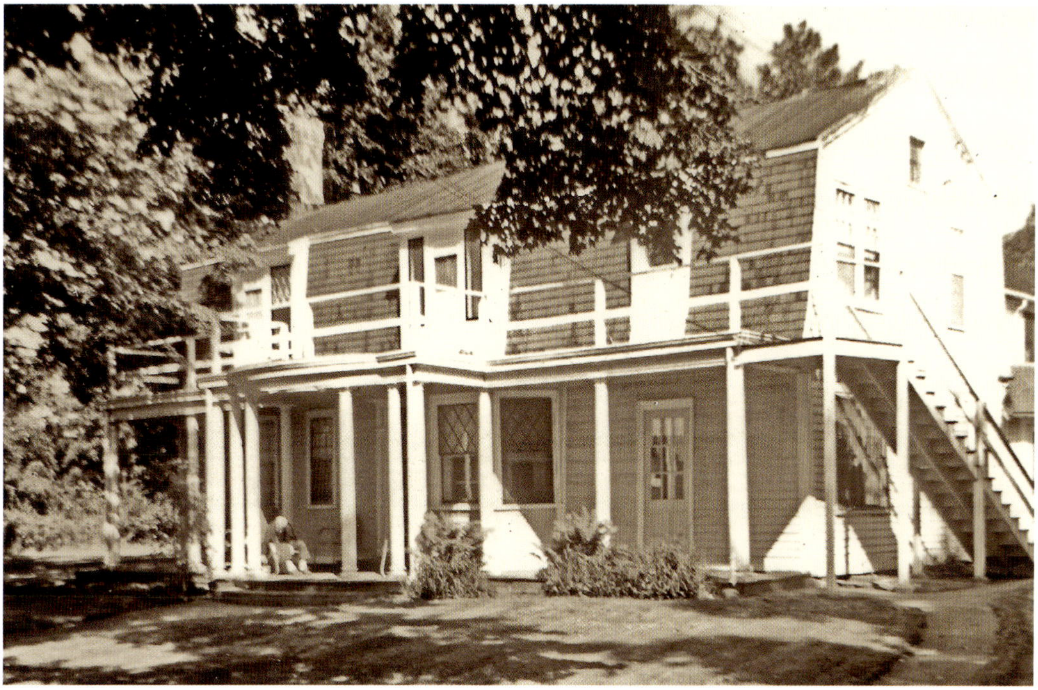

A HOME FOR MANY: For several decades special needs nursing and nursing homes occupied 9 Rice Avenue. As the Ann Judson Ross Home in the early twentieth century, it served the needs of retired women. Later it became a more general nursing home as Green Acres. Grown difficult to manage by the late 1960s, Green Acres was demolished, and a family home – the general type of housing in the 1980s – replaced it although it now fronts Whitney Street.

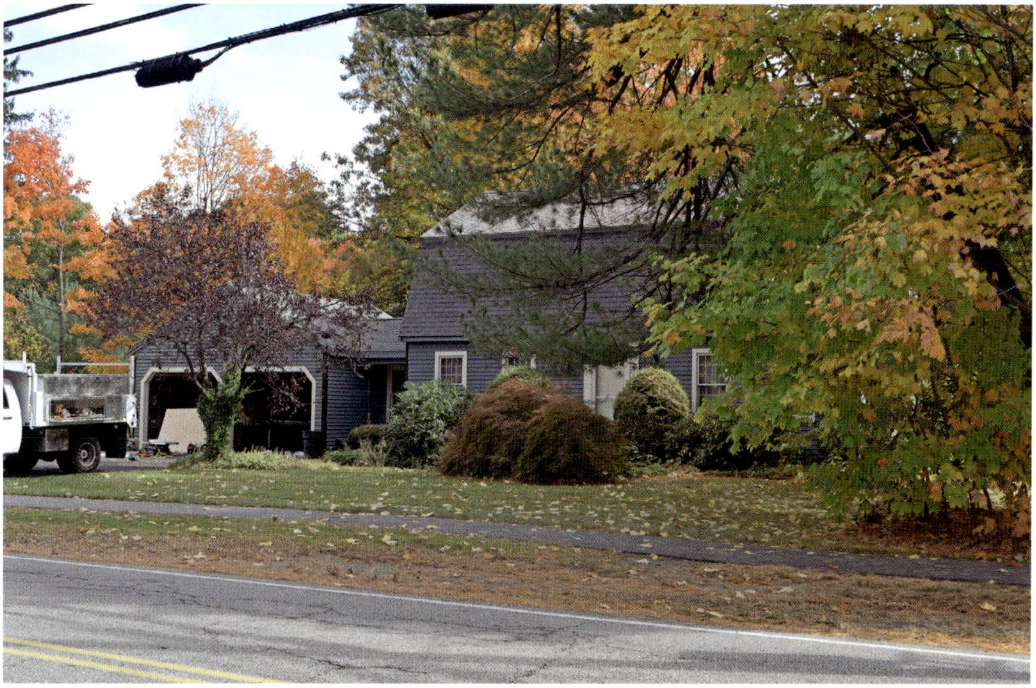

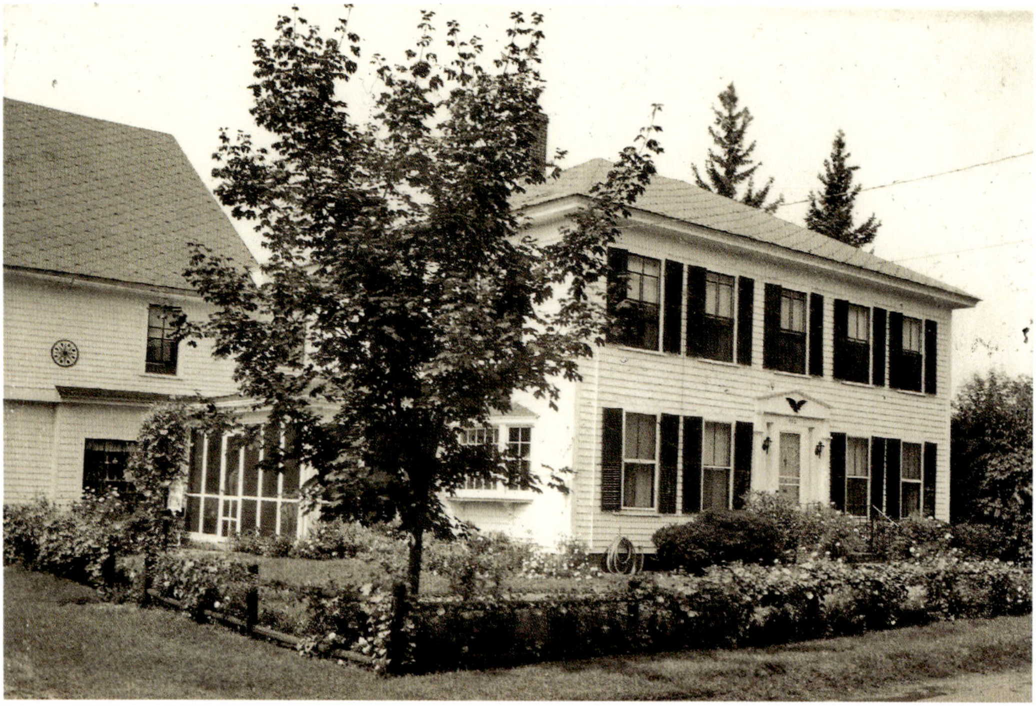

FARM TO DEVELOPMENT: The property at 155 Whitney Street provides one example of the trend in using space in the later twentieth century. As late as mid-century a farmer used his twenty-seven acres for a small herd of cattle and raised corn, asparagus, and strawberries commercially. By 1992 the house was razed and a substantial housing development, Treetop Circle, enclosed the acreage.

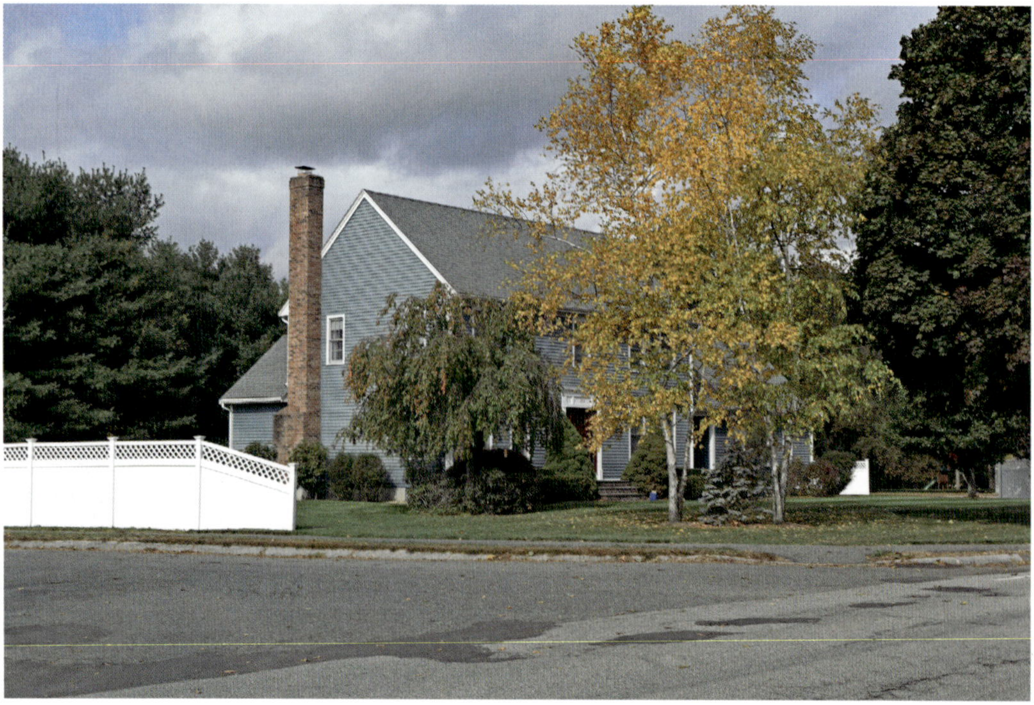

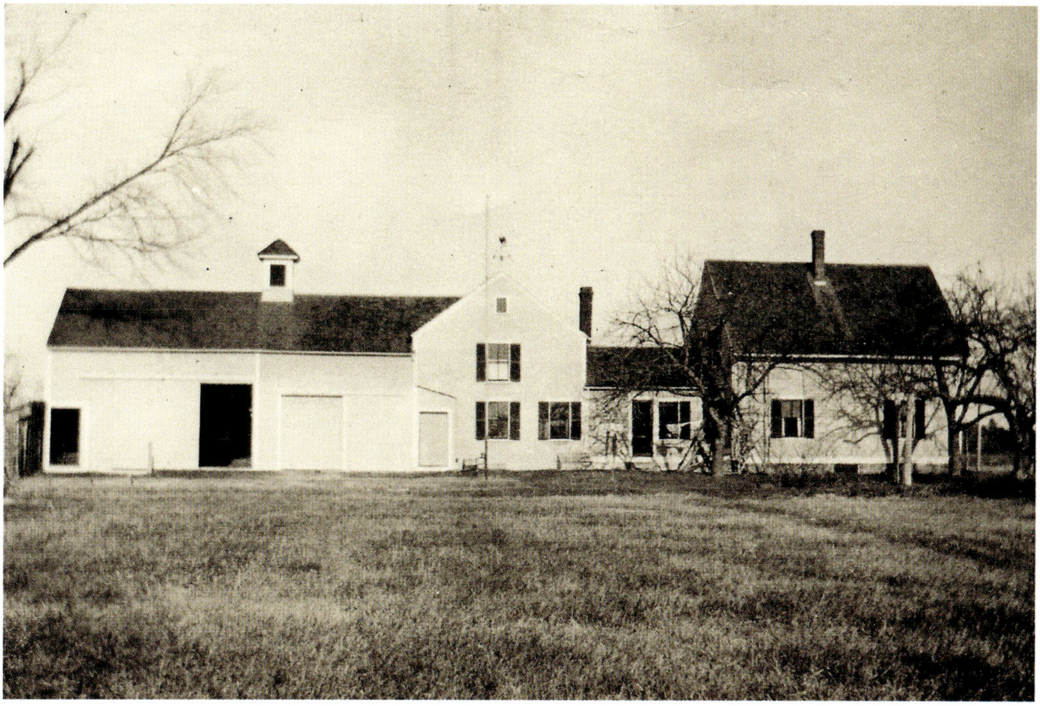

HOMES OF TWO CENTURIES: Helen Corey wasn't born when her father's house at 195 Whitney Street arose about 1850, but the first part of her more than one hundred years was spent there. She claimed that there were three wells on the property. In 1996 many trees and shrubs surrounded it; five years later, all had been removed along with the house for the construction of this larger home.

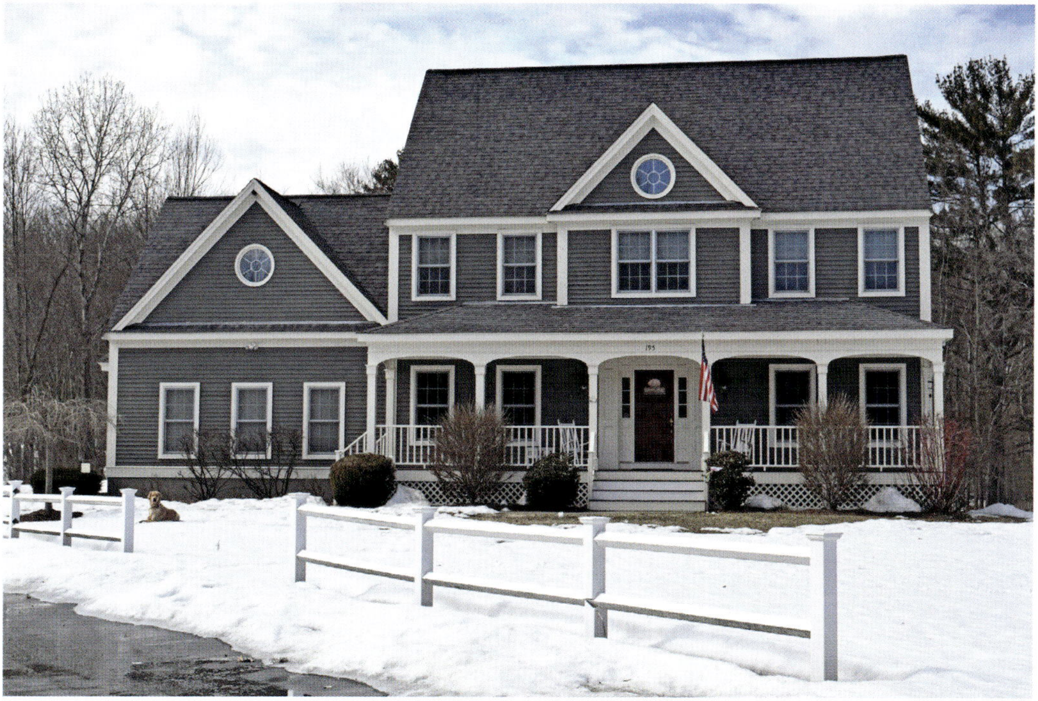

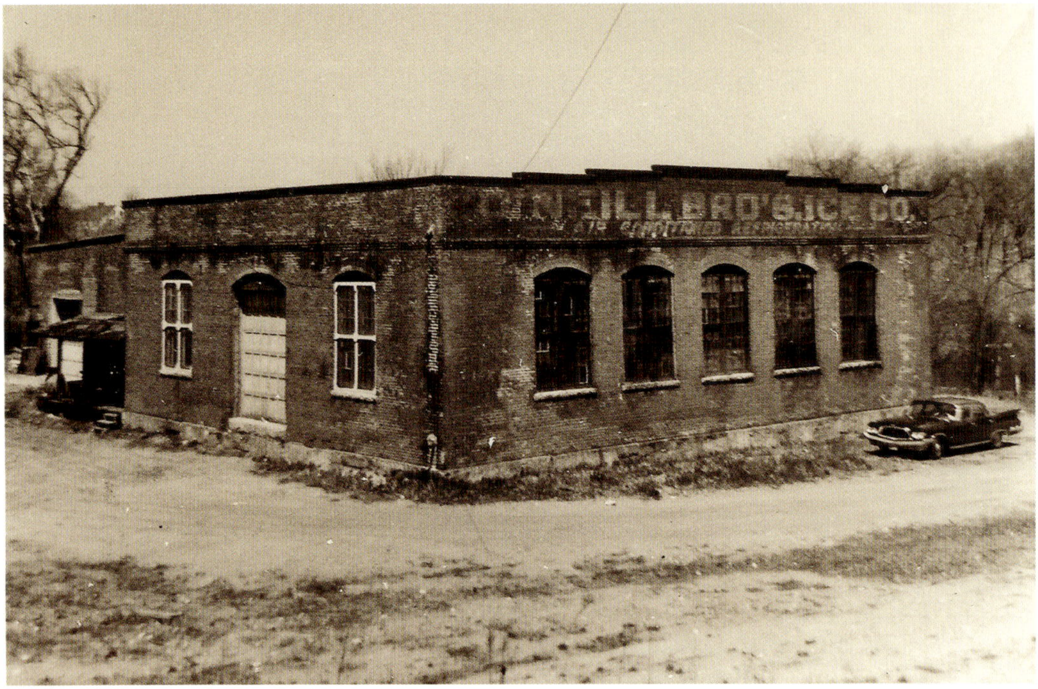

POWER, ICE, FOOD: This former power station for the Worcester and Marlborough Street Railway from the 1890s into the 1920s, found use as O'Neill's Ice House in the 1930s and '40s because it stood near a pond on 43 Hudson Street. It served the many families who then lacked refrigerators. After standing dismally empty for years thereafter, it came alive early in the twenty-first century as Peppers Fine Foods Catering Service.

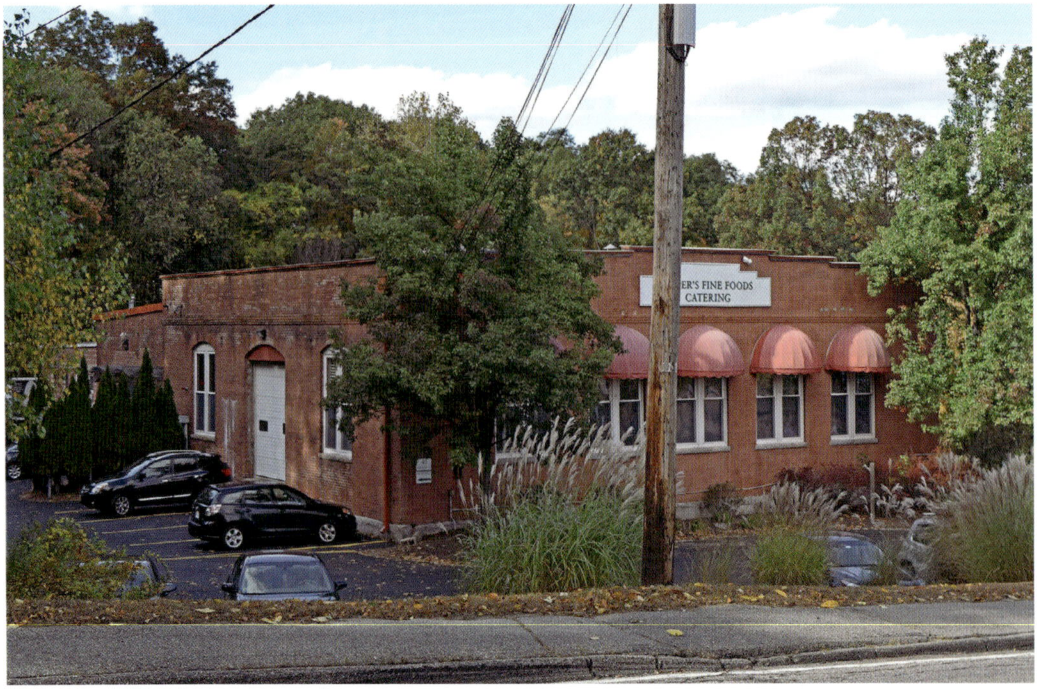

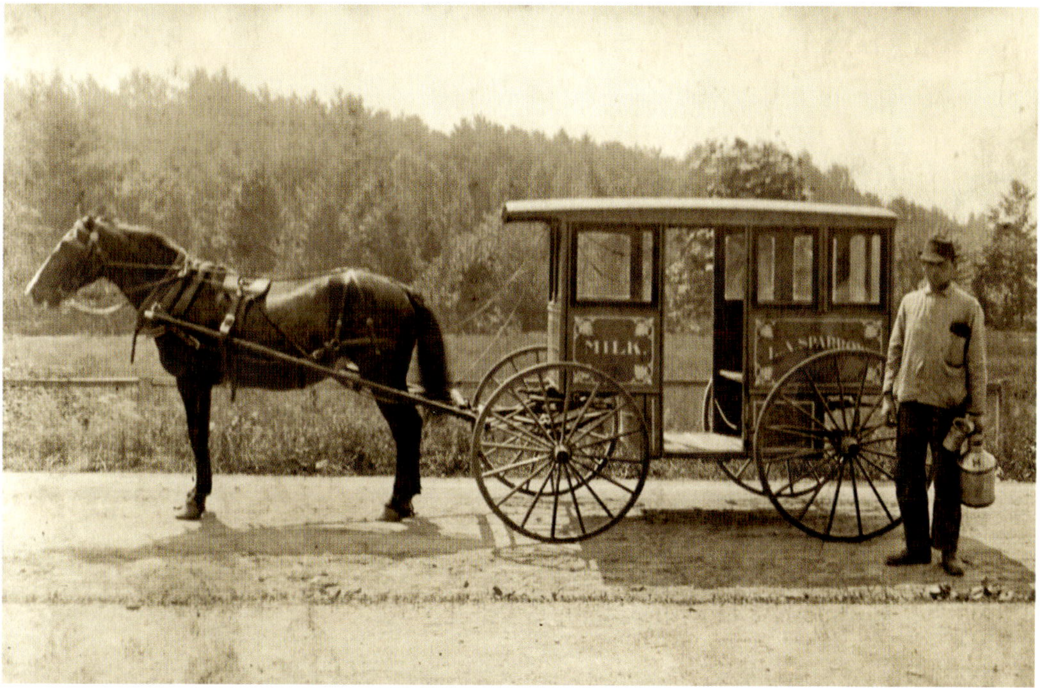

Making house calls: L. A. Sparrow's milk wagon delivered milk from his 250 acre farm on Colburn Street (see page 56). Three generations of the Sparrow family worked the dairy farm of 120 cows before moving to Vermont in 1970. Bearfoot Road now cuts through this property and supports many industrial businesses. In 2015 we have meals delivered from establishments such as Chris Singas' Northboro House of Pizza.

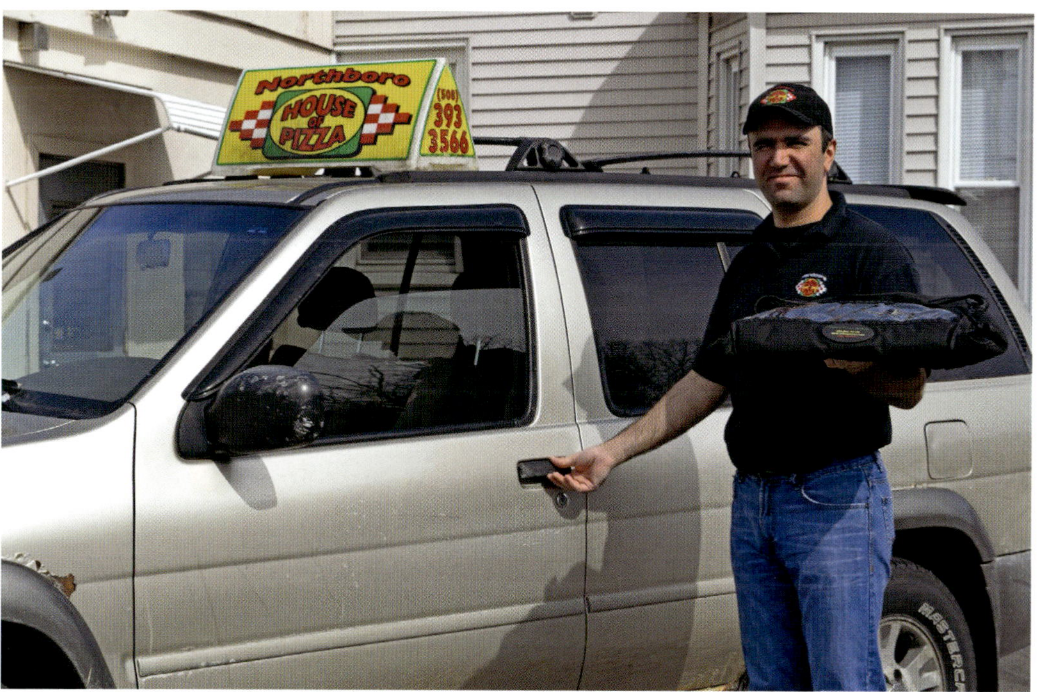

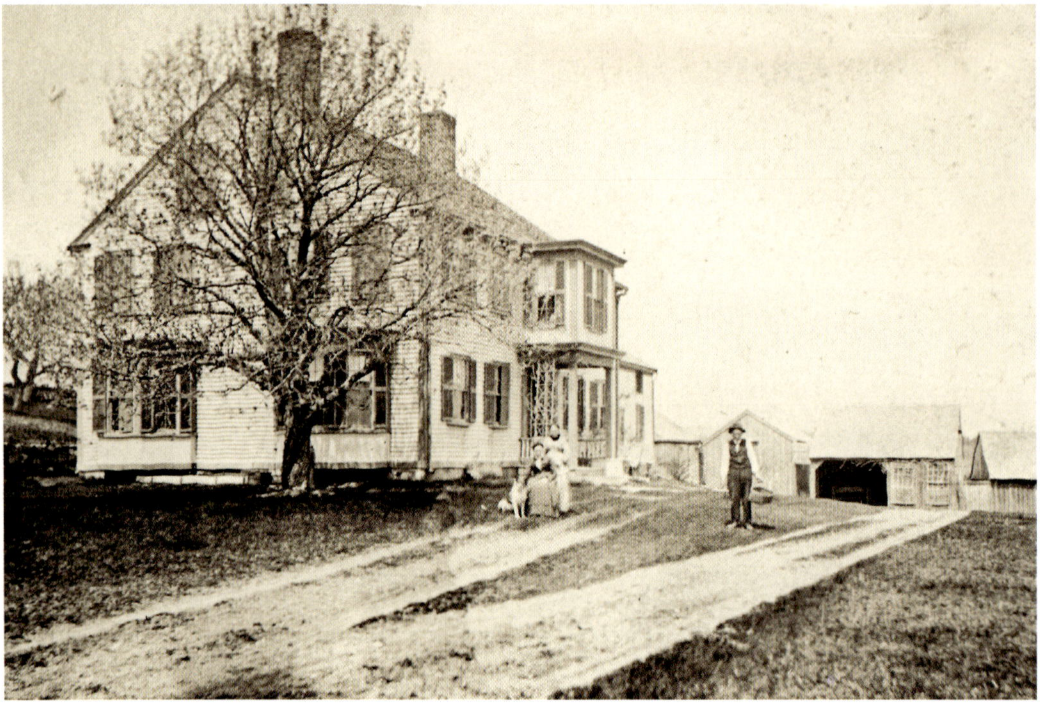

Colburn Street over the years: This street, named for an early family, served for two and one-half centuries as the setting for the Warren (and later) Sparrow farms. A short distance away, where Colburn leads into Bearfoot Road, the Northborough Senior Center has replaced another instance of rural Northborough, the Fish and Game Club.

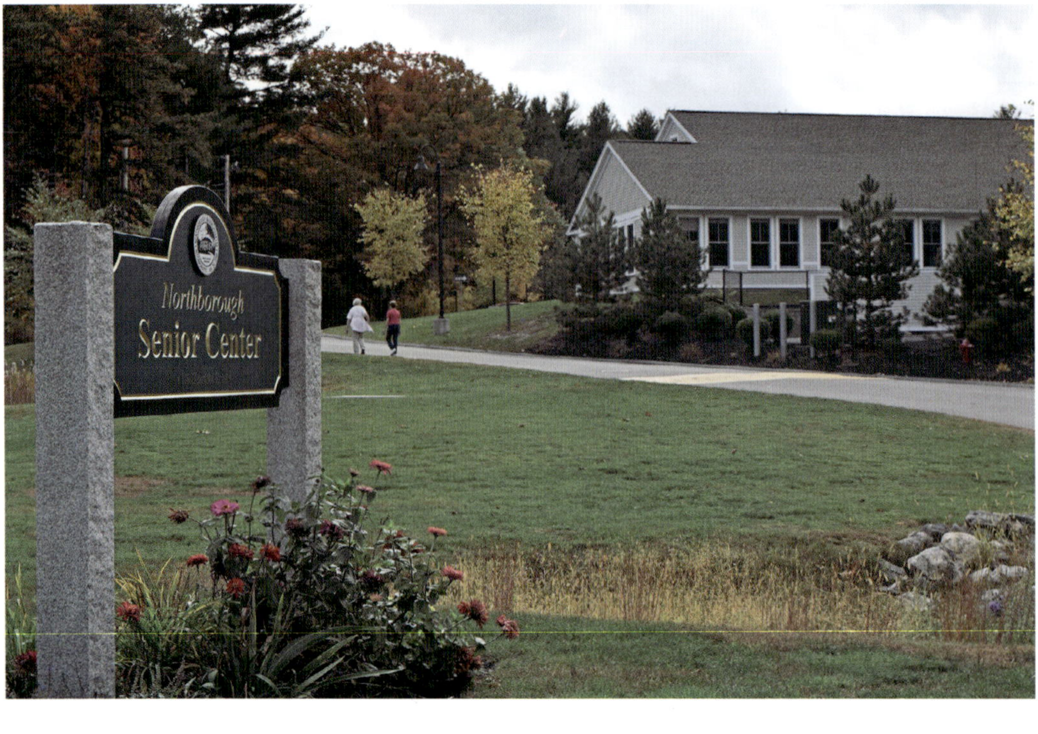

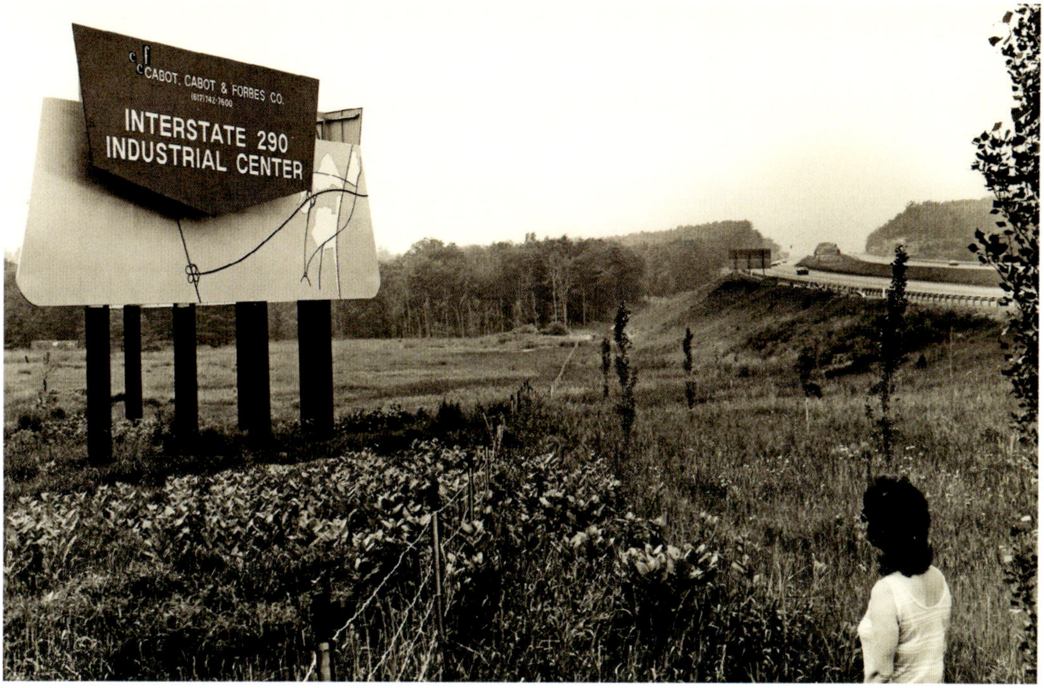

CHANGING LAND USE: The promise of a new commercial development in 1972 near the recently constructed Route I-290 gains the attention of a young woman, as captured by Gorchev & Gorchev Photographers. The woman may be aware of the history of more than two centuries of farming at this location. Several decades later, no one happens to be watching the prospect of more commercial activity at the same site, I-290 again in the background.

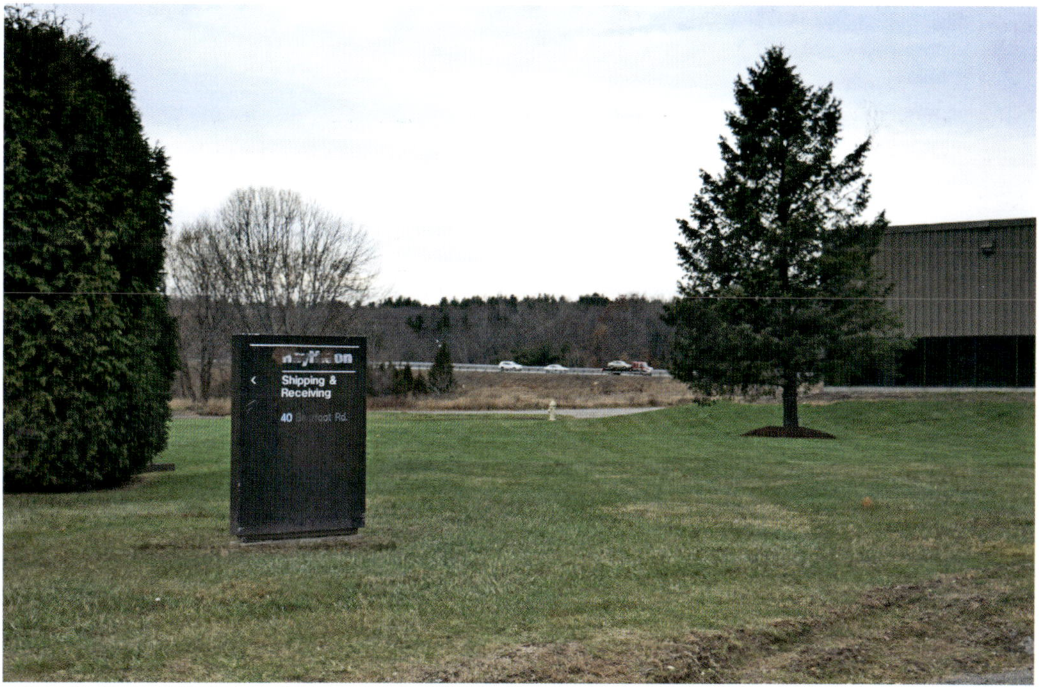

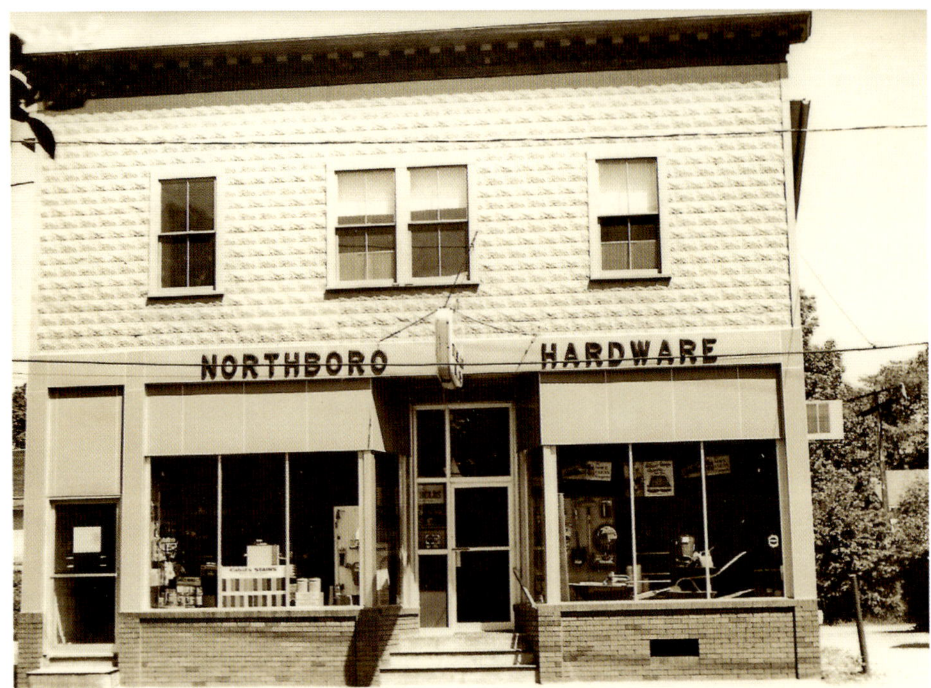

AN ADMIRABLE TRANSFORMATION: From its construction in 1907 until 1986 this building at 11 South Street housed a hardware store on its first floor; for much of this time its second-floor hall served various groups. Extensively restored thereafter, it was permitted to retain many of its original features. It became a physician's office and, on its second floor, as the air conditioners suggest, comfortable living quarters.

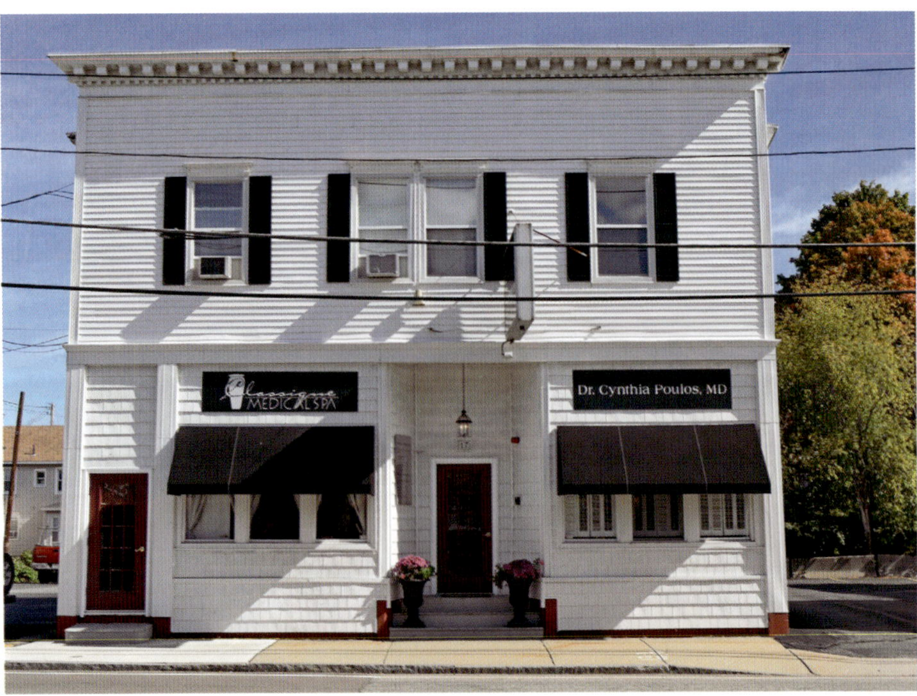

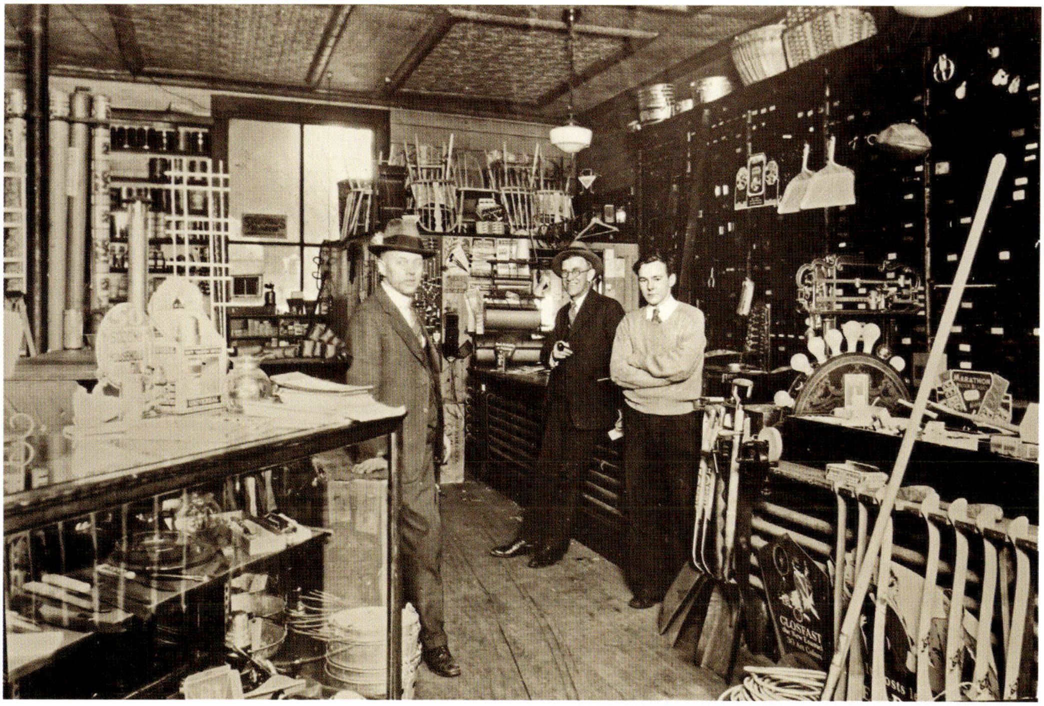

FAMILY BUSINESS: About 1940 John Fairley, seen at left, operated the hardware store he had acquired in the 1920s. In 1968 his son Arthur strikes a characteristic pose as he carries on this dispensation of household needs. By the 1980s the great multiplication of hardware items and the lack of parking space for this small but popular establishment had made it impossible to maintain on South Street near the center of town.

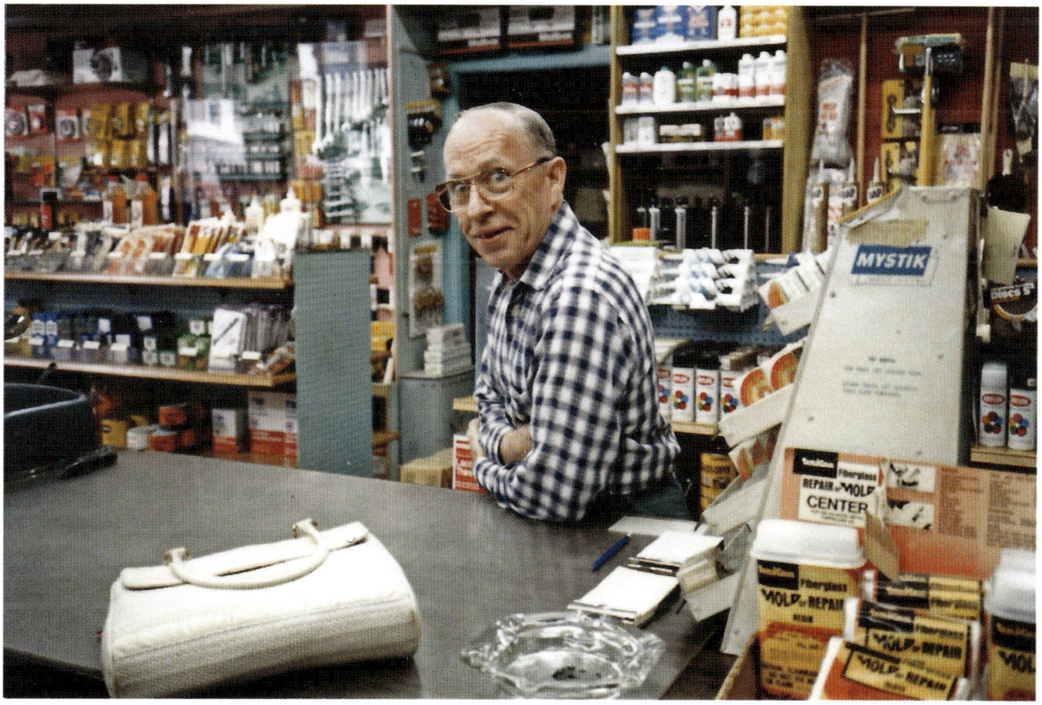

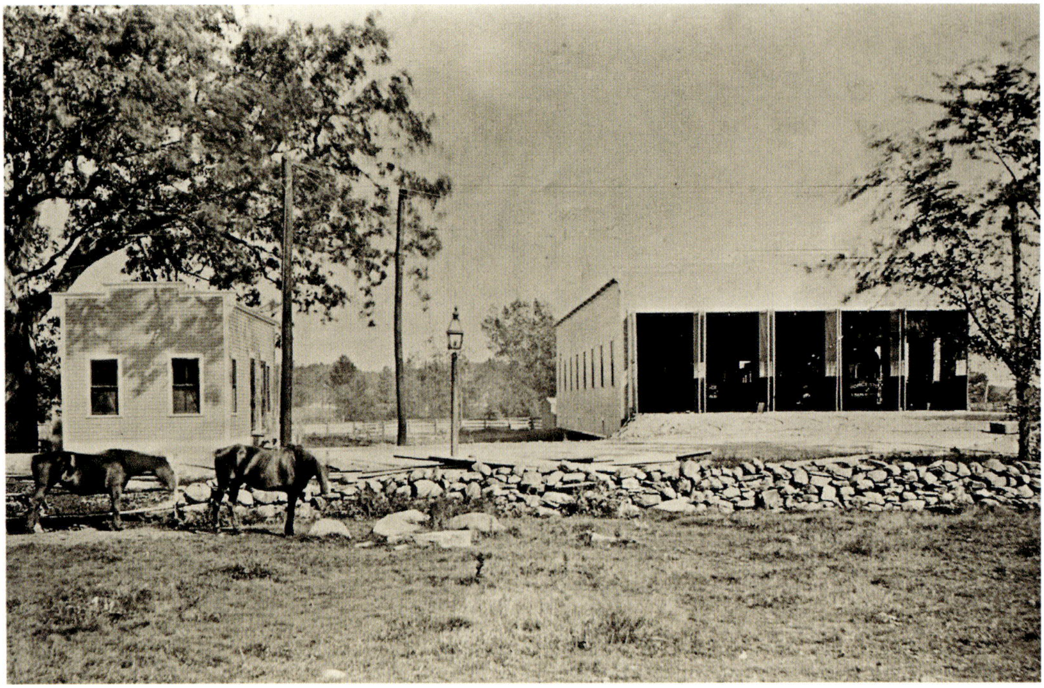

DAY TRIPPERS: The Worcester Consolidated Street Railway brought trolley service to Northborough in 1897 with tracks running from Worcester to Marlborough and on South Street to Westborough. This service brought many city visitors to Northborough on day trips to enjoy the country air and historic sites. The Car Barn with its office building, now gone, was located at 41 South Street, the home of Ken and Mary Hunt in 2015.

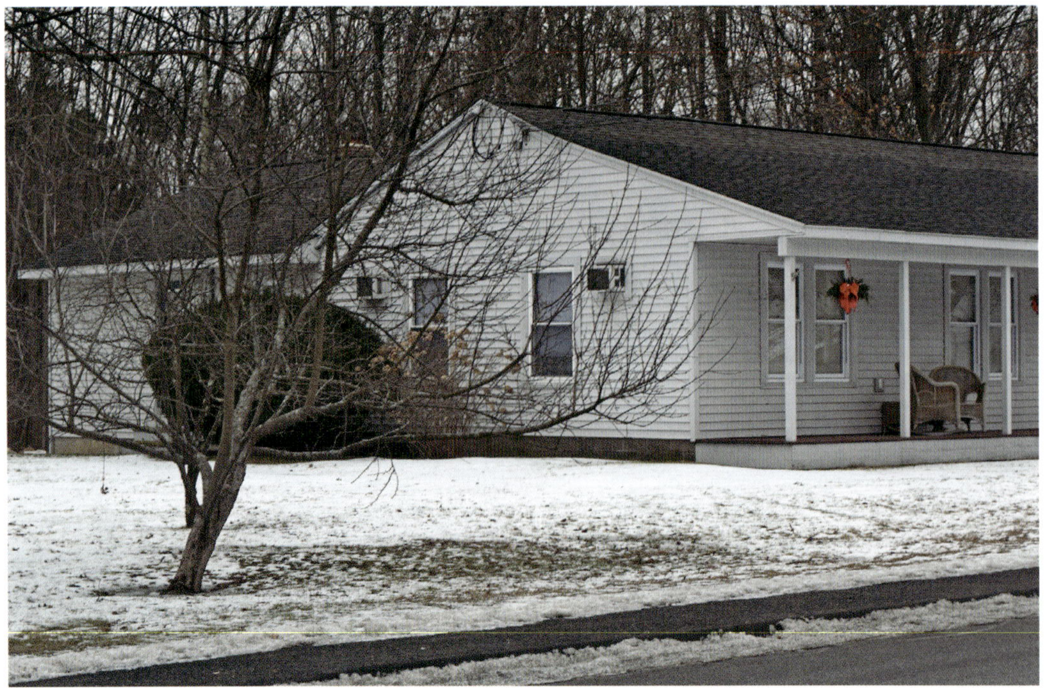

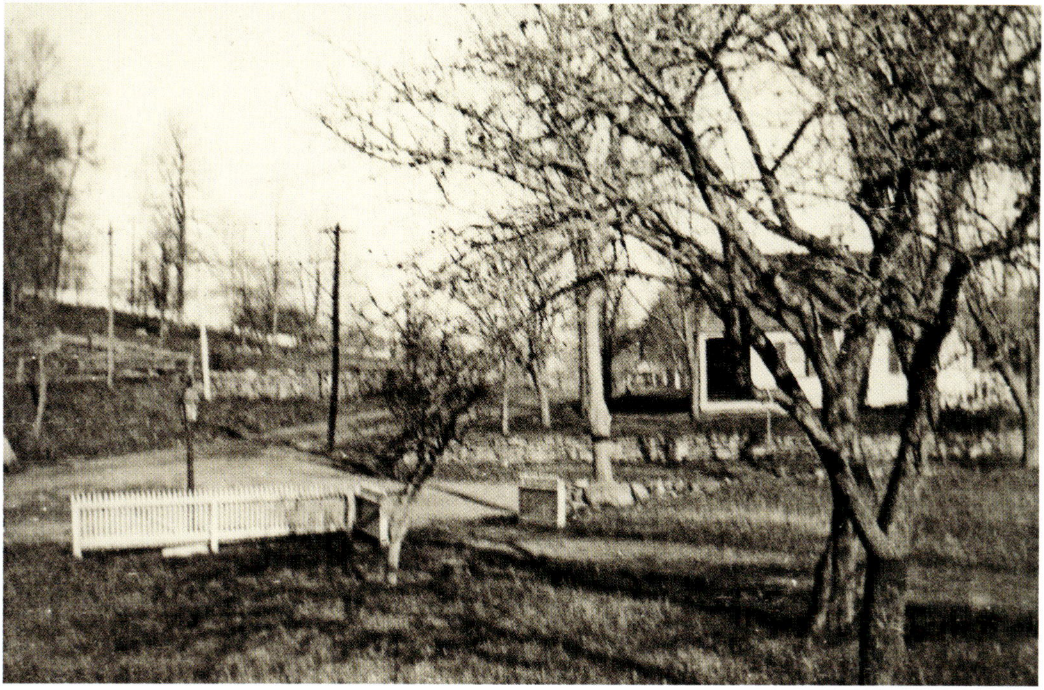

SHOP BECOMES PART OF HOME: In the early 1900s this house at the corner of Summer and South Streets included a nail shop from Seth Grout's home on Main Street across from the other end of Summer Street. Probably because in the early 1800s the Grouts housed area Baptists before they had a church building, it was called the "Gospel Shop." It eventually was moved and absorbed into the residential area of this house, still in use in the early 2000s.

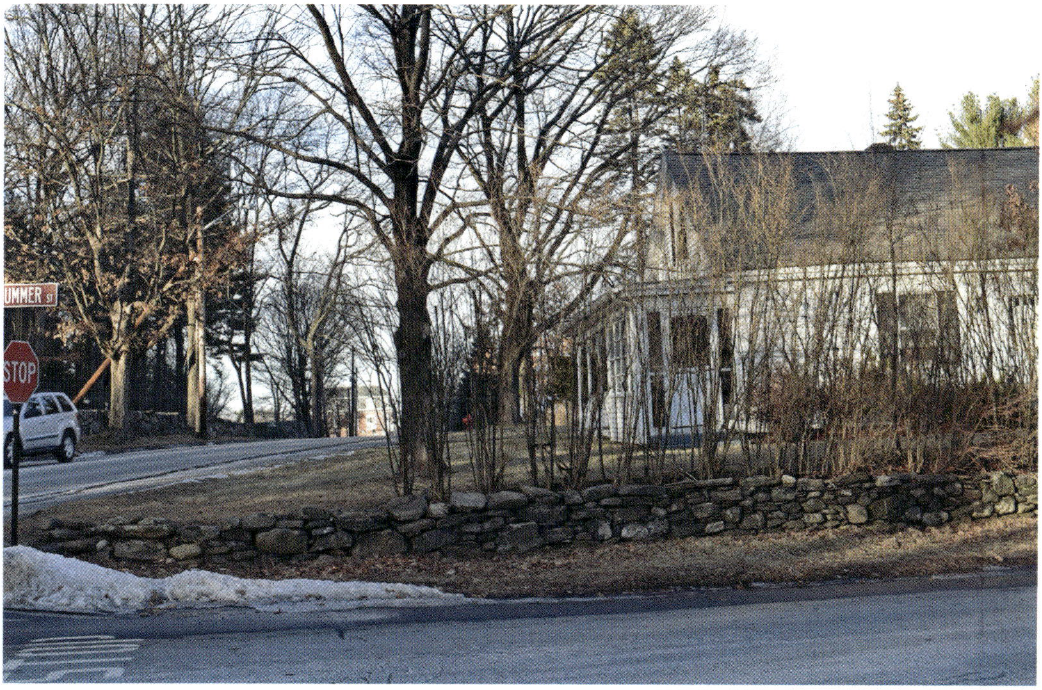

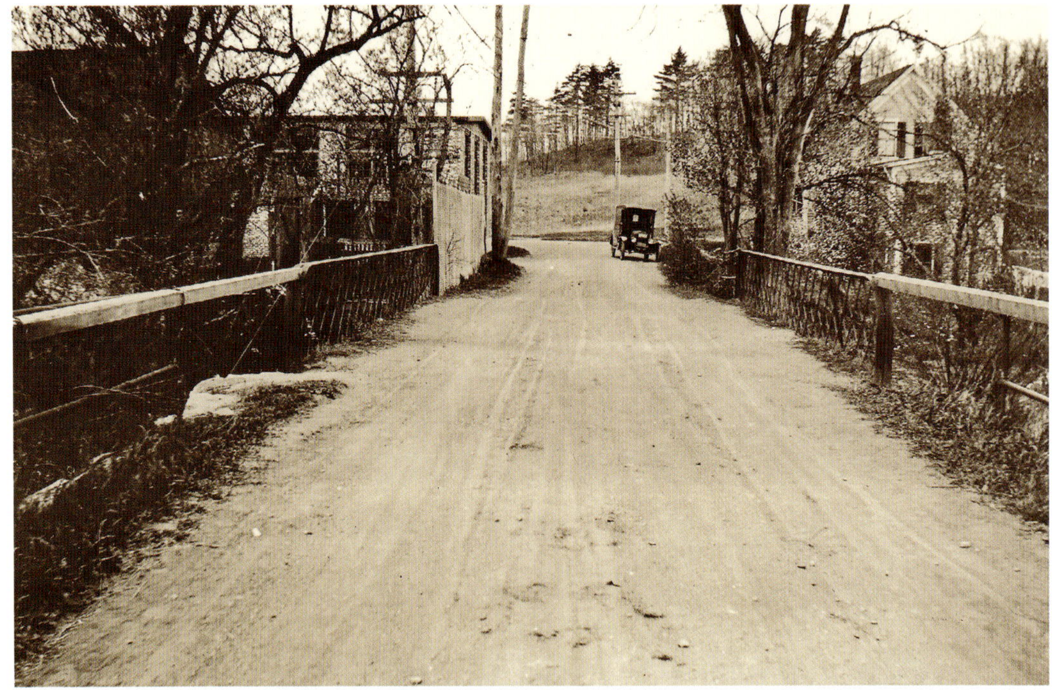

STREET BY THE RIVER: The Assabet River may be crossed in several places, one on River Street. In 1925 a prominent automobile of the time stands near a house later supplanted by a small parking lot for the business across the street. Its days as the last of Northborough's comb factories over, it had become the Arlington Shoddy Mills, but apparently no spinning or weaving – perhaps dyeing – was done there. More recently it has harbored other small manufacturing concerns.

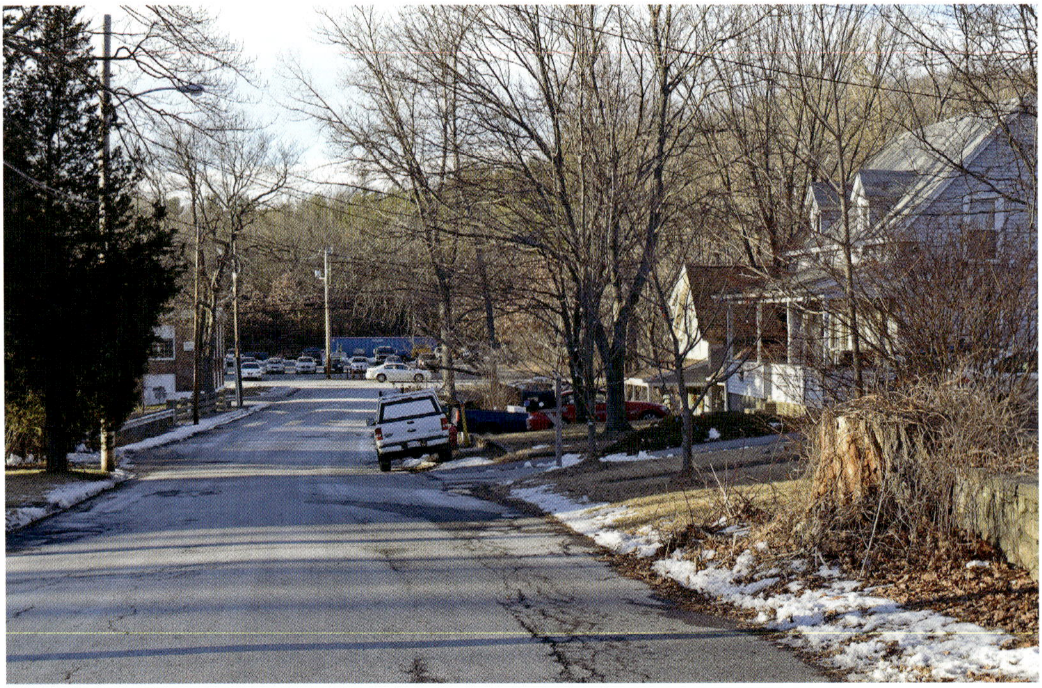

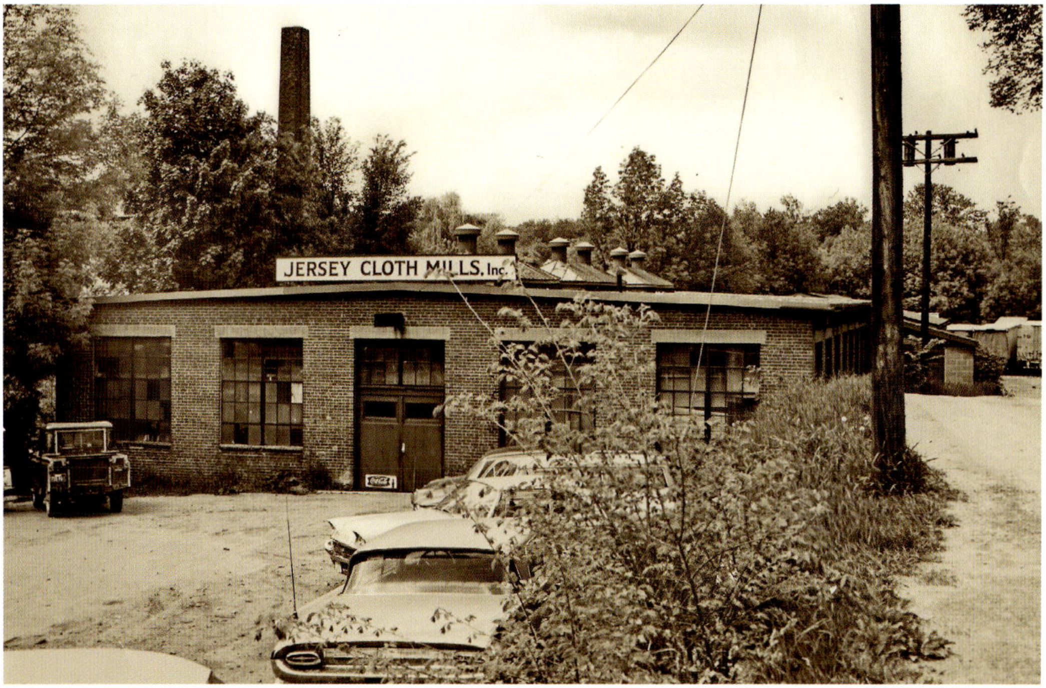

FABRIC-MAKING YIELDS TO CONSTRUCTION: Until April 6, 1970, when this building burned, cotton or woolen fabrics had been made in Northborough from its early days. The Jersey Cloth Mills, a remnant of this activity along the Assabet River, then employing twenty people, made knitted fabrics for hospitals and industrial outwear. The site, close to housing on Allen Court built for an earlier fabric mill, remained industrial.

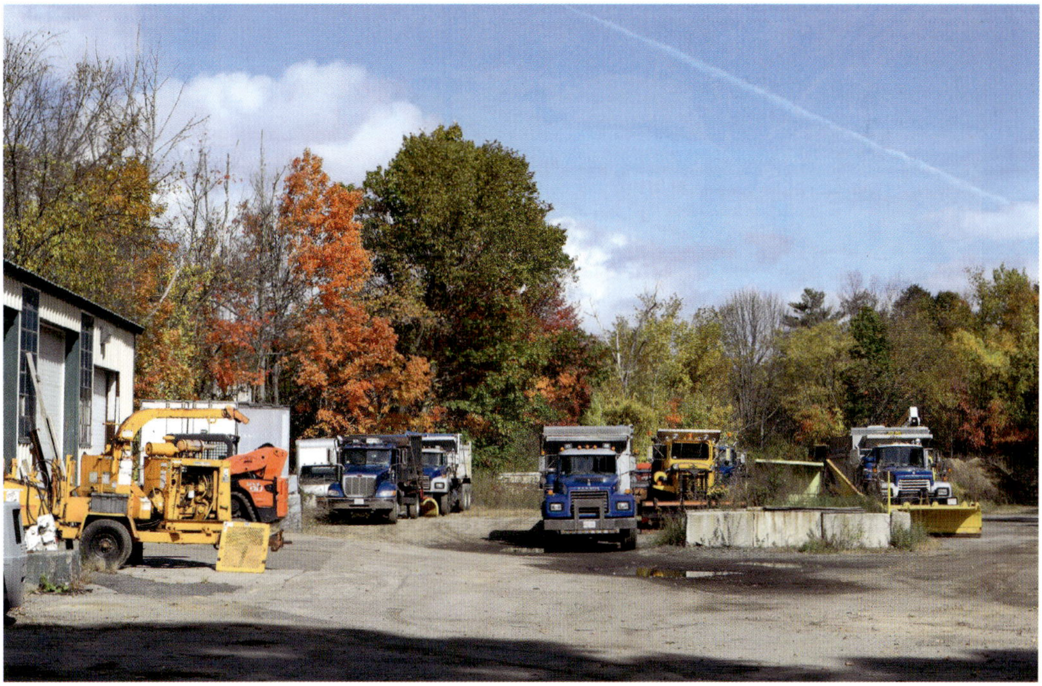

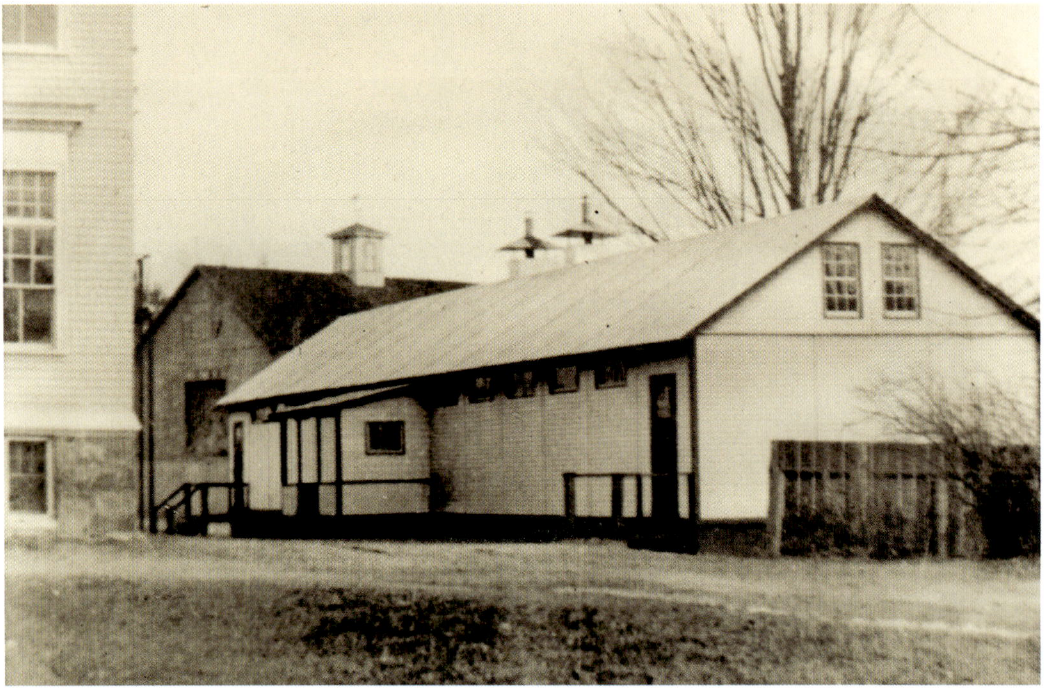

THEIR SCHOOL WAS PORTABLE: The gathering of more than fifty children from two grades into one of the four classrooms in the Hudson Street School in the 1920s presaged the necessity that as the local population increased something had to be done. The temporary response was a portable school which enabled adjoining grades to be separated. A new high school eventually also provided elementary space. Senior housing now occupies the space nearby.

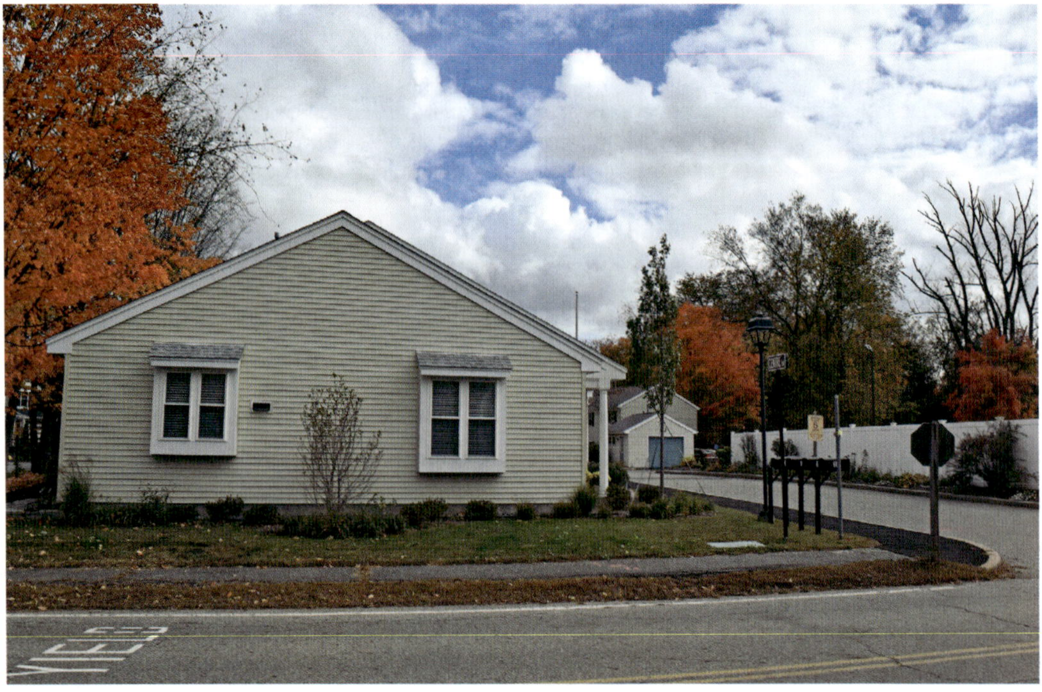

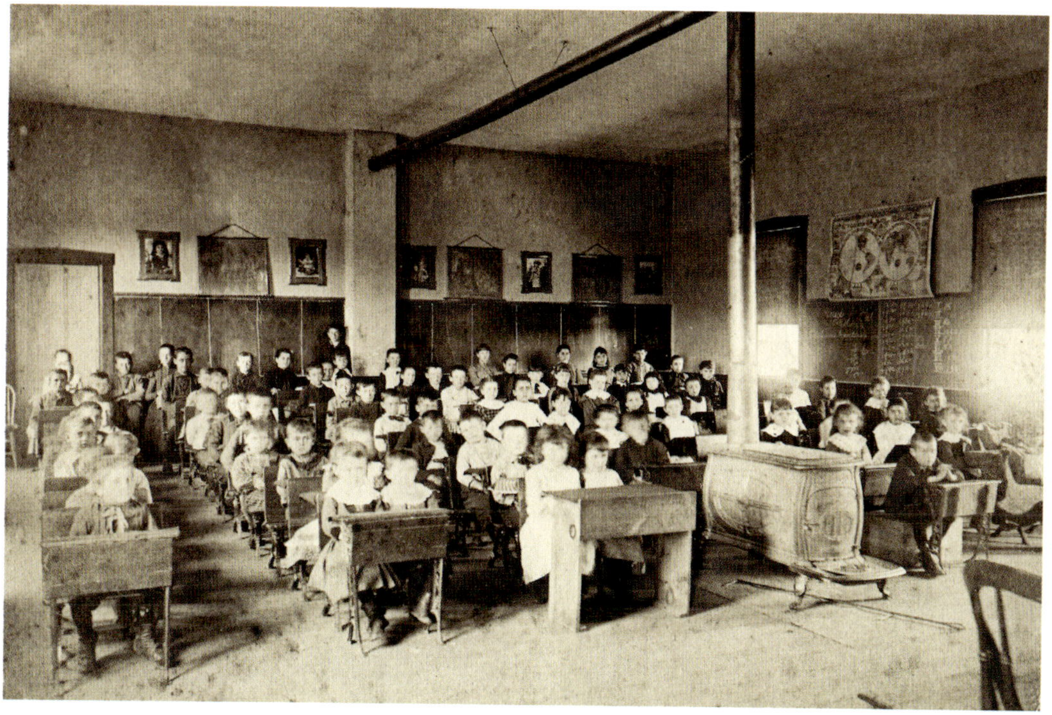

CREATIVE LITTLE MINDS: This overcrowded schoolroom seats two small children to a desk with ages ranging from six to teens. This must have been a trying experience for child and teacher alike. The central stove kept some warm and toasty while others in the corners were chilled. By 1958 conditions had improved. Mrs. Betty Schleyer's first grade class at Zeh School was spacious for age appropriate learning.

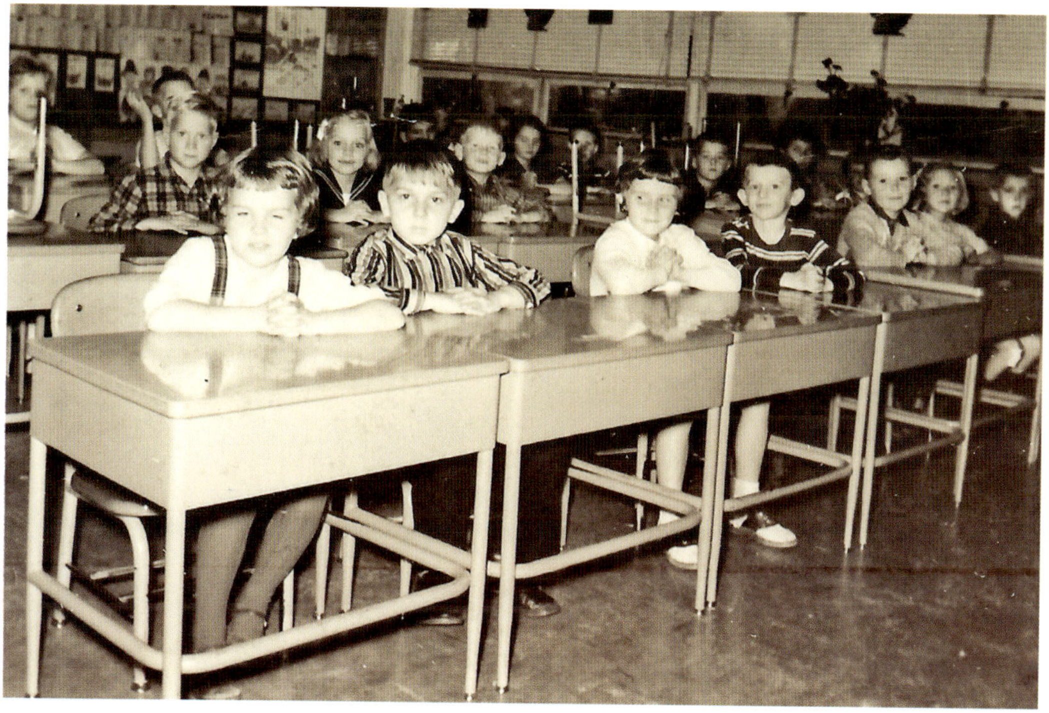

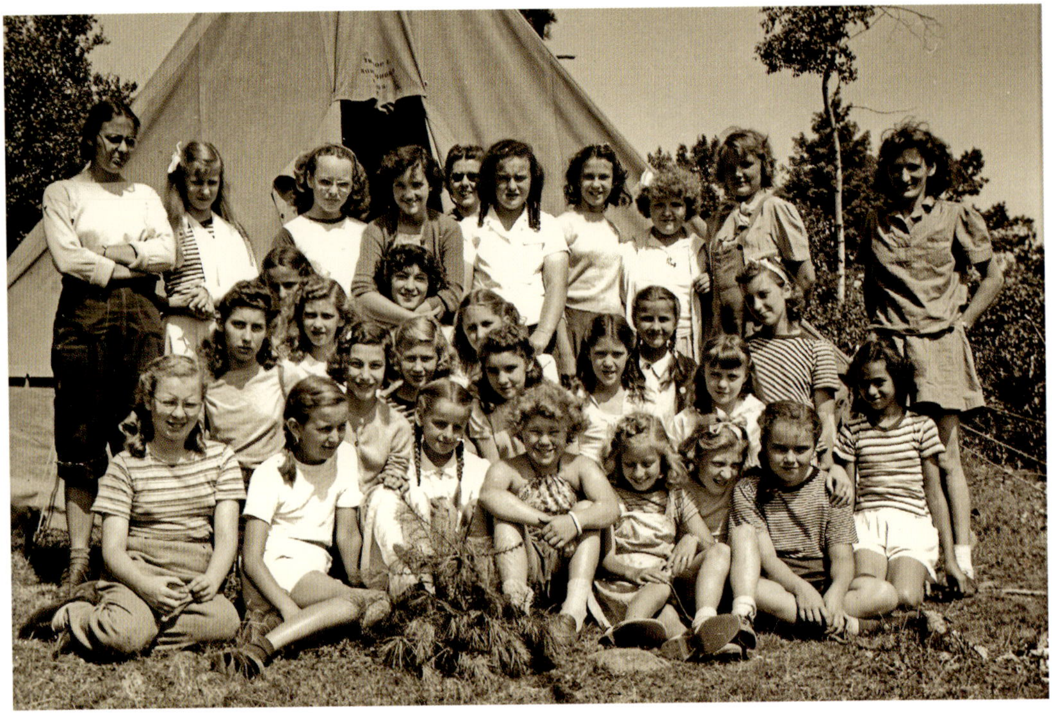

GIRL SCOUTING: In 1945, the Northborough Girl Scouts sponsored a day camp on Mt. Assabet that was enjoyed by many Northborough girls. Co-leader Pat Proctor MacFarland is on the left. The Girl Scouts celebrated their 100th anniversary in 2012 and Meredith Rubin captured Northborough's contribution for posterity.

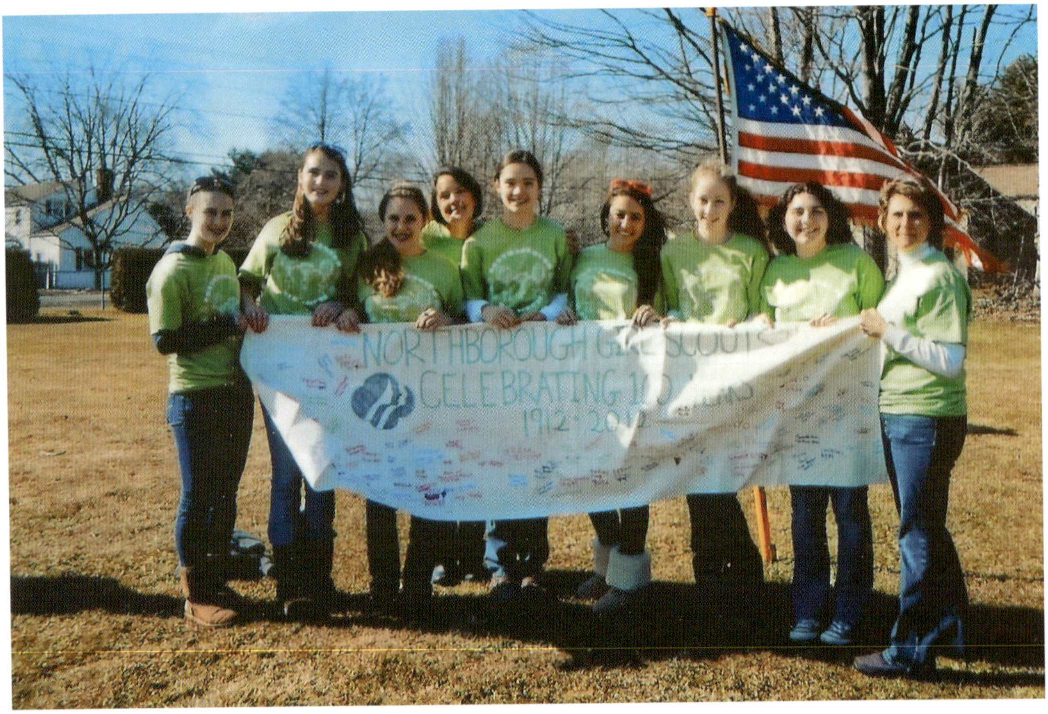

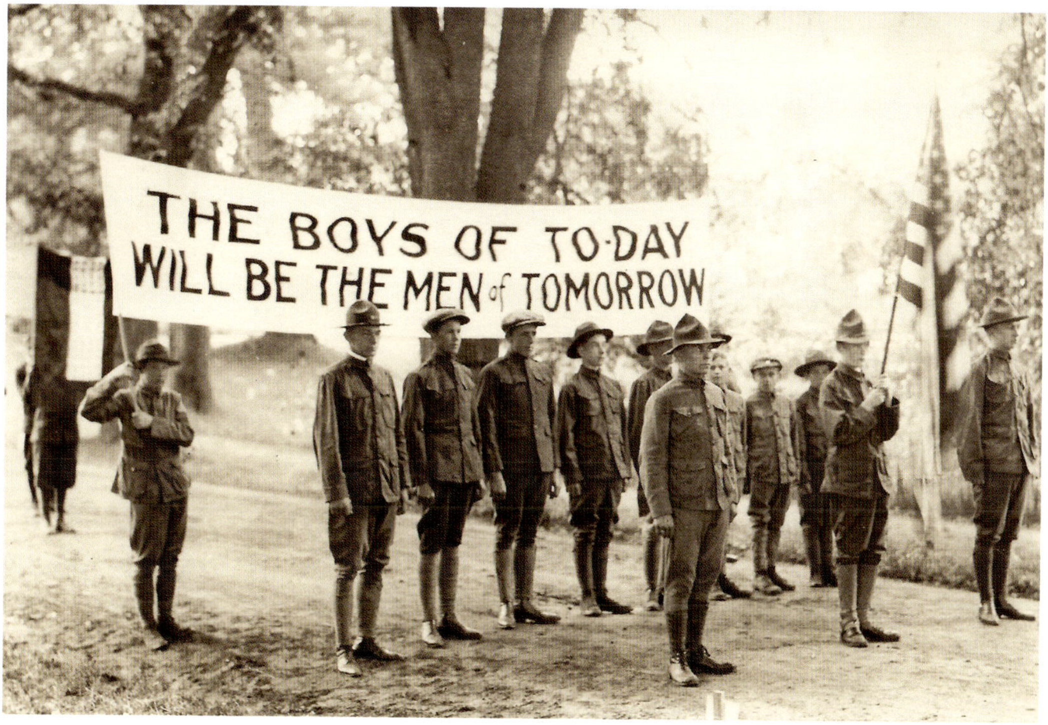

BOY SCOUTING: Troop 1 marched in the town's 150th anniversary parade in 1916. During the four day celebration they ran errands, helped with crowd control and cleaned up after the festivities. Perhaps some of today's young scouts from Troop 101 will participate in our town's 250th anniversary in 2016.

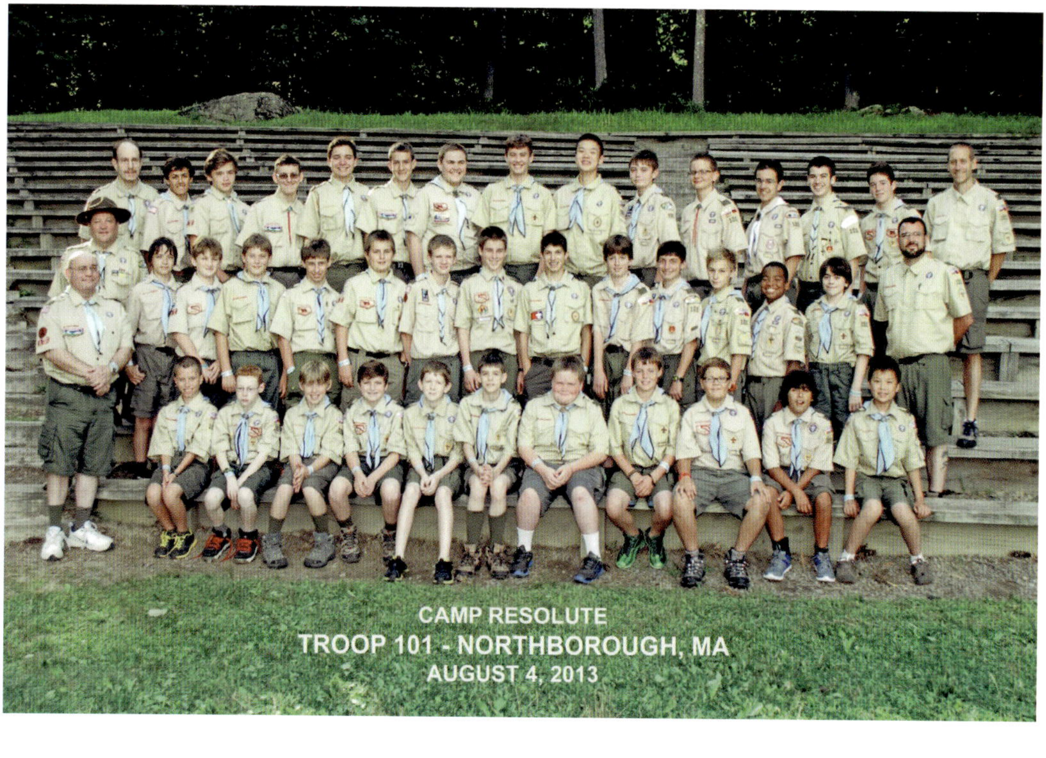

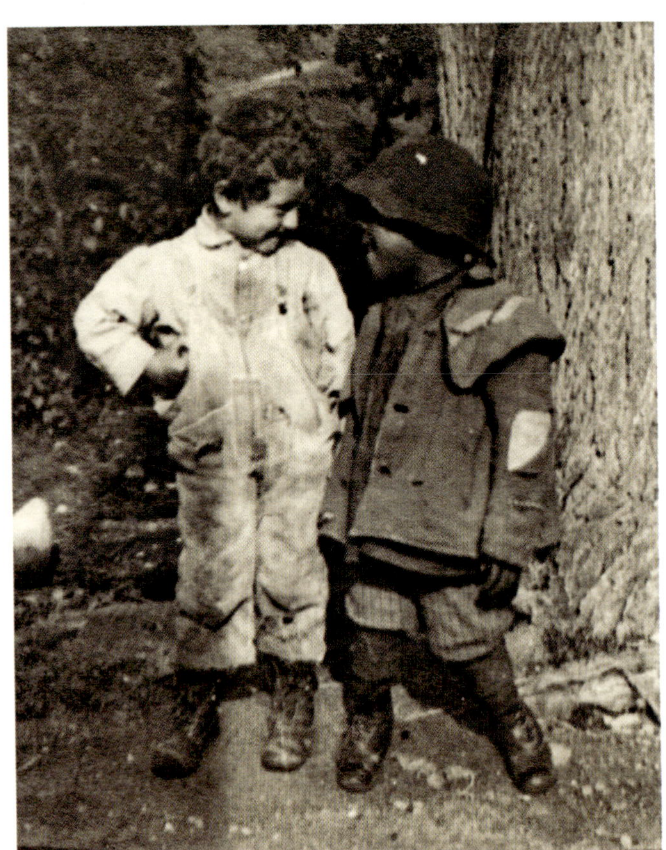

A YOUNG PHOTOGRAPHER: In 1910 Northborough had 1,713 white residents, including Tony Dabardo, probably Italian, and nine blacks, among them Tommy Cobb. Clarence Nelson, seen with his bicycle in 1908 at the age of thirteen, captured these friends. Nelson earned a Silver Star and Purple Heart in World War I. After his wife died, Nelson, a lover of birds and other animals, living in a cottage he fashioned close to a lake, sought to emulate the life of Henry David Thoreau.

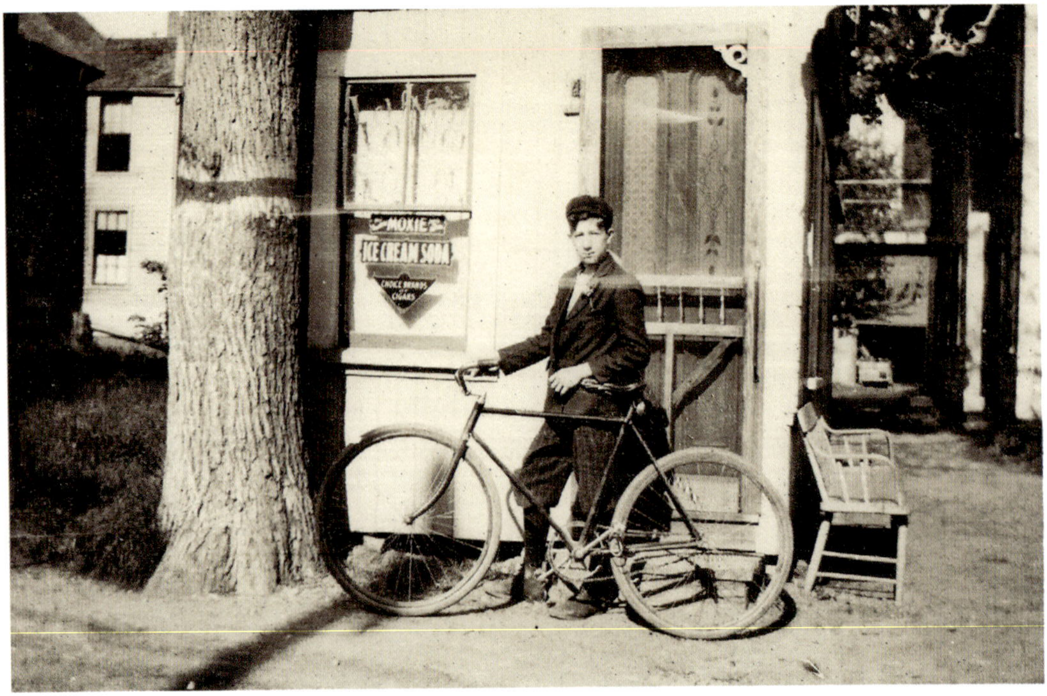

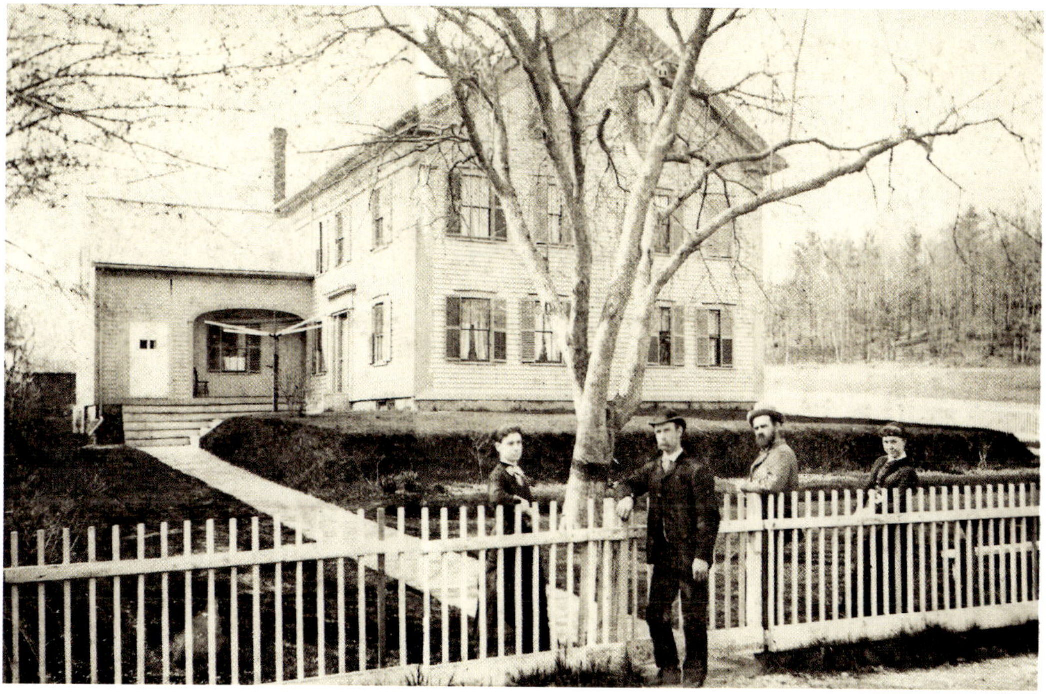

ONE FAMILY, FOUR FAMILIES: The Harringtons pose near their picket fence on 59 Hudson Street in the later nineteenth century. Francis, the gentleman at the gate, had kept a journal through such events as the Battle of the Crater at Petersburg in the Civil War, and would become Northborough's town clerk in the early years of the twentieth century. After much deterioration of the Harrington's former home, these four affordable homes replaced it.

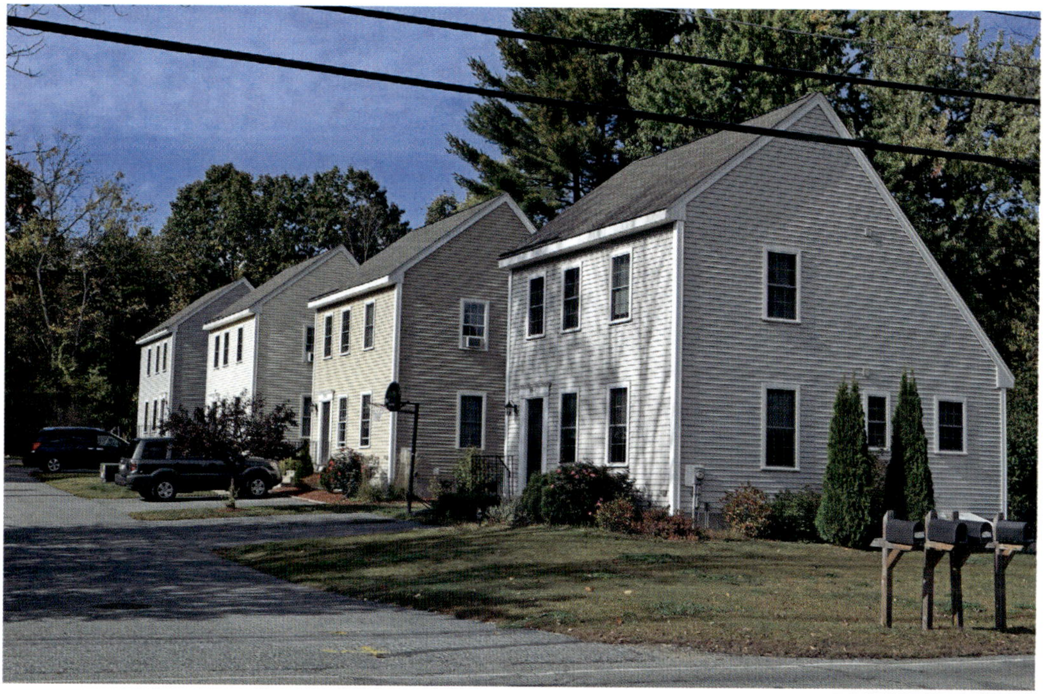

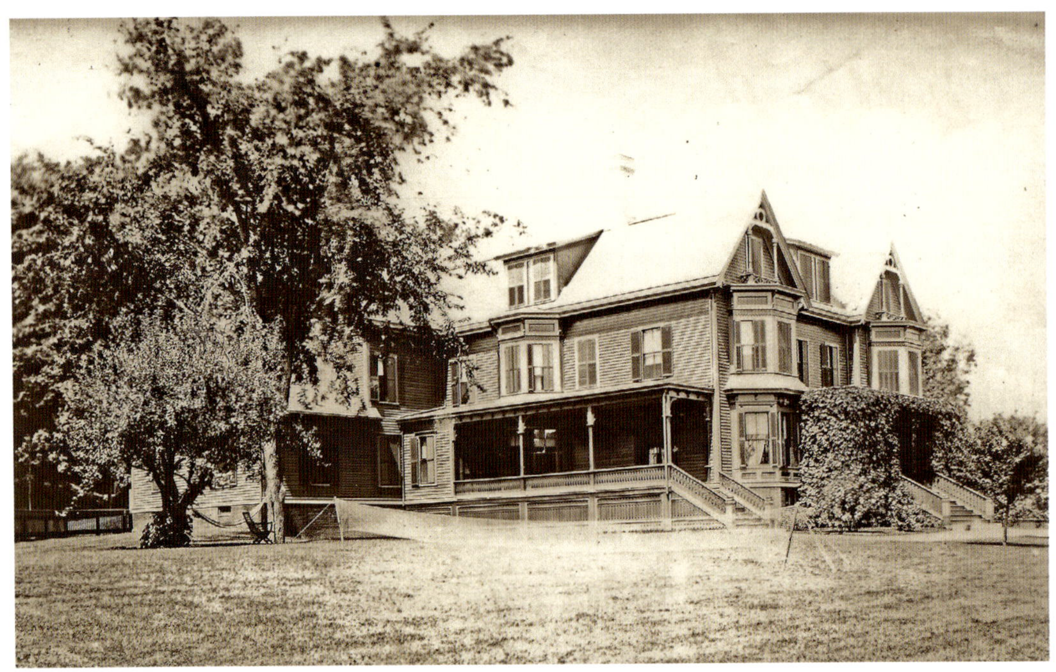

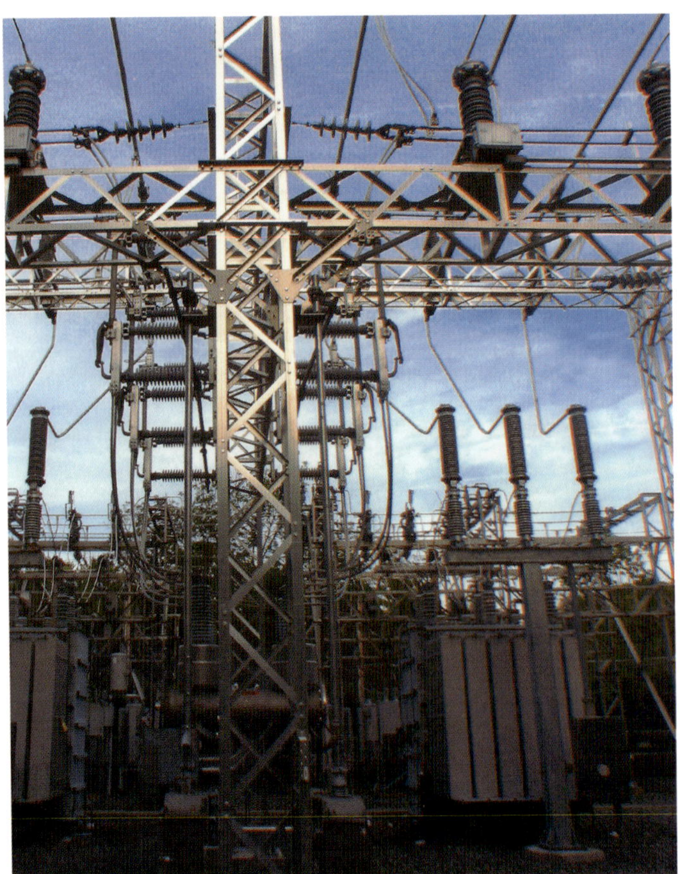

Two scenes in woodside: This fine nineteenth-century house of David Wood reminds us of a time when an entrepreneur, as well as his work force, usually chose to live near his workplace. It stood across the street from his Woodside fabric mill until the house burned in the 1930s. The electric substation that replaced it has been strikingly photographed by Geoff Wilson. Many people still live nearby, however, in the building that used to be the mill.

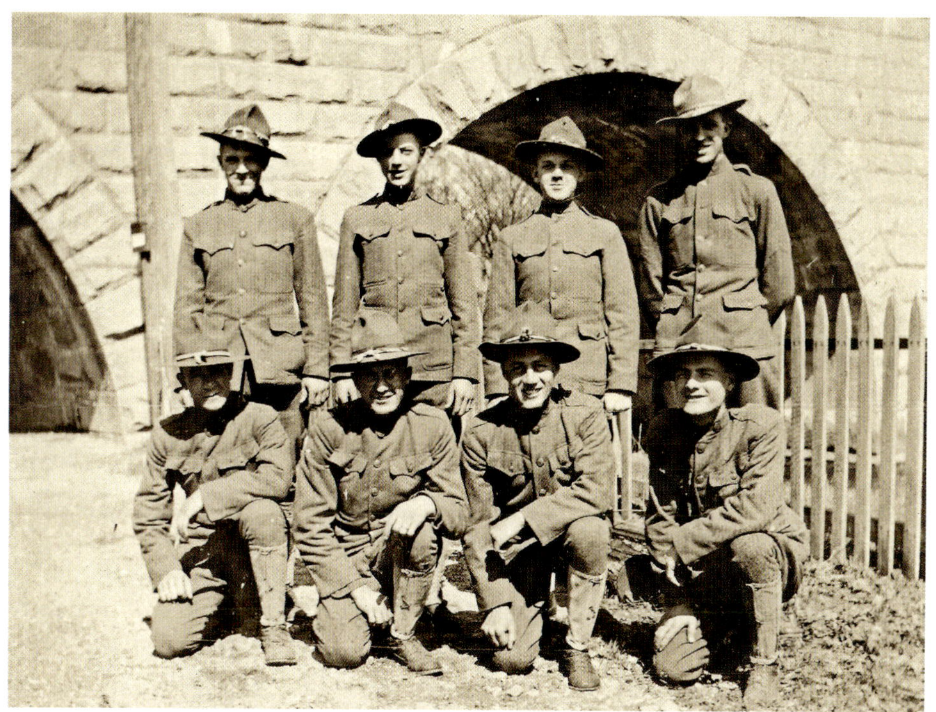

GUARDING A TREASURE: Twenty days after the United States entered World War I, one sergeant and seven privates were guarding this seven-arch bridge, built in the 1890s, as a crucial link of eastward water supply from the Wachusett Reservoir across the Assabet River. Some years later persistent leakage from the first arch onto Hudson Street made it necessary to pipe the water beneath the river. More recently the nonfunctional bridge persists as one of the most photographed structures in town.

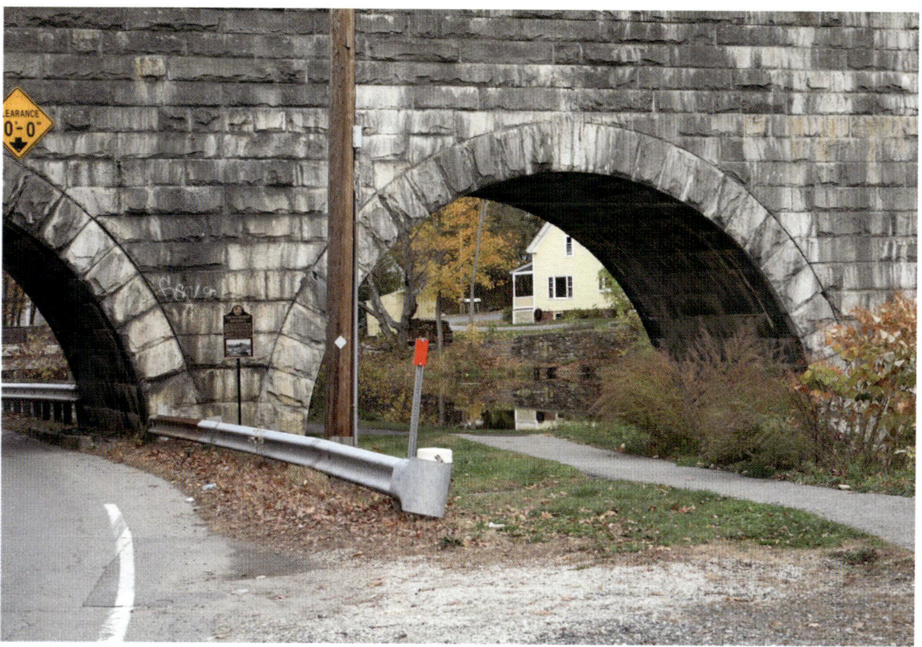

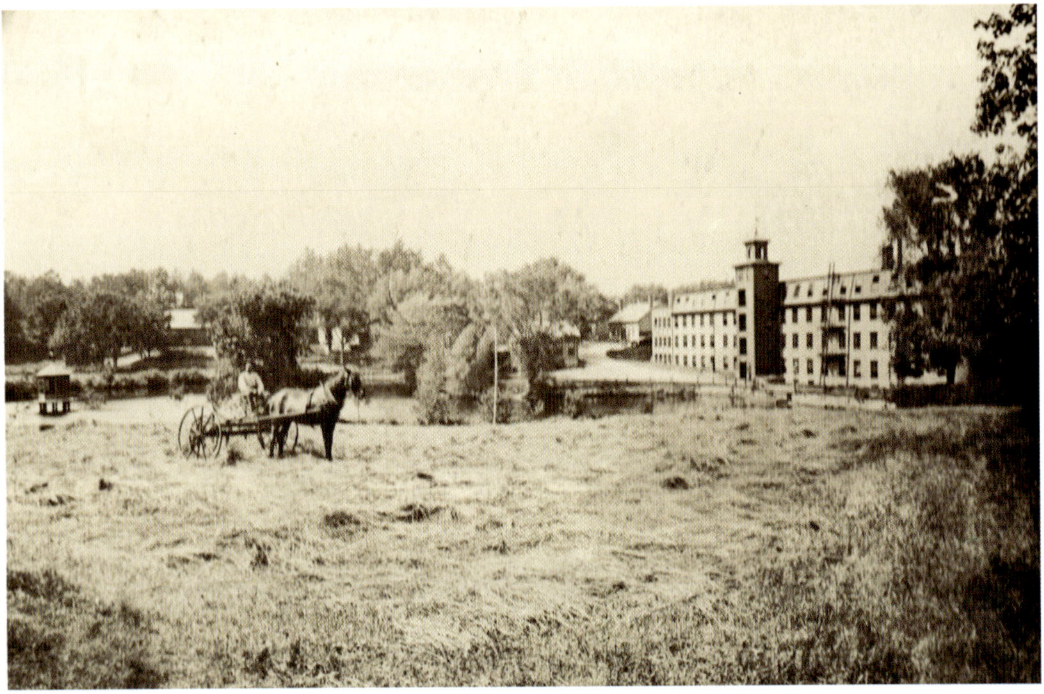

THE HEART OF CHAPINVILLE: In the late nineteenth and early twentieth centuries the largest employer in Northborough, the Chapin fabric mill, its owner's name applied to this industrial section of town, ran on power supplied by water funneled from the Assabet River beyond the hay field. The road immediately in front of the mill remains as Chapin Court. Only a large cellar hole and remains of its foundation persist to the right of the road.

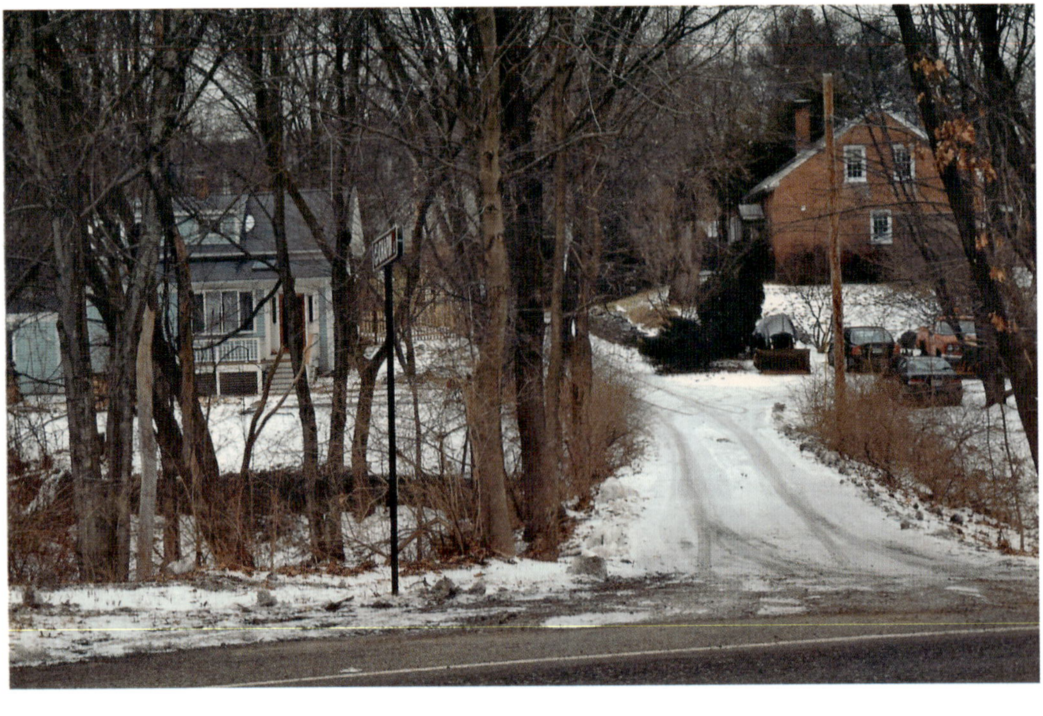

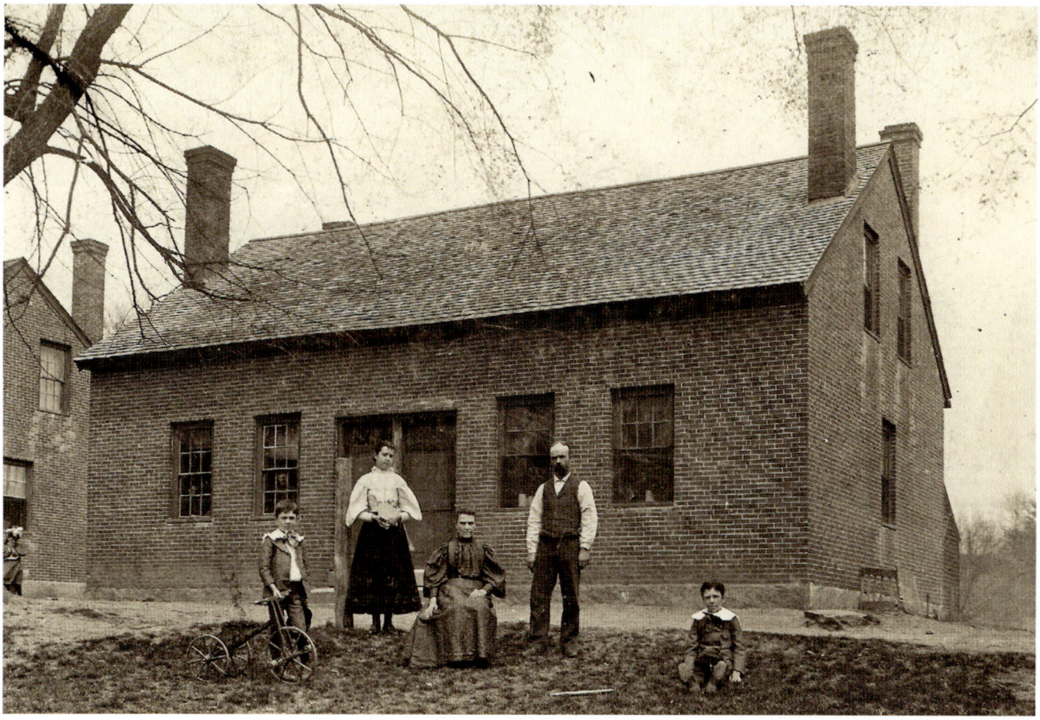

THEY REMAIN AND SERVE: The Collard family gathers outside their house around 1916. It and two identical houses on Chapin Court were constructed by the developers of a fabric mill, eventually called the Chapin Mill, which employed hundreds of Northborough (or "Chapinville") people from the 1830s until well into the twentieth century. Over the generations these distinctive houses have persisted as residences with only one remaining as a duplex.

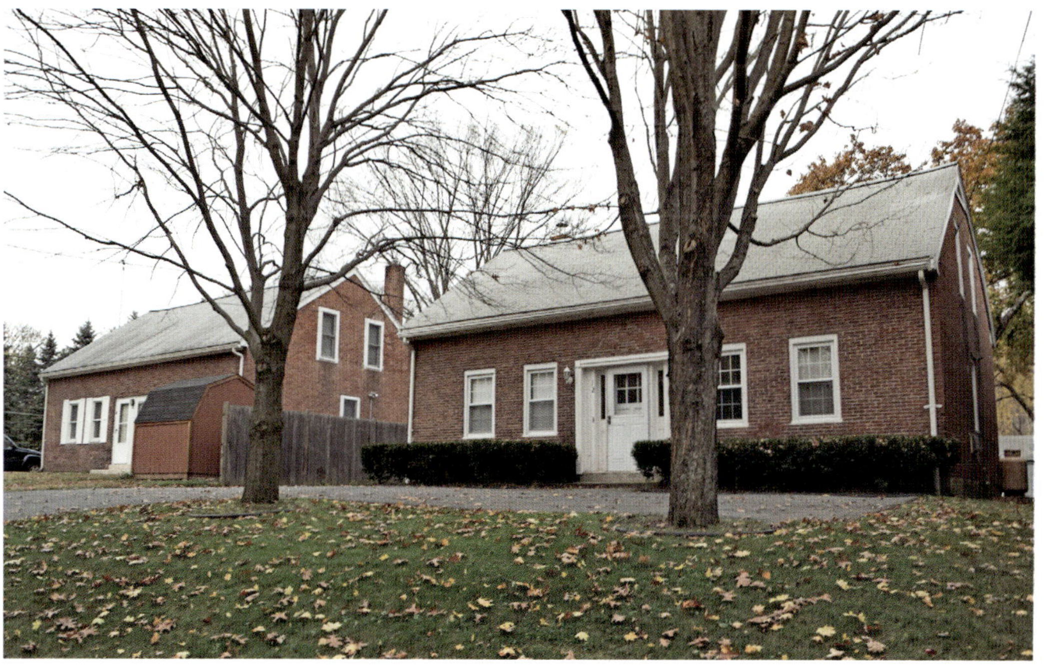

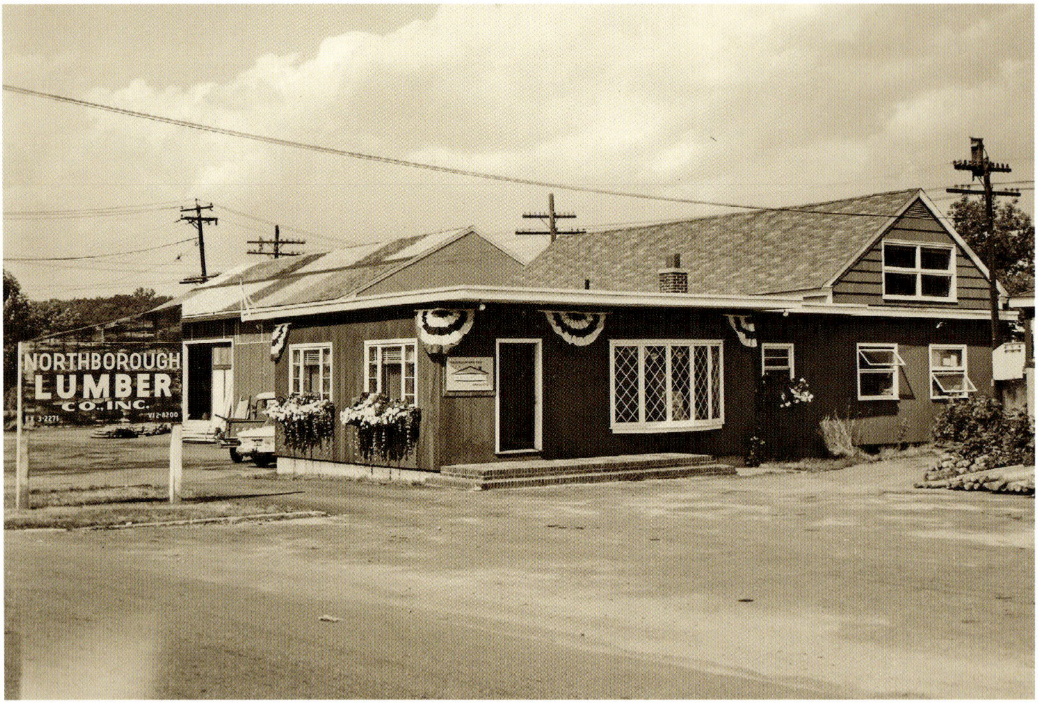

FROM LOGS TO DOGS: Through most of the twentieth century a lumberyard was operated from this building at one corner of Blake and Pierce Streets. The roof exemplified various types of materials. The advent of large home improvement stores ended Northborough Lumber and other similar businesses. More recently dog owners could have their pets kept, groomed, or trained on part of this complex.

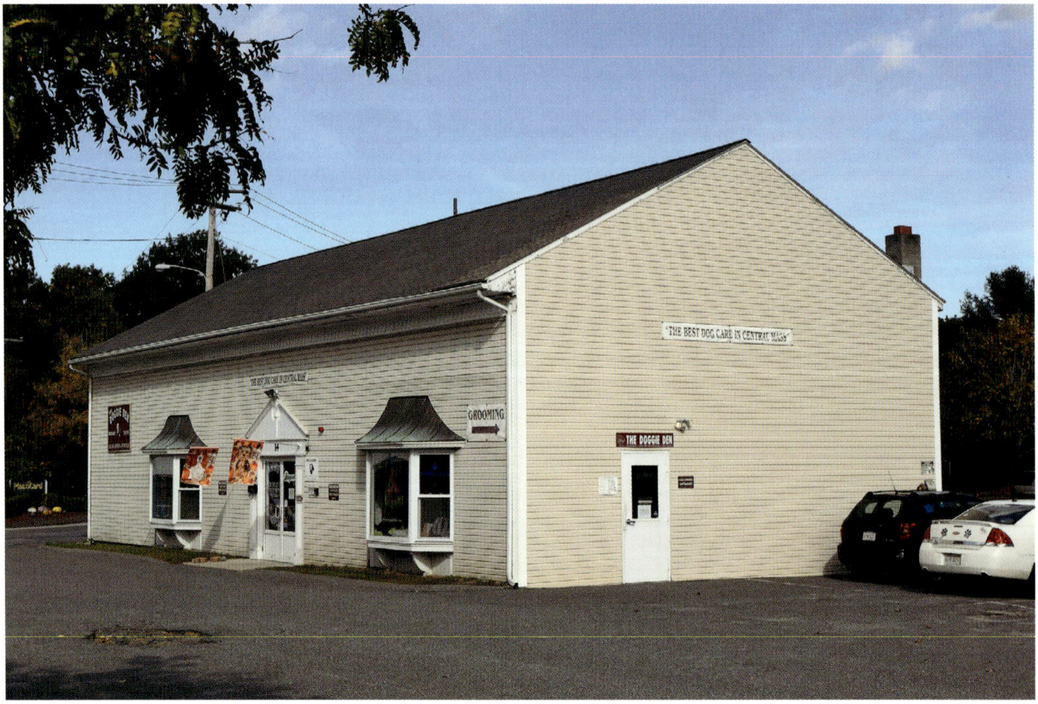

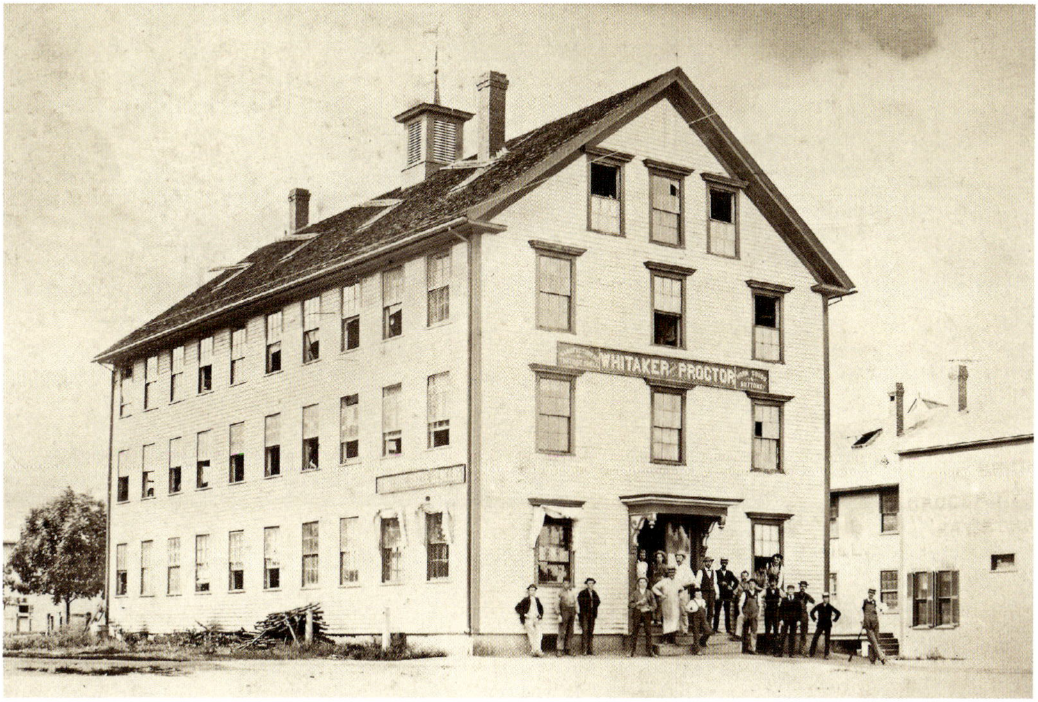

FROM BUTTONS TO BOWLING: Contrary to appearances, these photographs depict the same building on 11 Blake Street. The Whitaker and Proctor button factory of the end of the nineteenth century, its work force on deck (*c.* 1885) becomes, after a devastating 1948 fire and a determined restoration, a popular bowling establishment. The main clue is the row of ten windows on the second floor.

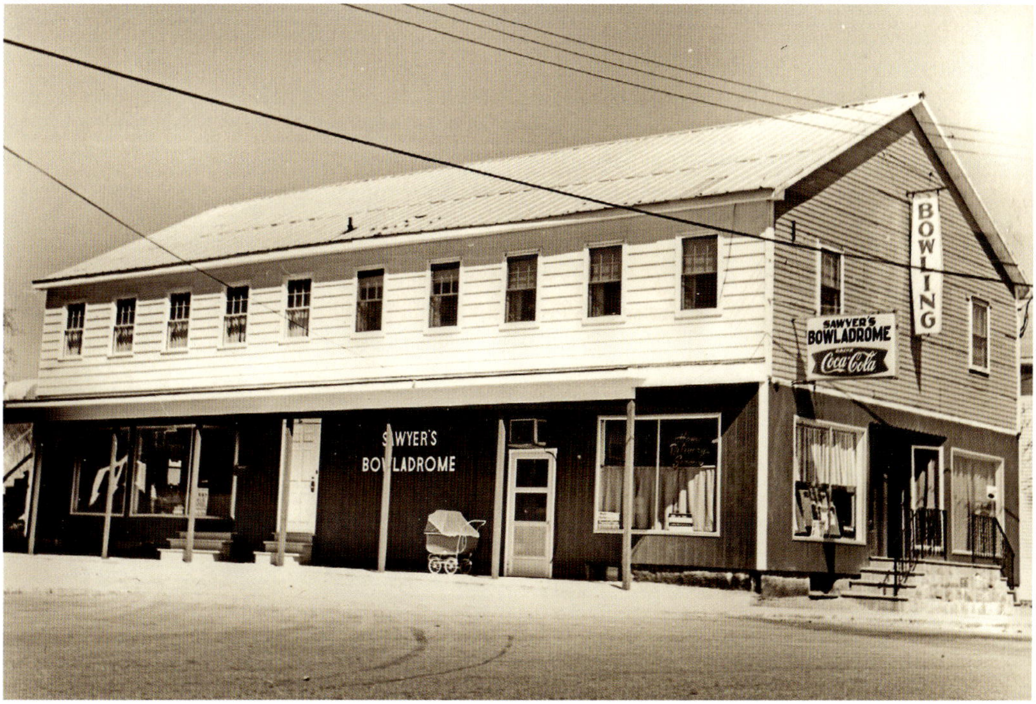

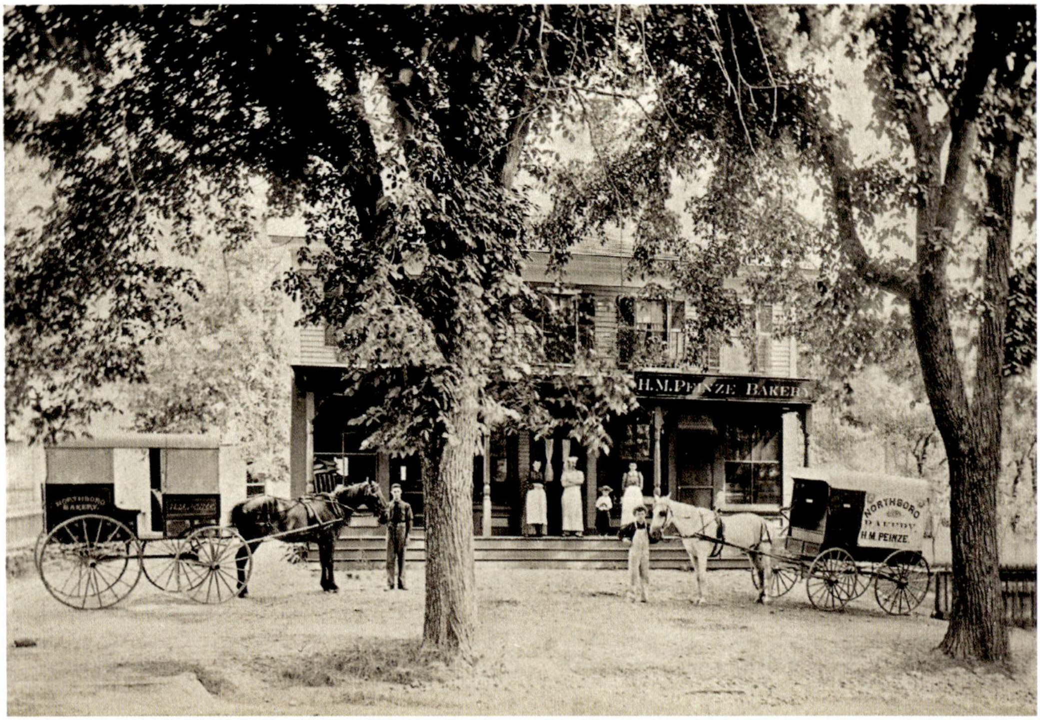

A LONG-LASTING COMMERCIAL BUILDING: All humans and animals posed for this picture of Peinze's Bakery on 19 Blake Street in the late 1800s. The building remains in use, but all liveliness seems to have departed.

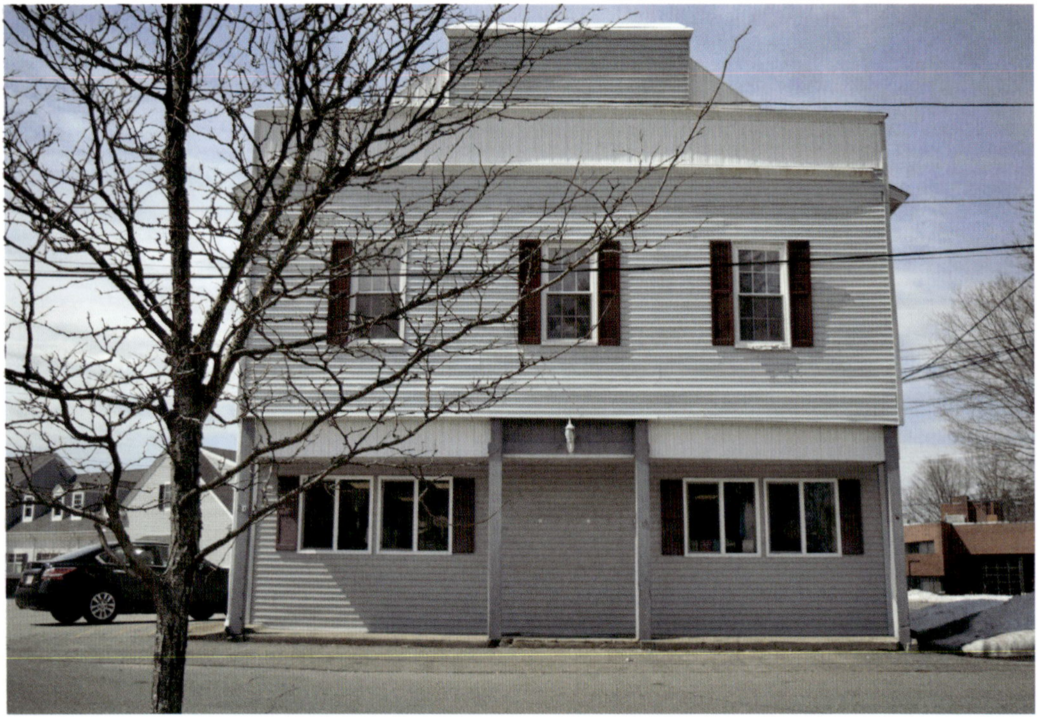

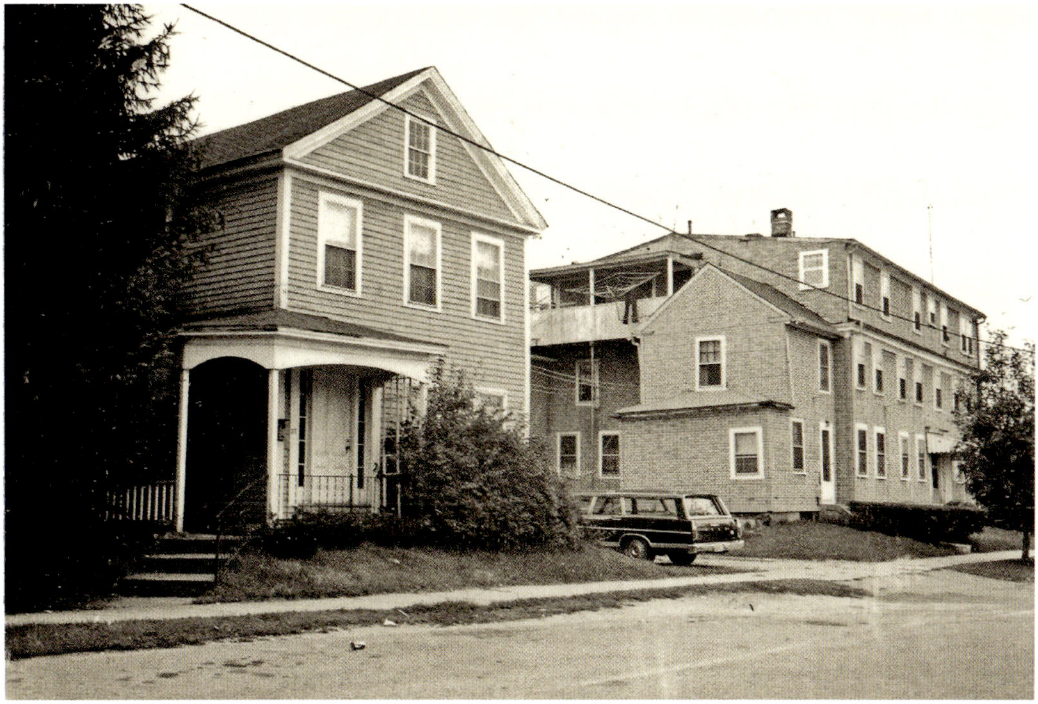

A COLONIAL TAVERN VANISHES: In the 1860s Northborough moved the centrally located Munroe Tavern (on the far right) from its place at the town center to one corner of Blake and Pierce Streets to make space for a new town hall. A stopping place once familiar to Revolutionary War soldiers became a tenement. Worn down over the decades, it was removed for a twenty-first century apartment building.

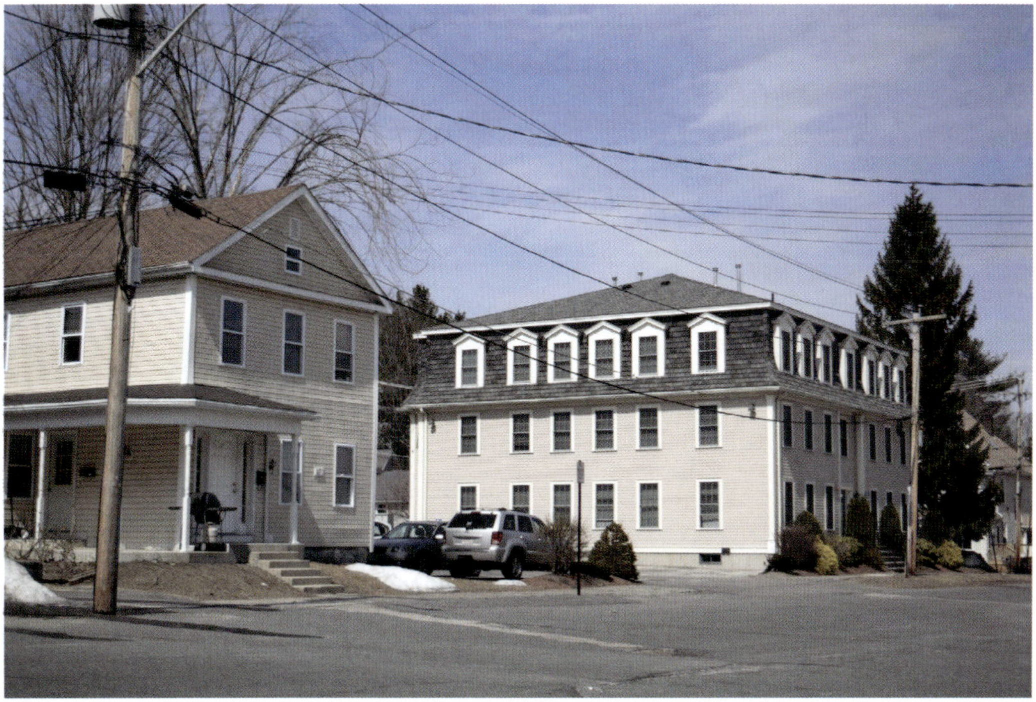

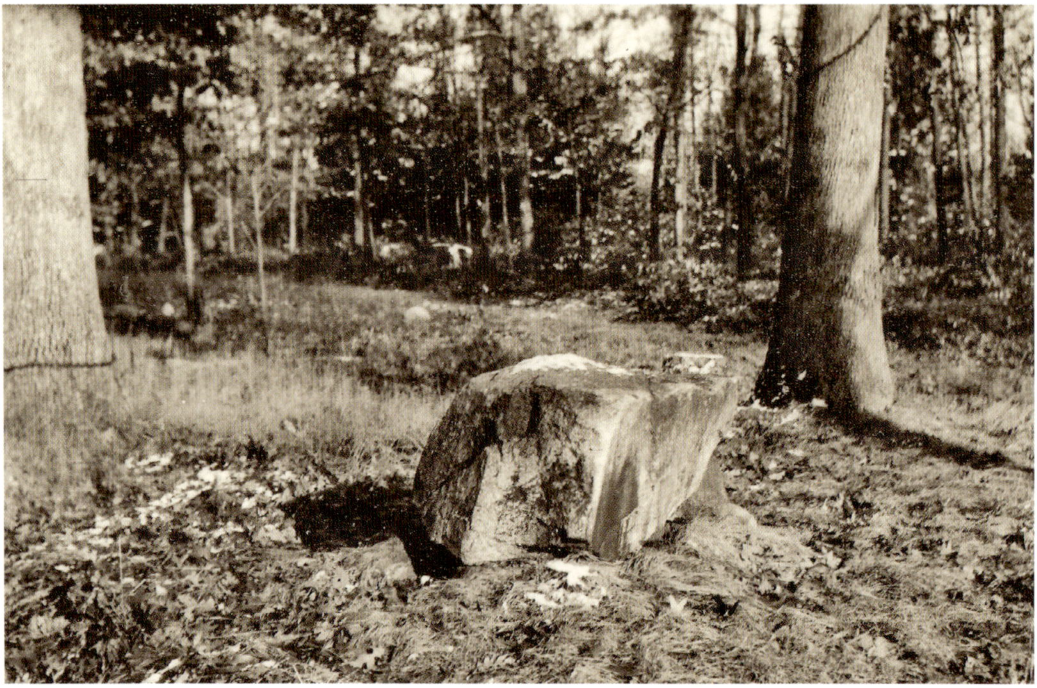

STONES REMAIN, TREES GROW: These gravestones of the Wheeler family in Northborough's first cemetery on Brigham Street, far from the Westborough churchyard, were considered illegal. After burying people here during the first half of the eighteenth century, Northborough, free from Westborough after 1766, made a cemetery behind its First Church. The stone pictured above was an aid to mounting and dismounting a horse.

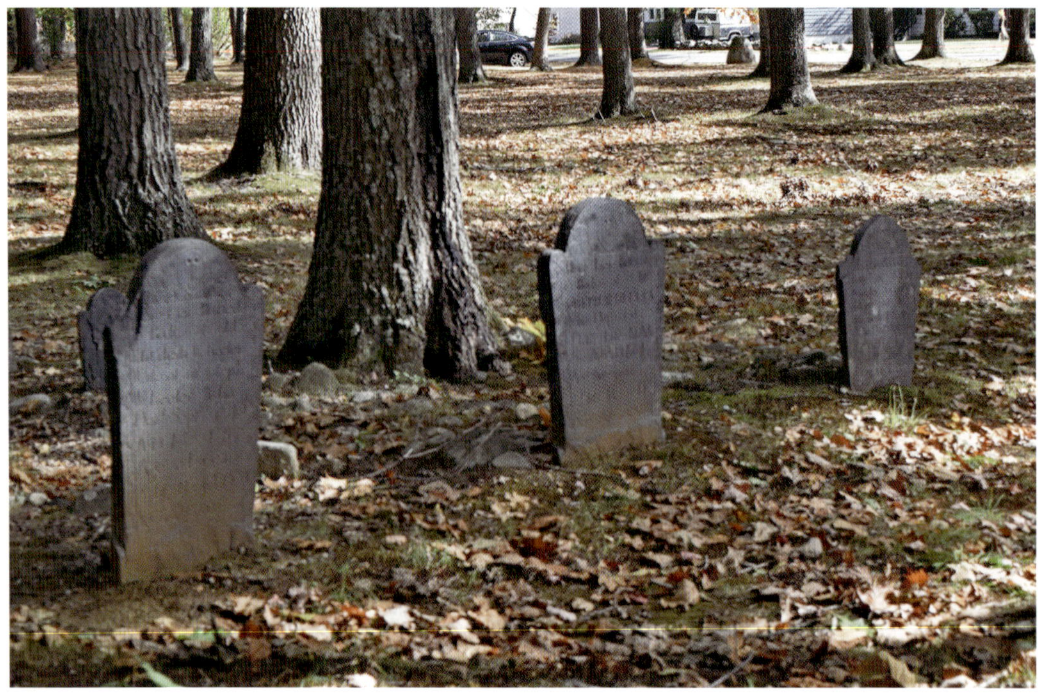

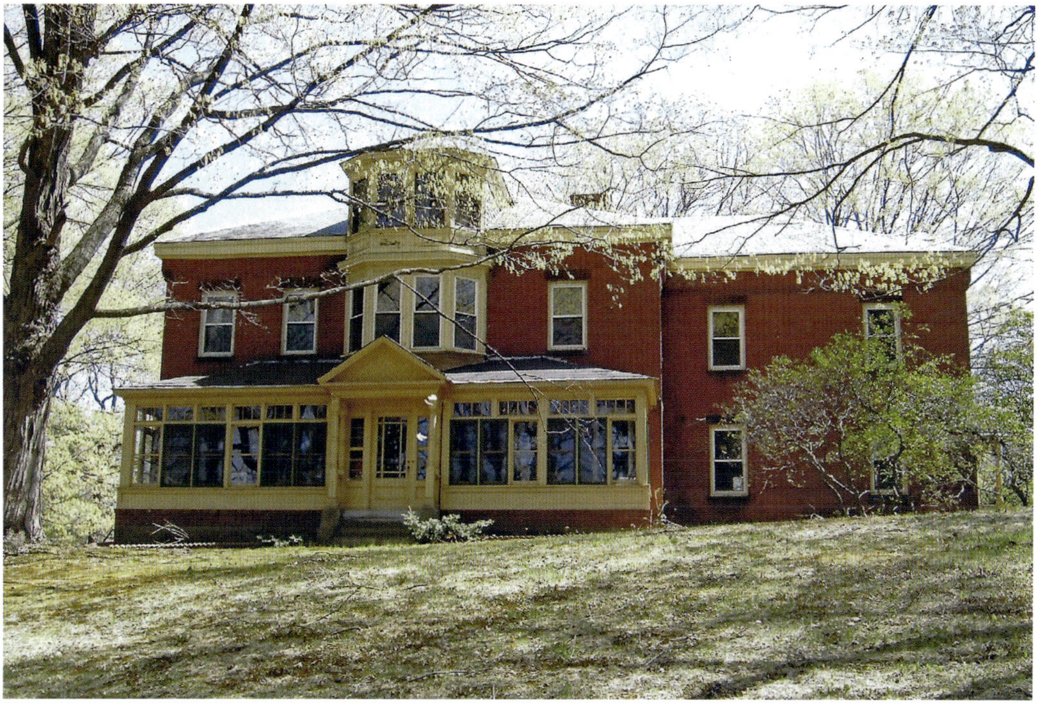

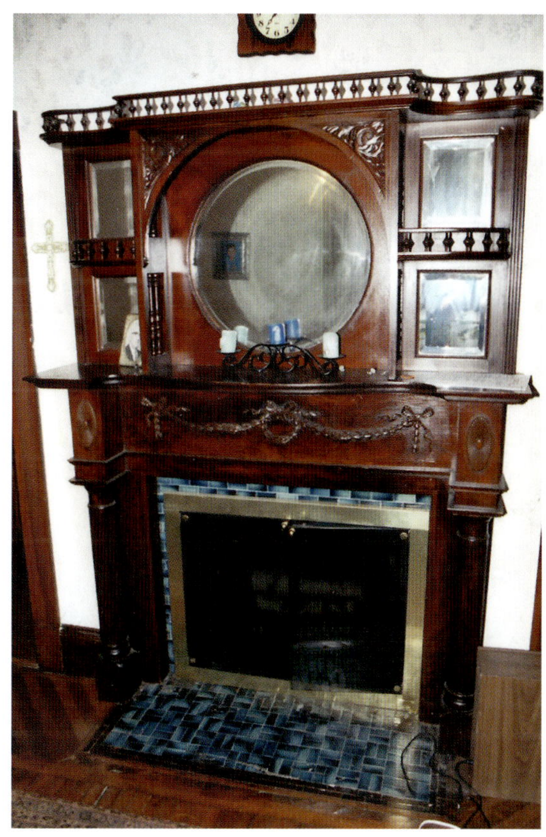

A MANSION GOES: This imposing brick mansion was built in 1870 by Charles H. Winn for his new wife, Maria E. Hunt. The interior showcased heavy oak paneled doors, hand-carved fireplaces, parquet floors, built-in cabinets and an apartment on one side for boarders. It was razed in 2006 and replaced by several duplexes and a memorial plaque at the site.

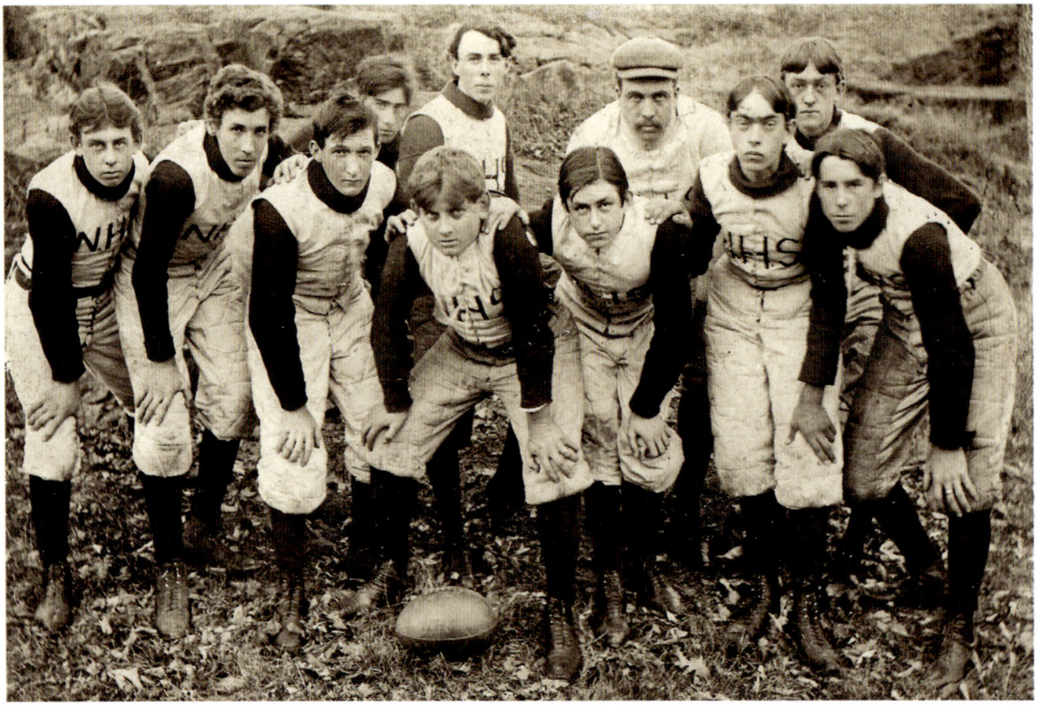

PUT ON YOUR GAME FACE: These Northborough High football warriors, a year or two before the end of the nineteenth century, are few in number, but they look rugged and determined. Equipment and uniforms changed considerably by the time their counterparts from the much larger Algonquin Regional High School squad of 2003 played Holy Name High School.

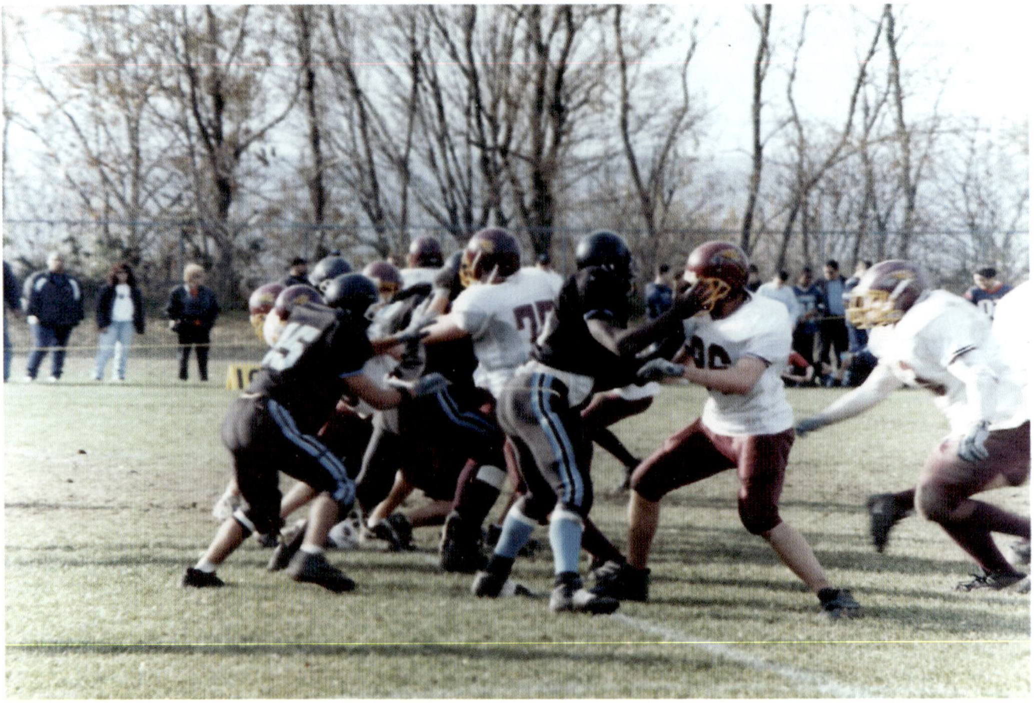

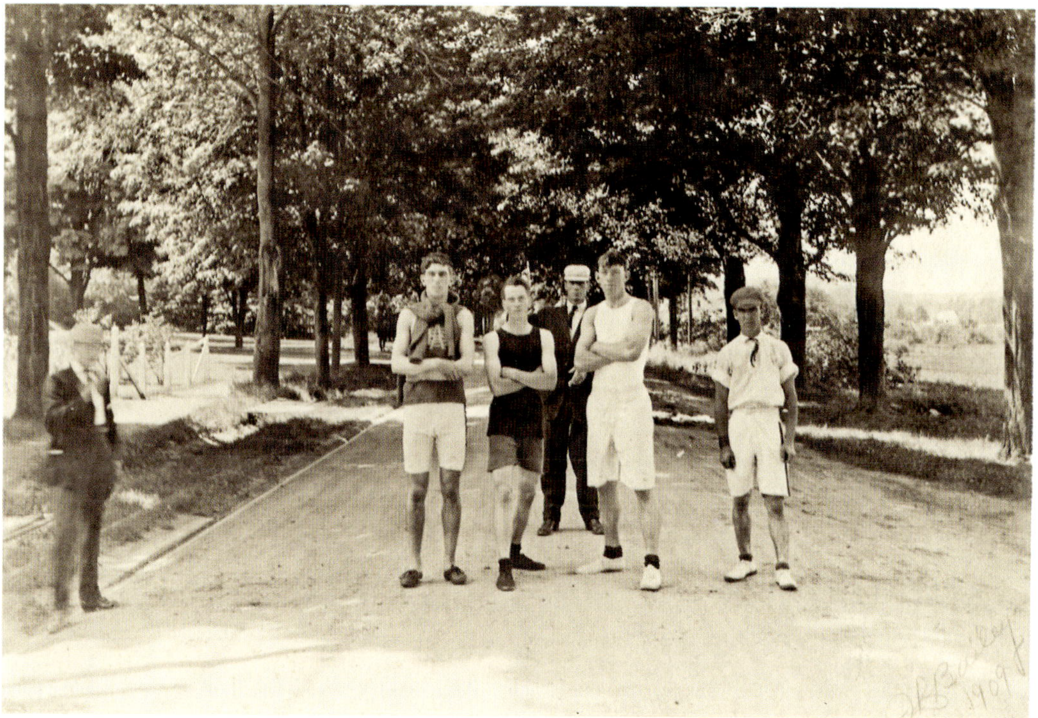

RUNNERS IN TWO CELEBRATIONS: The four runners photographed for a race on July 4, 1909 were all young males. At Applefest on September 20, 2014, the runners were old and young, male and female. On that date more people were participating in this five-kilometer race than watching it.

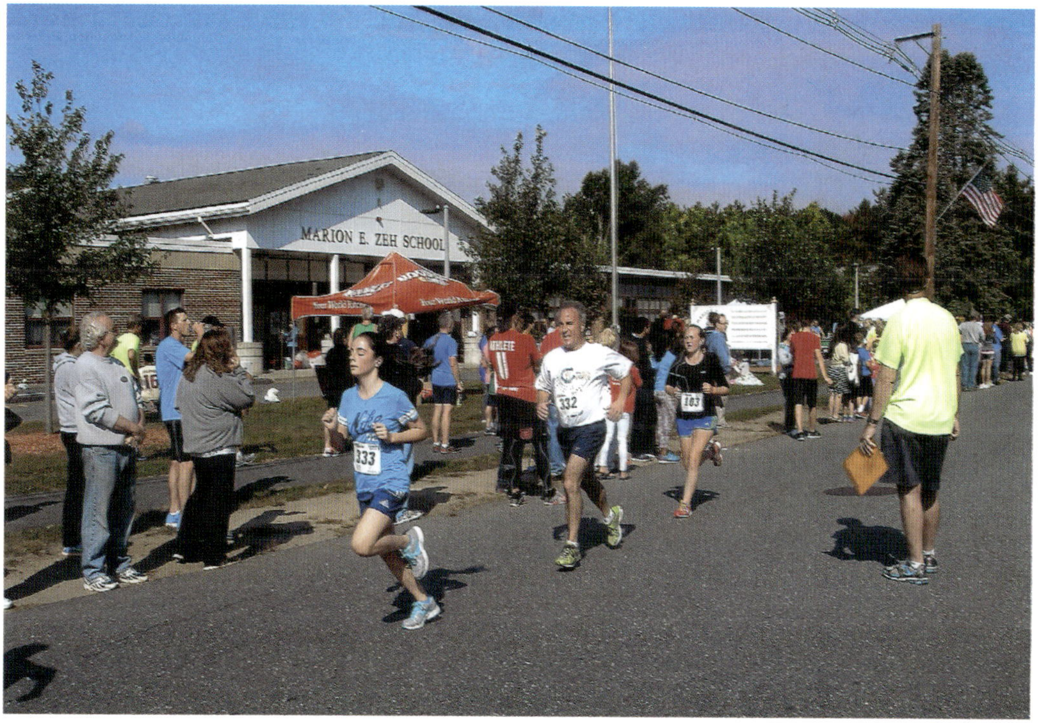

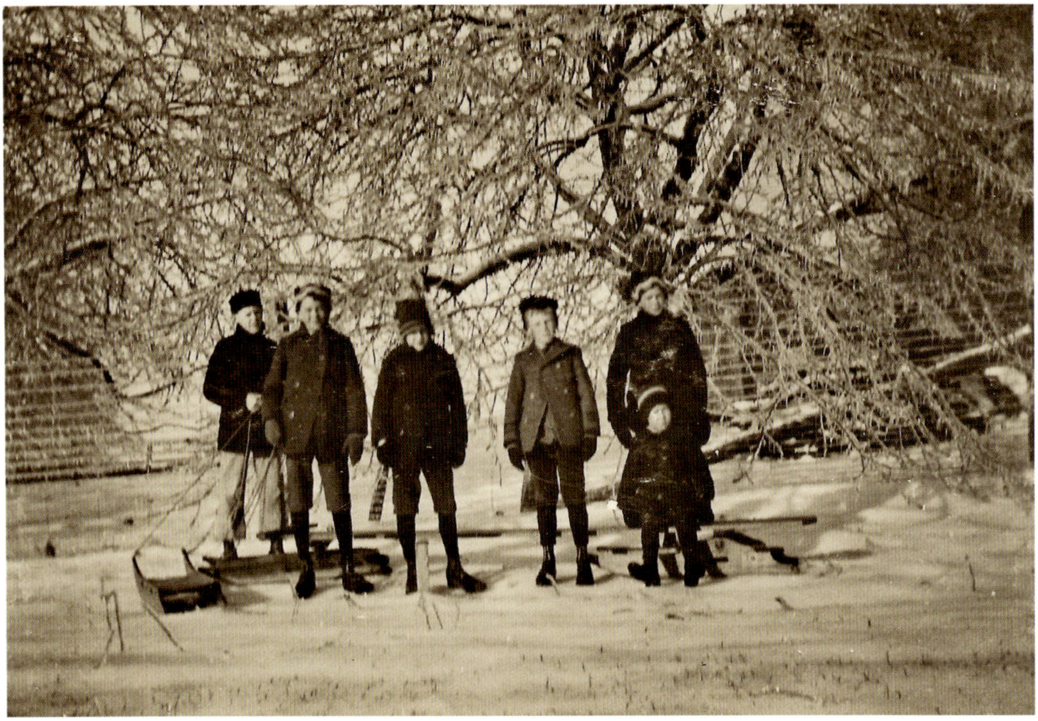

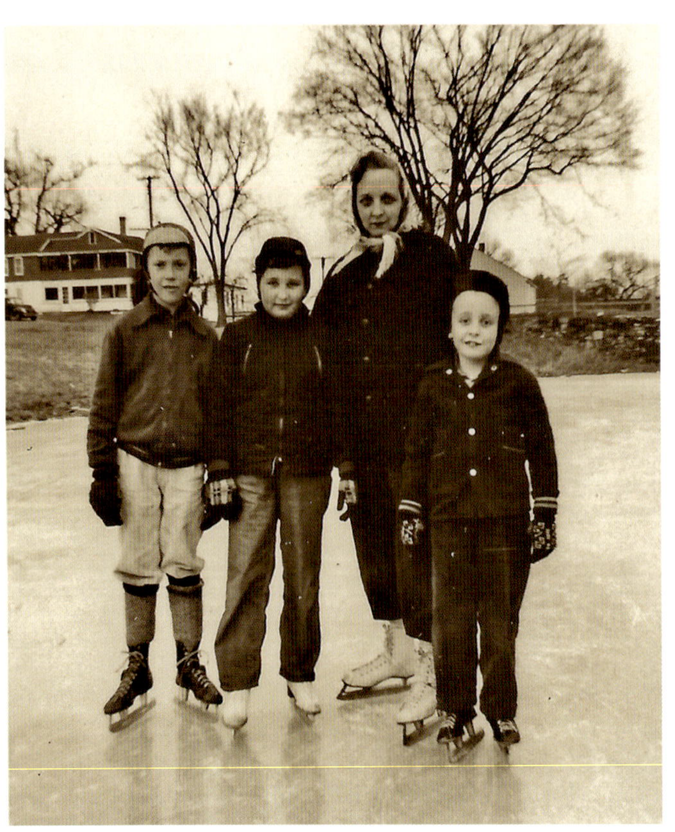

SIX BOYS, TWO SLEDS: Sharing equipment means sharing fun in Northborough during the winter of 1899. In 1951, Bob Stone, Carol Schleyer Bostock, Betty and Jackie Schleyer take time out from skating to capture the moment on Stone's Pond located on Rice Ave.

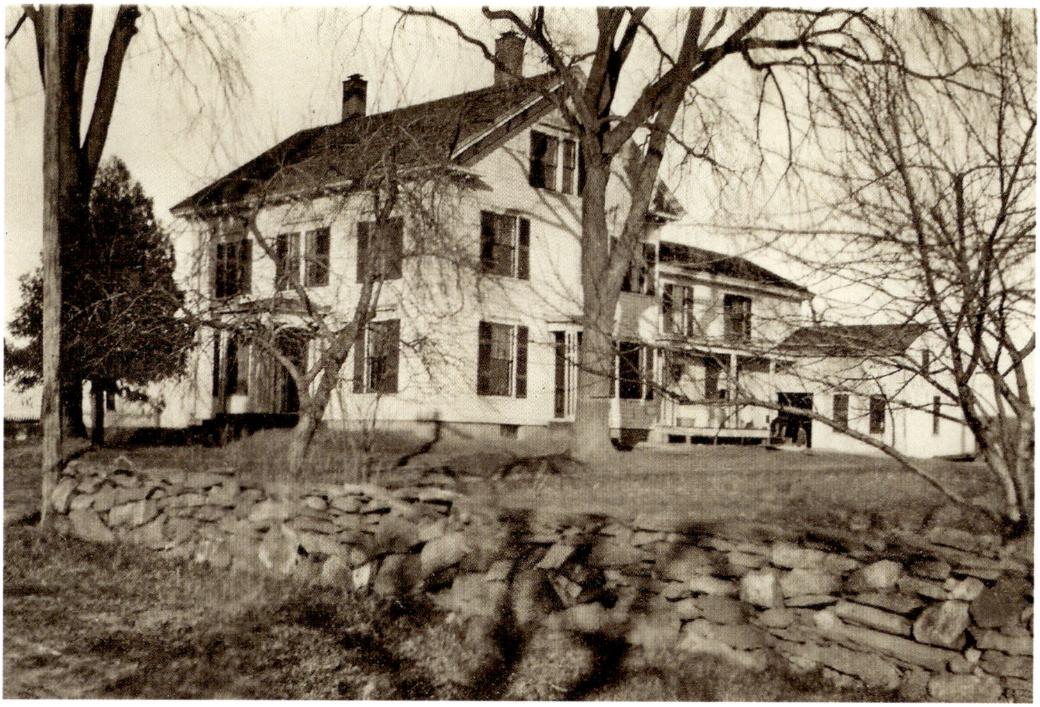

LYMAN STREET: The Norcross house, as it was known, was the seat of a farm. Farms were the main features of this street until well into the twentieth century. Large commercial buildings have replaced the Norcross farm and other nearby farms, but a short distance away a tunnel for cows to cross the road still exists.

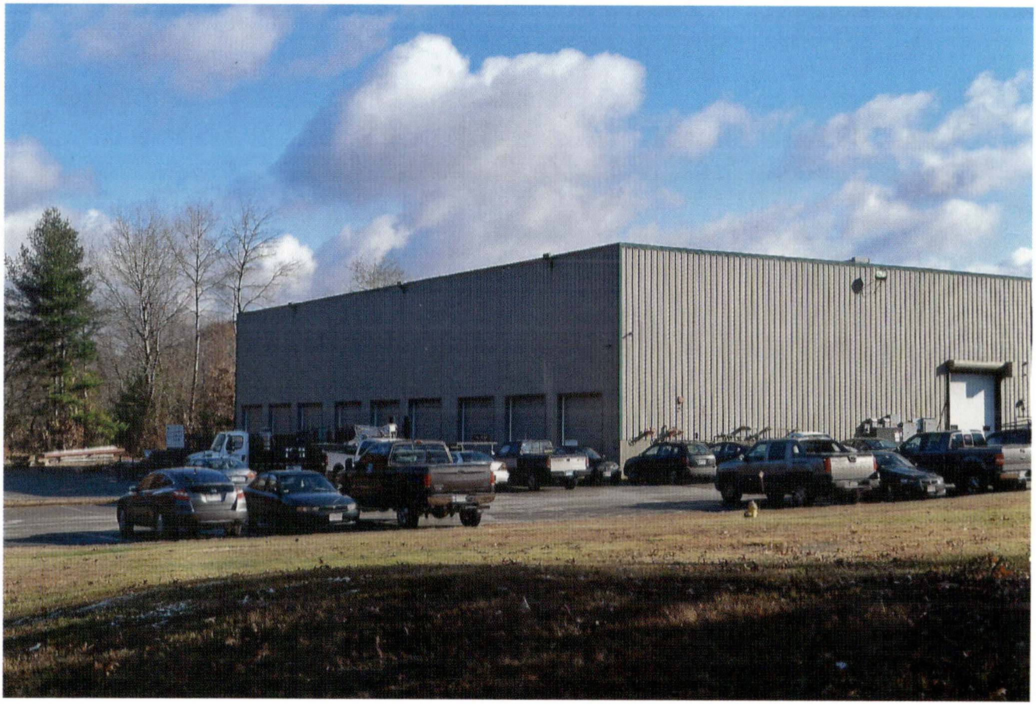

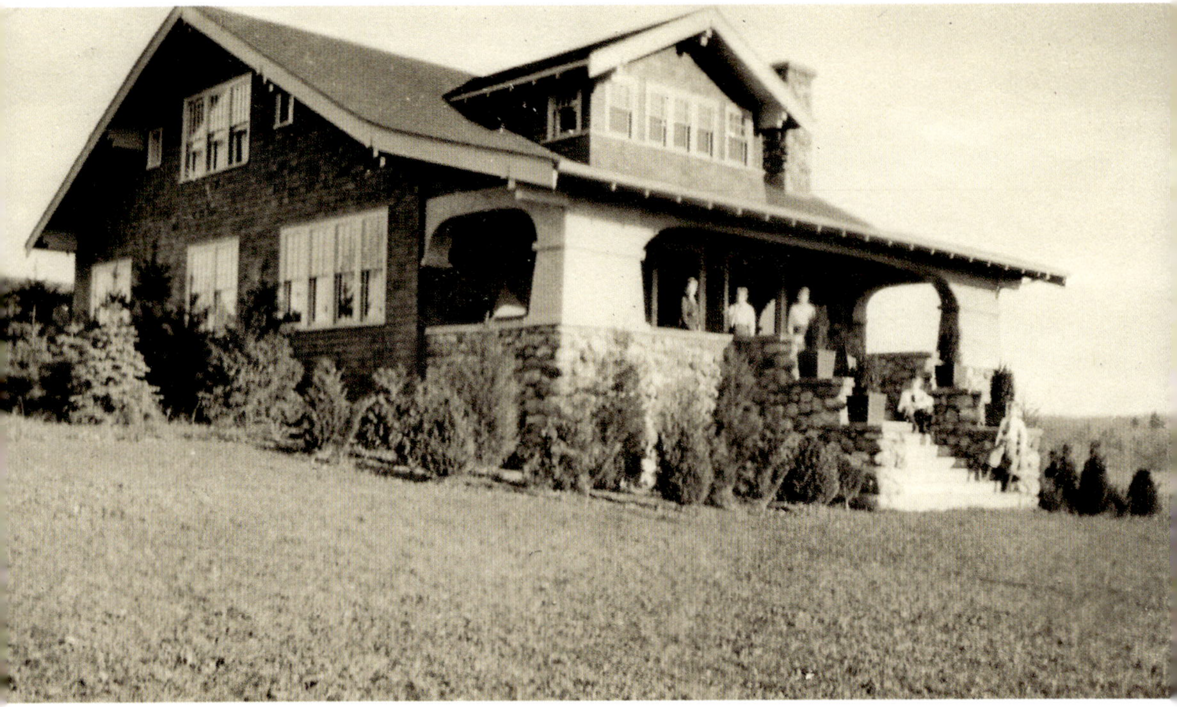

Did a century go by? This house has changed more in designation than appearance. In 1914 it was considered to be on Bartlett Street, in 2014 on Stirrup Brook Drive. Very little – not even the extensive fenestration of the gable – has been altered. The modern family shares the fondness for coniferous shrubs. Whatever the interior is like, the later residents apparently saw no reason to alter the exterior.

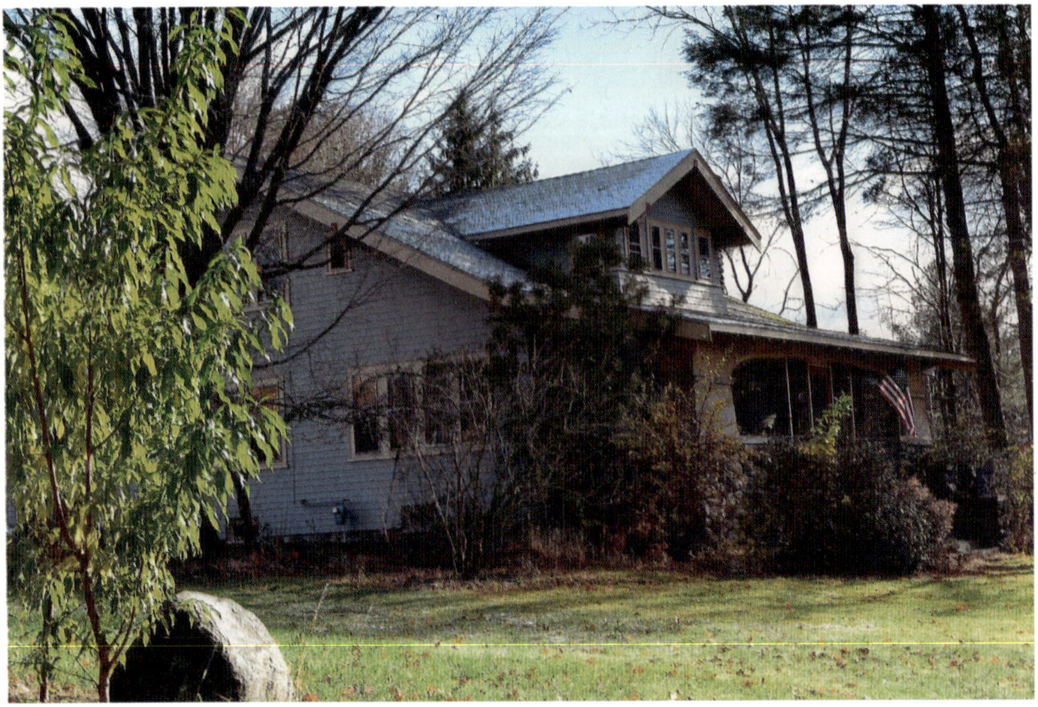

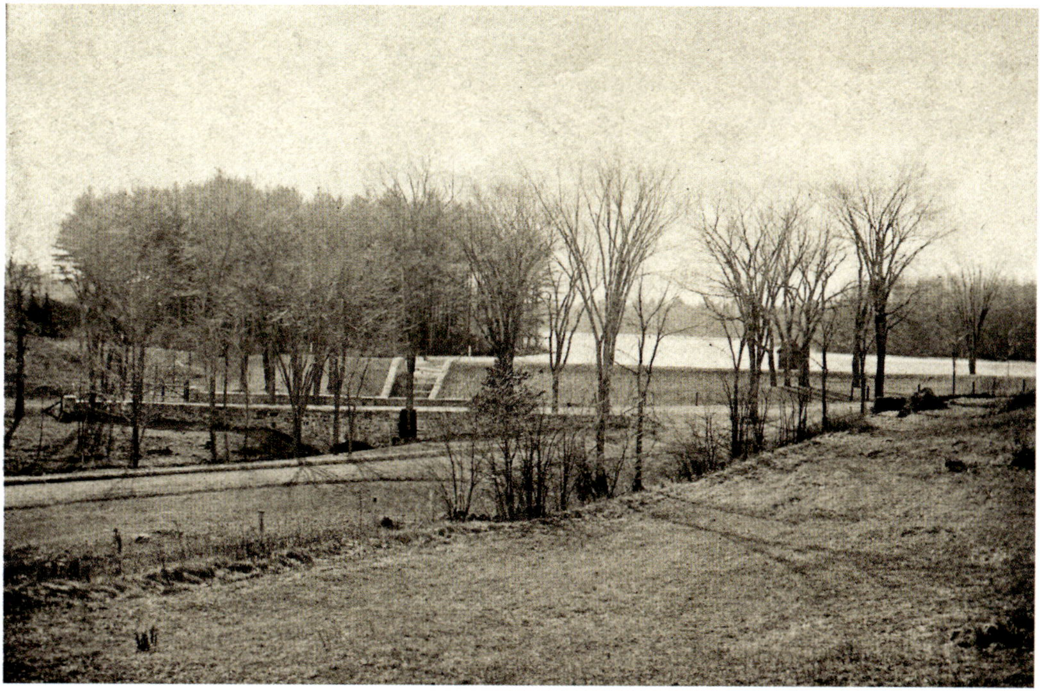

HOME-GROWN POND: Bartlett Pond was fashioned by damming Stirrup Brook, which boasted no pond but powered a saw mill at Bartlett Street in 1830. An 1855 map shoes a modest pond. It grew subsequently, providing the town new recreational opportunities, particularly when firearms manufacturer Daniel Wesson raised the dam in the early 1880s for the sake of a pump house further down the brook to water his mansion. We see it, probably just afterwards, and again in 2014.

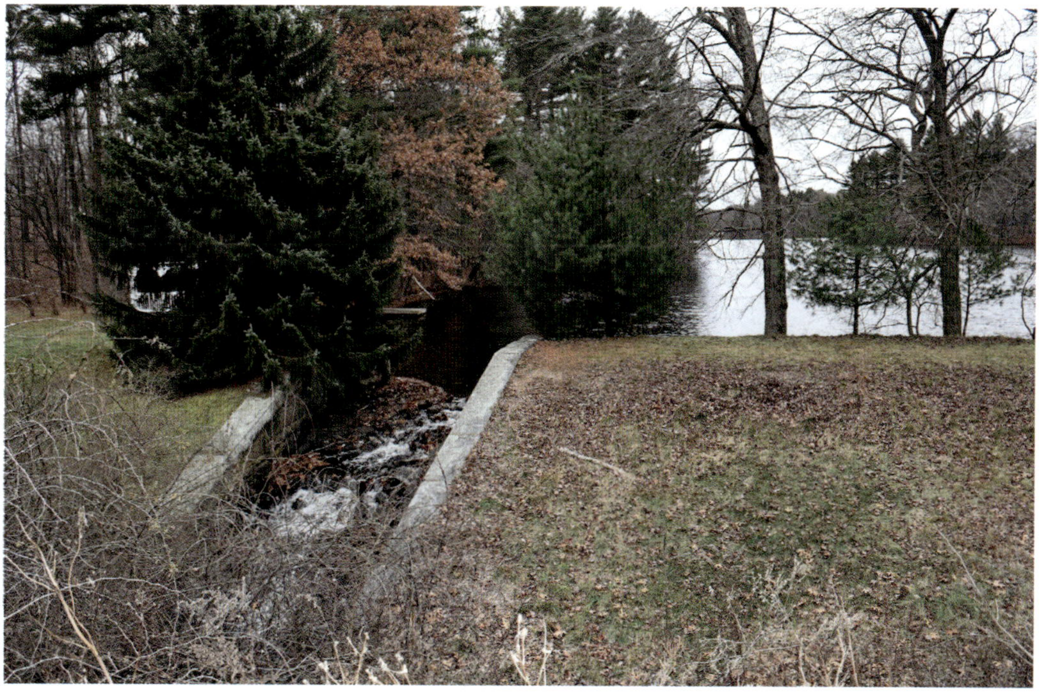

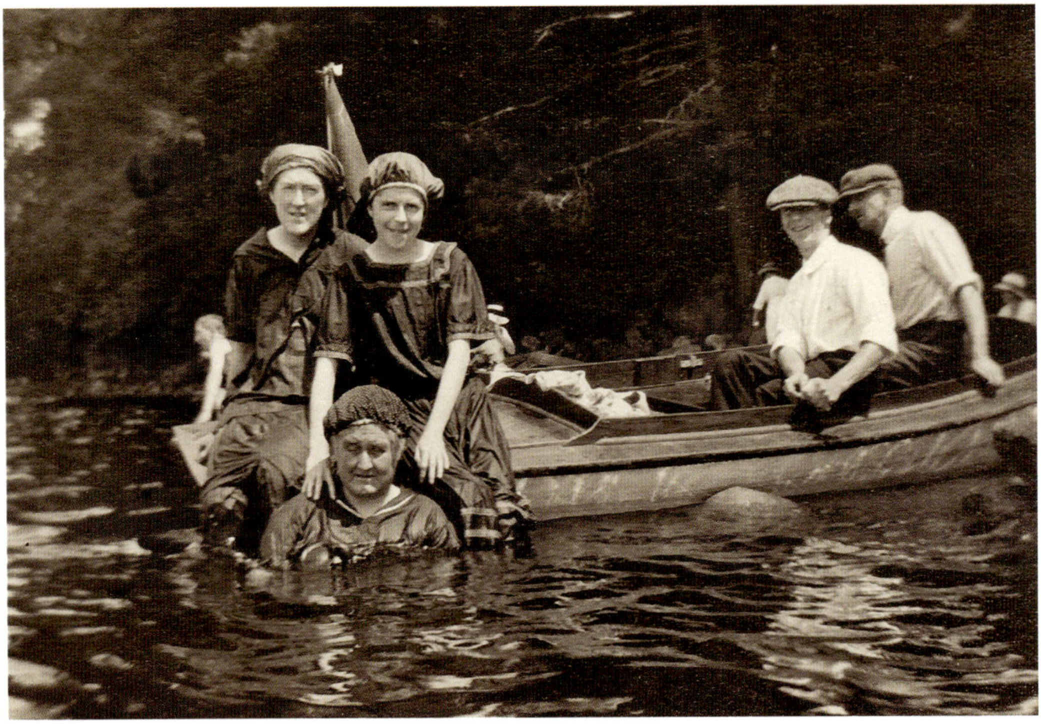

FUN TO BE HAD: Swimmers and boaters alike enjoy the summer day at Bartlett Pond, about 1900 including Marjorie Haskell. Some fifty years later, swimmers with more comfortable clothing spent the day at Solomon Pond behind the Grille Restaurant in the 1960s.

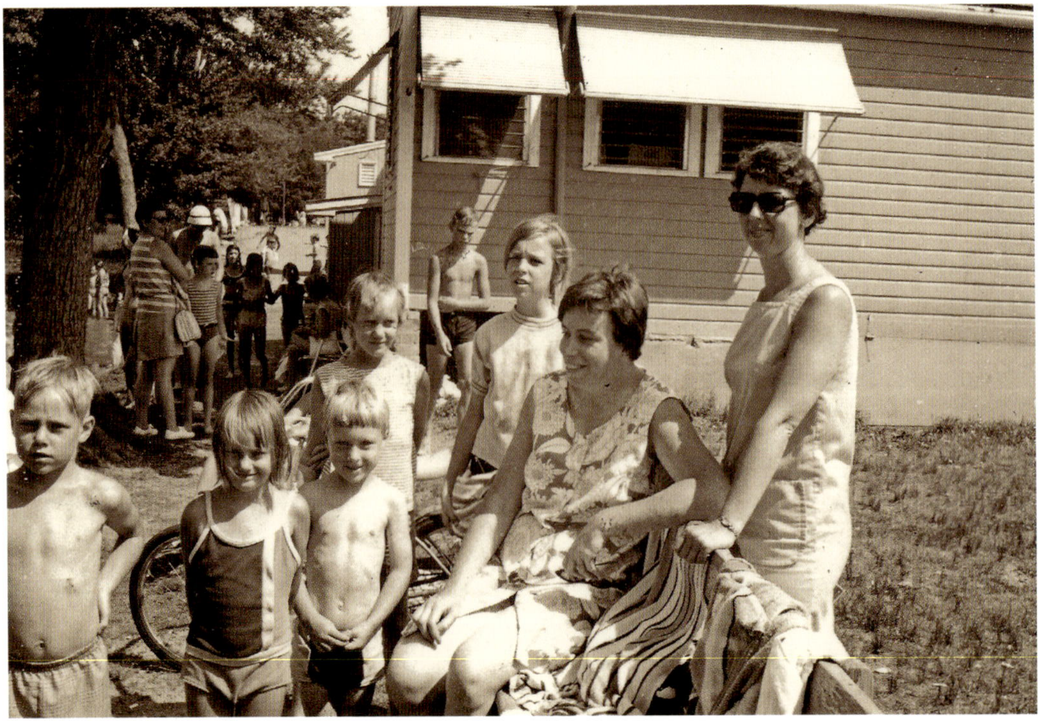

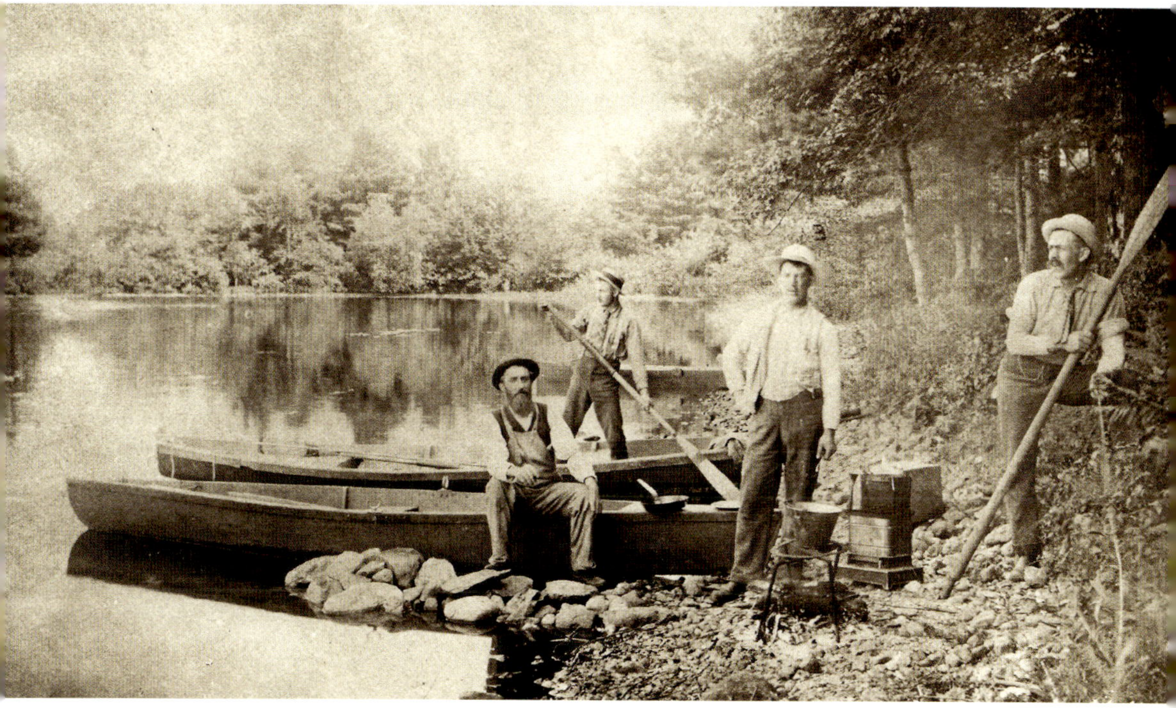

FOUR PLAYERS, YOUR MOVE: It is a bit difficult to determine what the four men are doing at Bartlett Pond around 1900. No fishing gear is in sight, and they are not making their paddles work. Perhaps it is best to say that they are doing just what the four birds are doing at the same pond over a century later – relaxing and enjoying. Betty Tetreault captured the photo of the swan family.

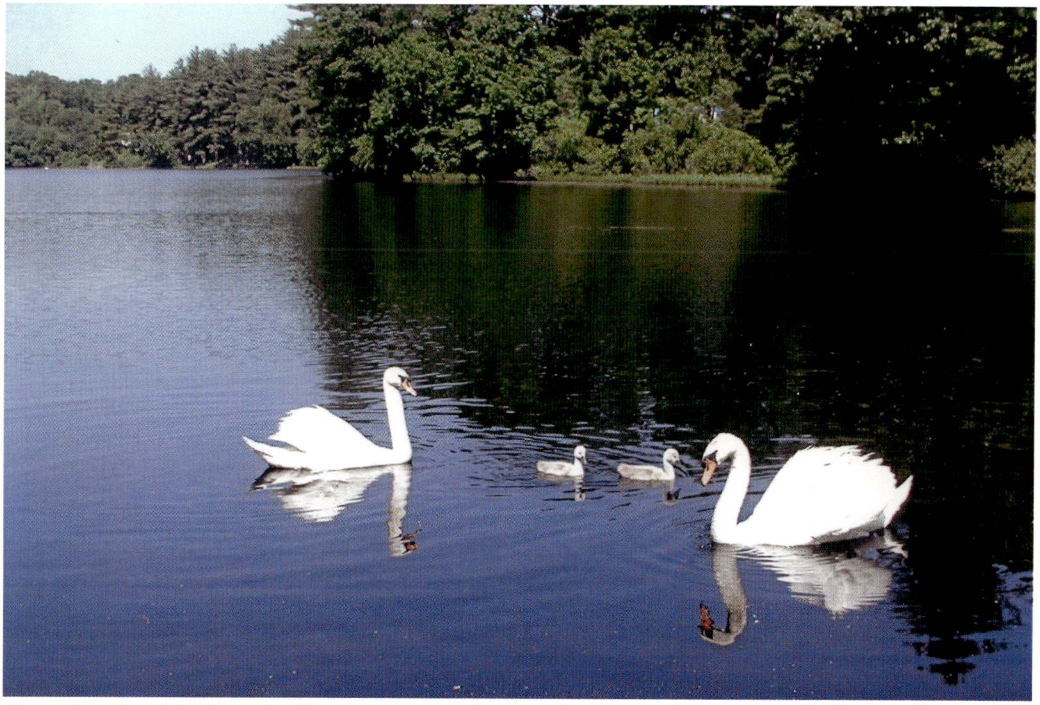

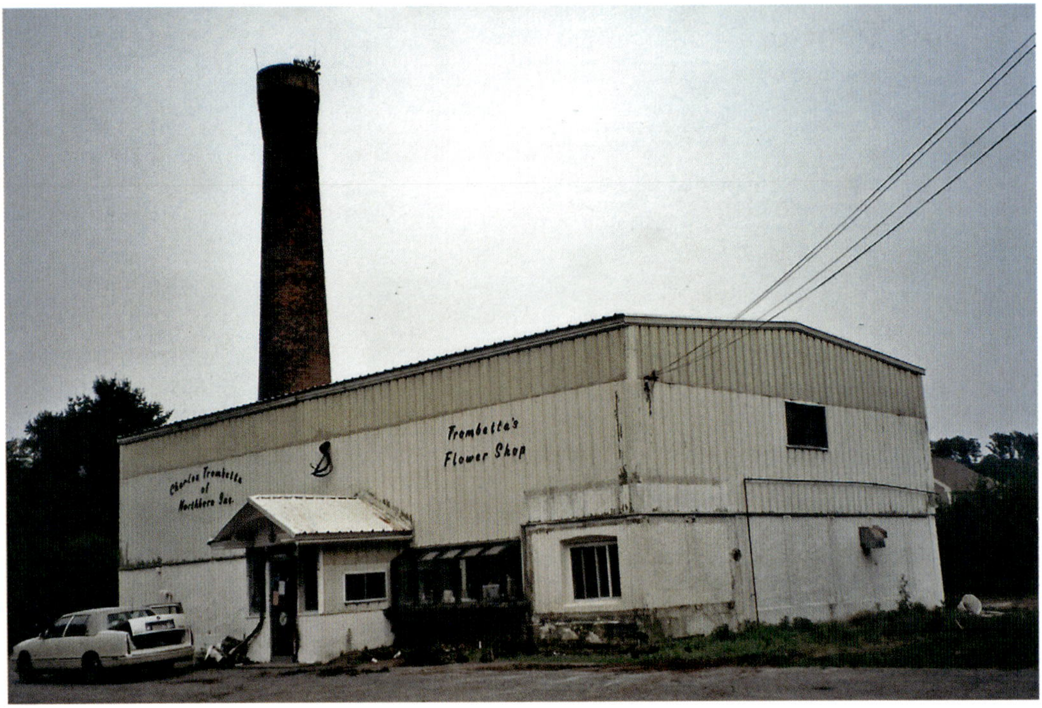

A DEFLOWERING: For many decades florists – Ralph Wadsworth, Oren Whitney, Allison Schofield, and finally Joseph Trombetta – occupied 73 Pleasant Street. Trombetta's establishment faced demolition at the time of the picture, 2002. It was the only business on this residential street, but its absence meant that all of a sudden it became difficult, if not impossible, to purchase flowers in Northborough.

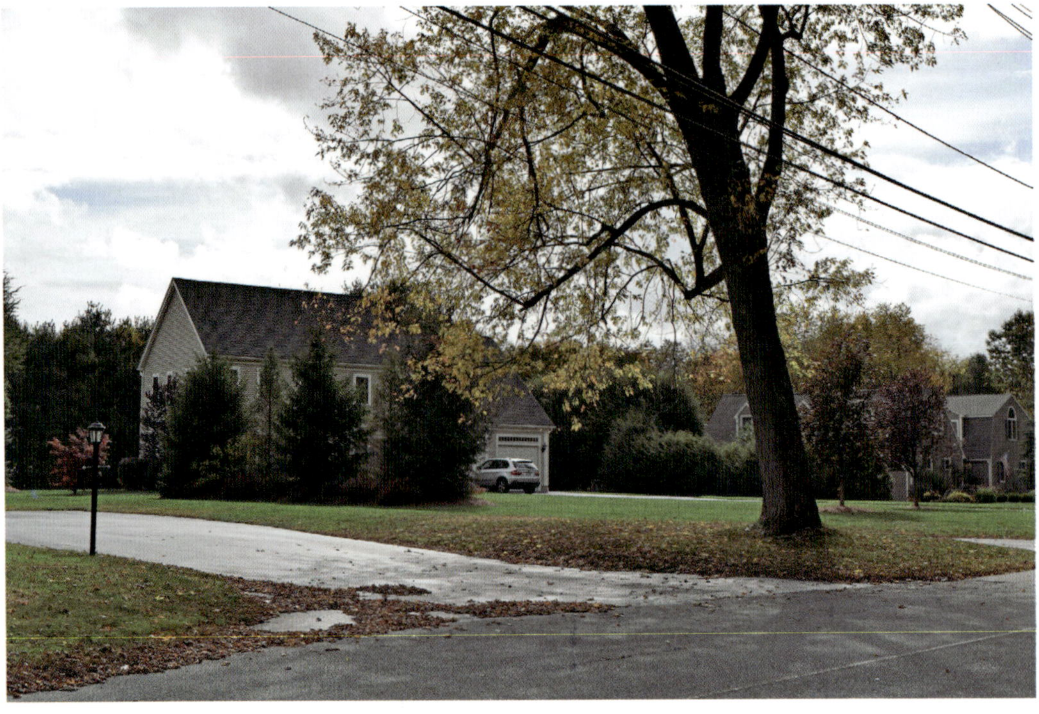

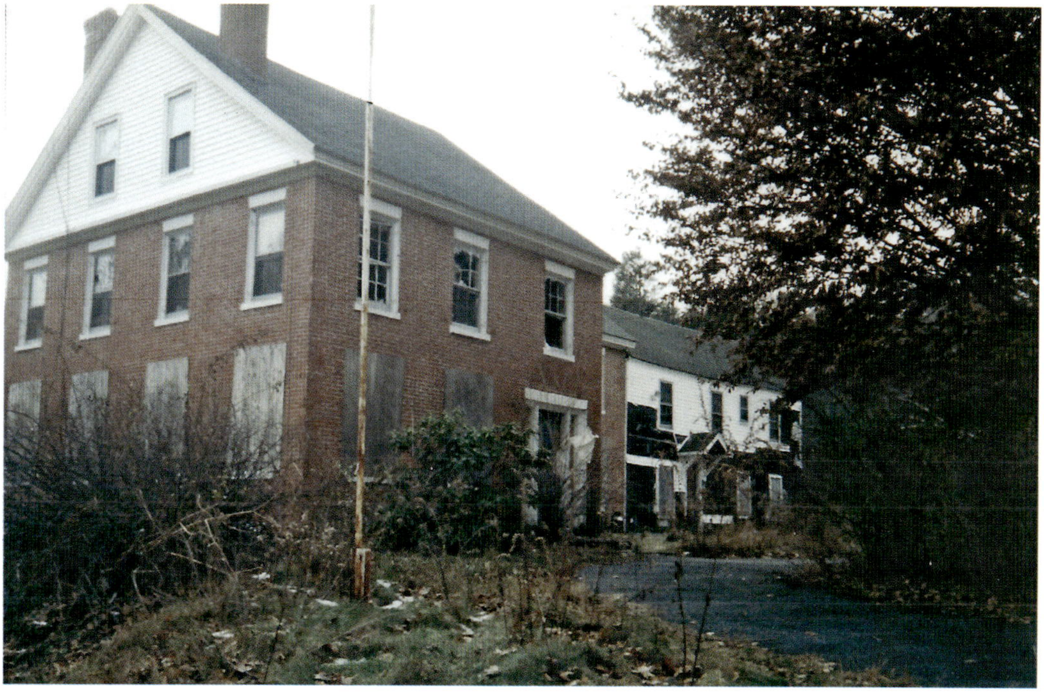

25 Rutland Road: In Northborough's early days Rutland Road was an egress to the west but probably fell out of use even before the automobile arrived on the scene. The nineteenth-century brick house owned by the Lincoln family and later by the Rich family was the only known residence on that road. Abandoned in the 1980s, the home became a centerpiece for a housing development early in the twenty-first century. Closed off at both ends, the road continued its basically hidden existence.

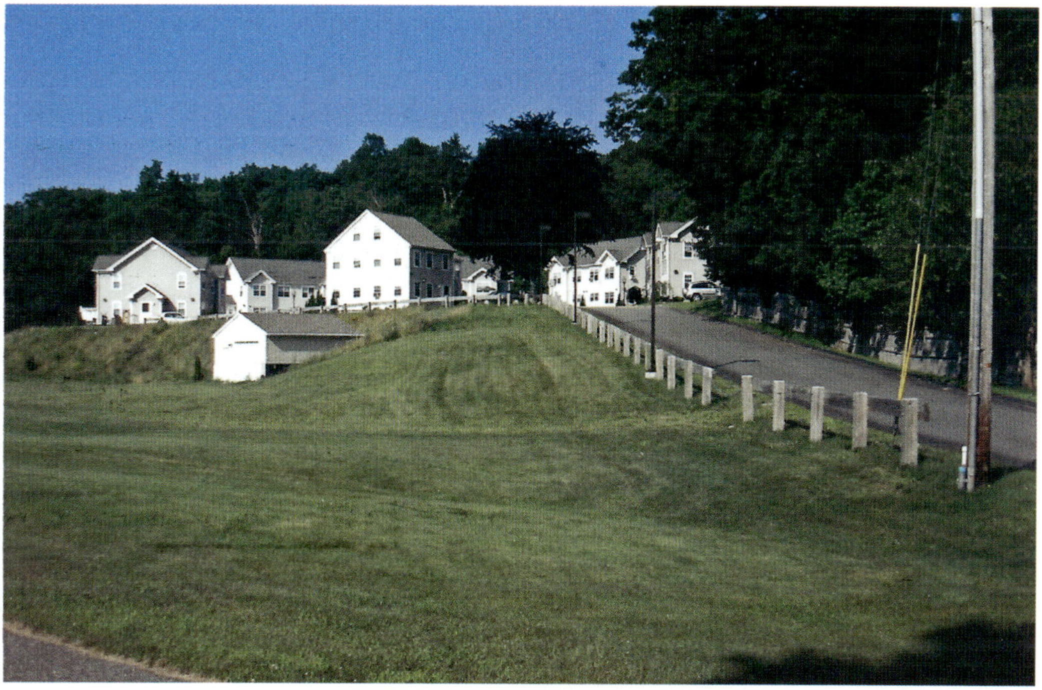

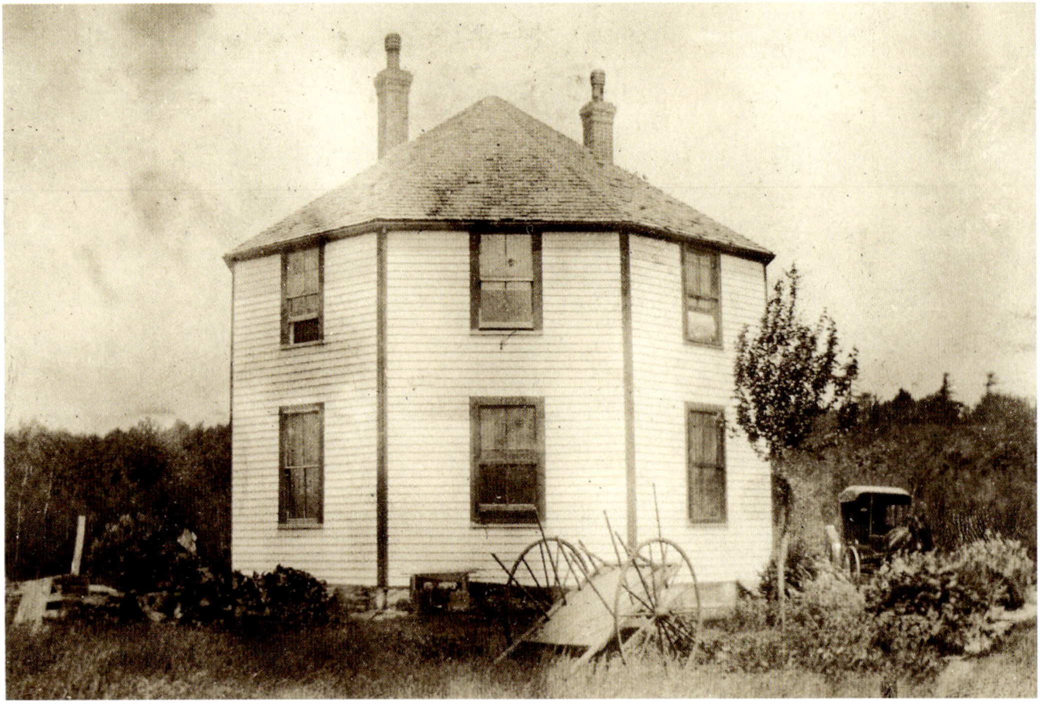

Distinctive woman, distinctive house: Alice Fisher's apparently hexagonal house stood on her eighty-two acre lot near Northborough's Oak Avenue. Considered an eccentric, she once berated a local minister out on a walk for thus profaning Sunday. She died in 1911 at age eighty. On April 17, 1926 firefighters were called to the address but could not save the house. The area has remained one of natural beauty.

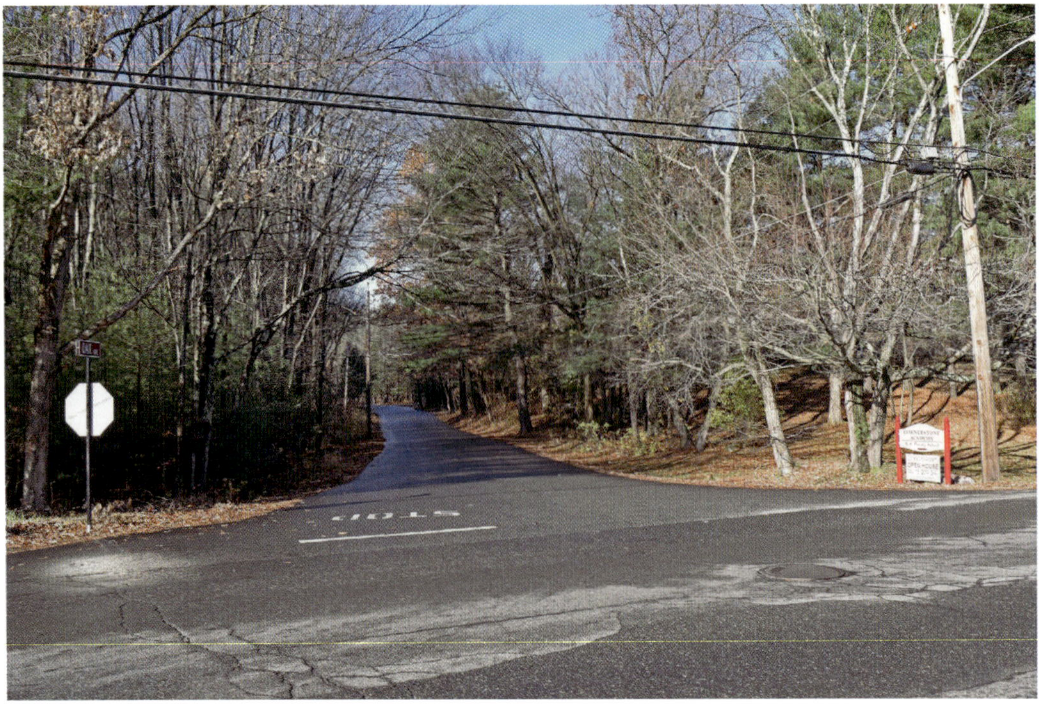

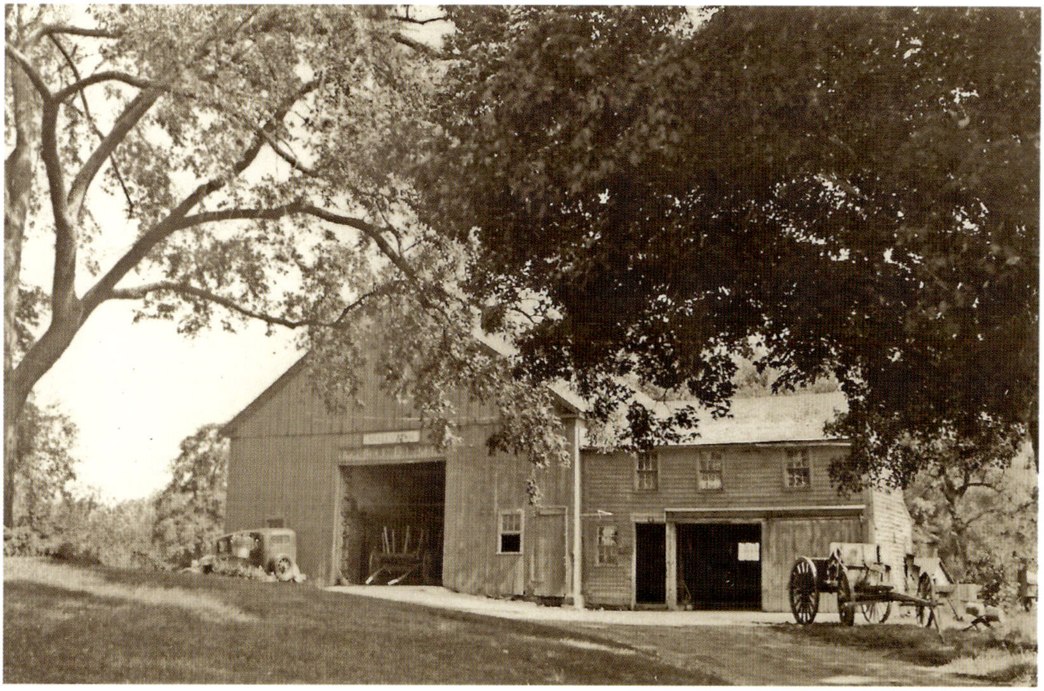

EDUCATION IN THE COUNTRYSIDE: Around 1840, before the barn was built, the structure to its right served as Elmer Valentine's private school. In Boston before coming to Northborough he had taught the future great Massachusetts senator, Charles Sumner, and other luminaries. His specialty was writing – calligraphy, that is. He and his wife had fifteen children and usually about twenty-five student boarders. The building exists no longer, but the former Valentine home remained a residence at the time of writing.

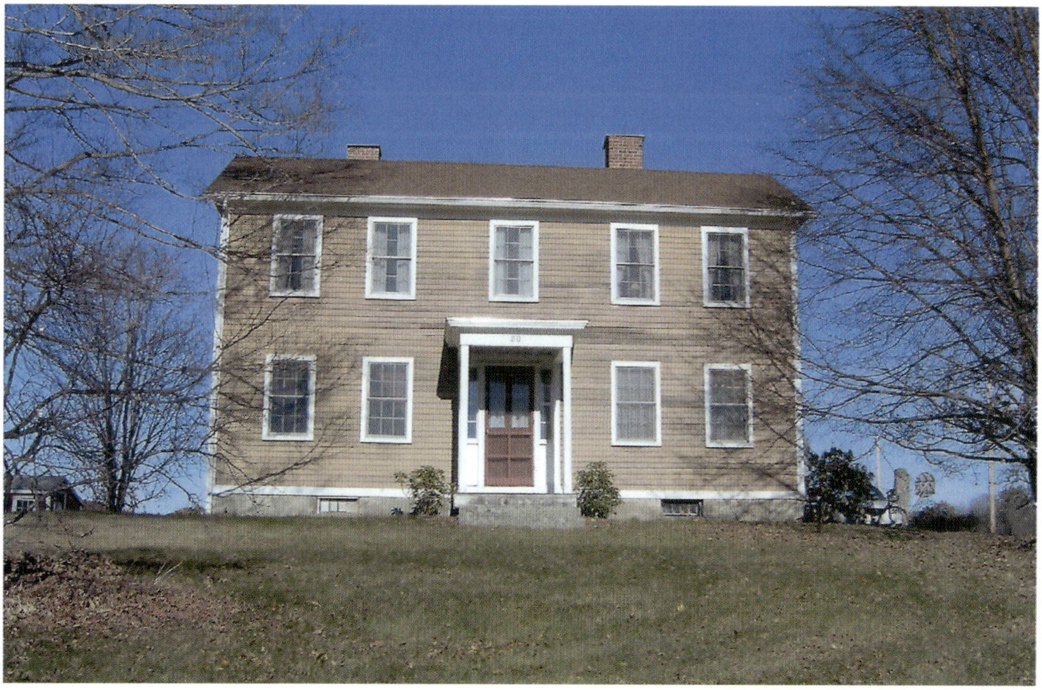

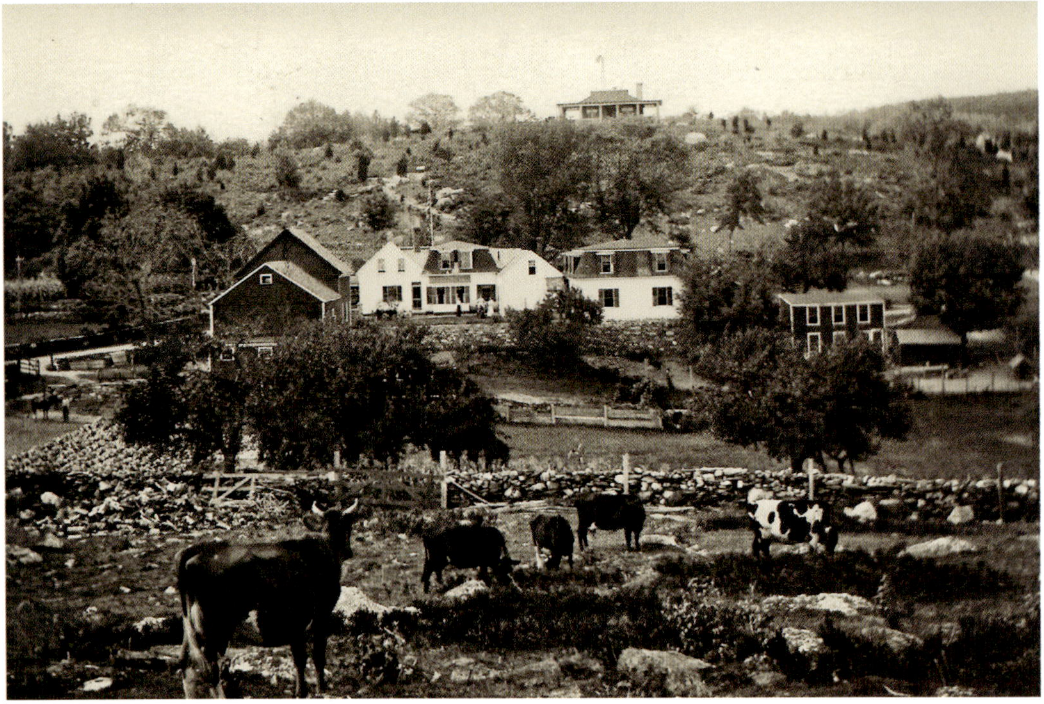

300 Howard Street: The Mentzers gather at the 1744 Joshua Townsend house that is surviving from the eighteenth century. Looking toward Howard Street one can see on top of the hill beyond a bungalow built by one of the Mentzers. It has been replaced by a much more elaborate residence called Whipsuppenicke. In the twenty-first century the hill is heavily wooded.

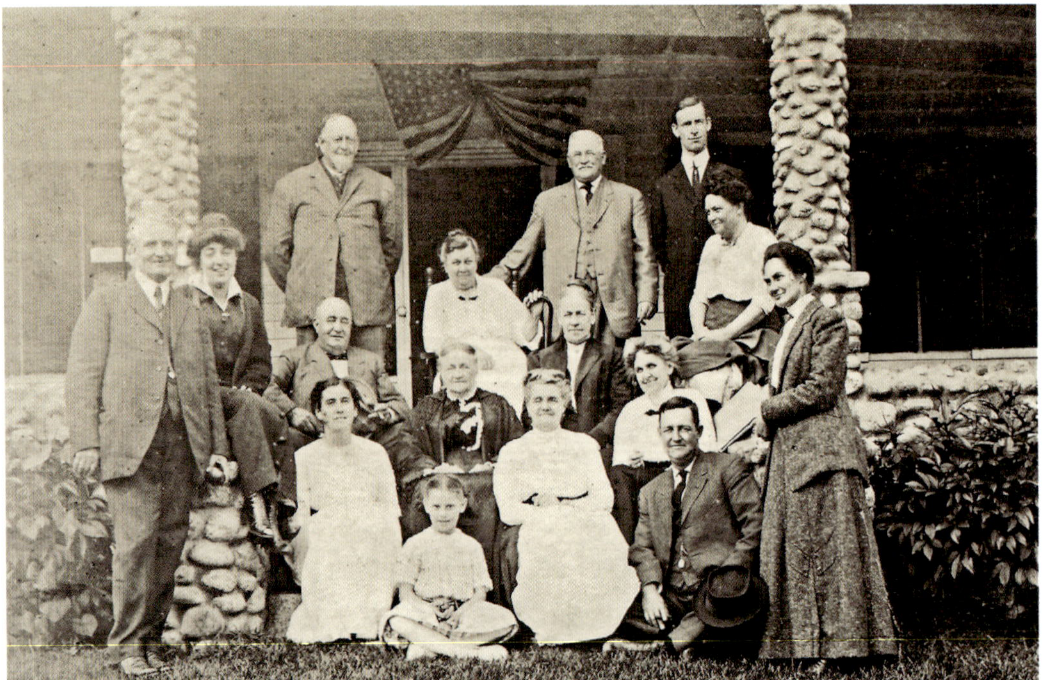

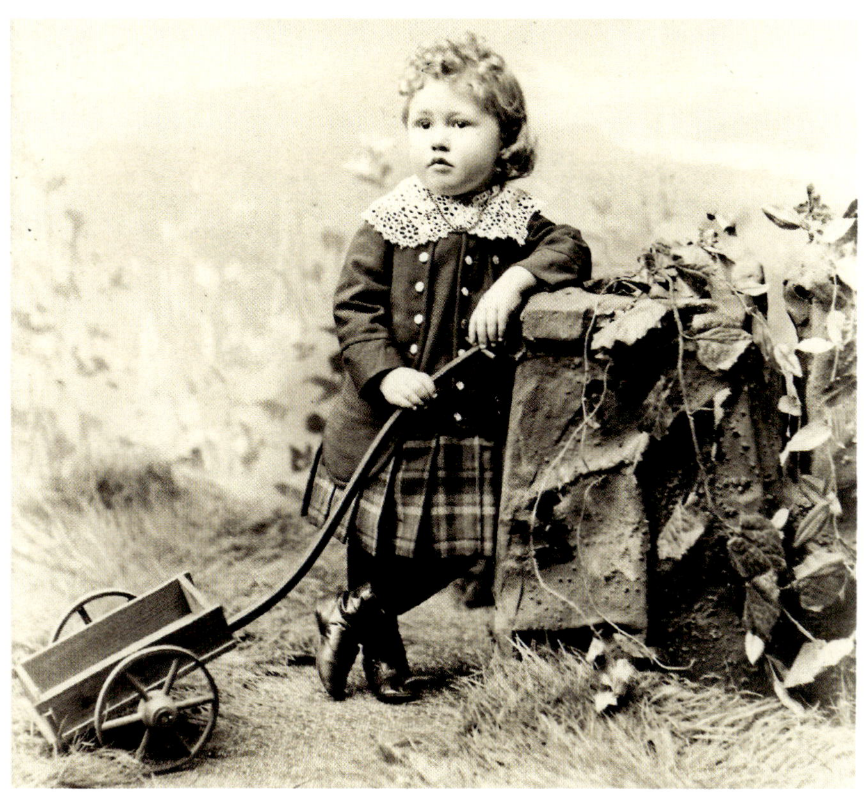

ARE WE DONE YET? Posing for the camera is hard work. William Wadsworth (b. 1882) is in a dress, typical of the era. No doubt he was eager to graduate to knickers and stockings at about age four and into long pants around age thirteen. William continued in the family's tradition as store owner on West Main. Below, Everett, only two years old, is keeping with comfortable current styles that allow him to be a challenge for grandparents Dave and Cathy Cairns.

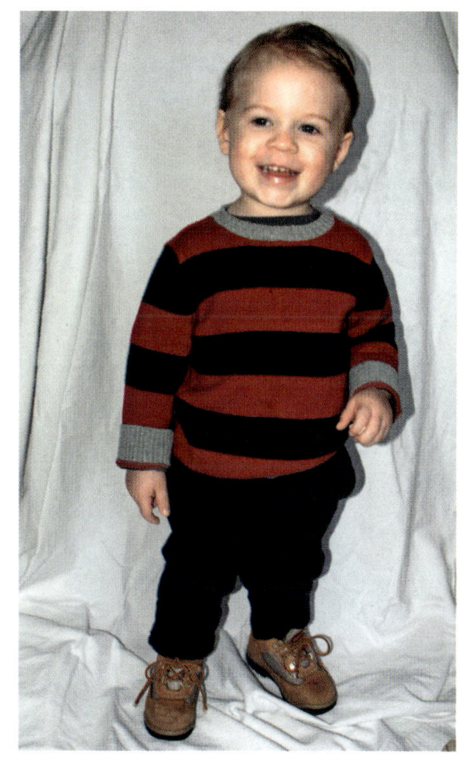

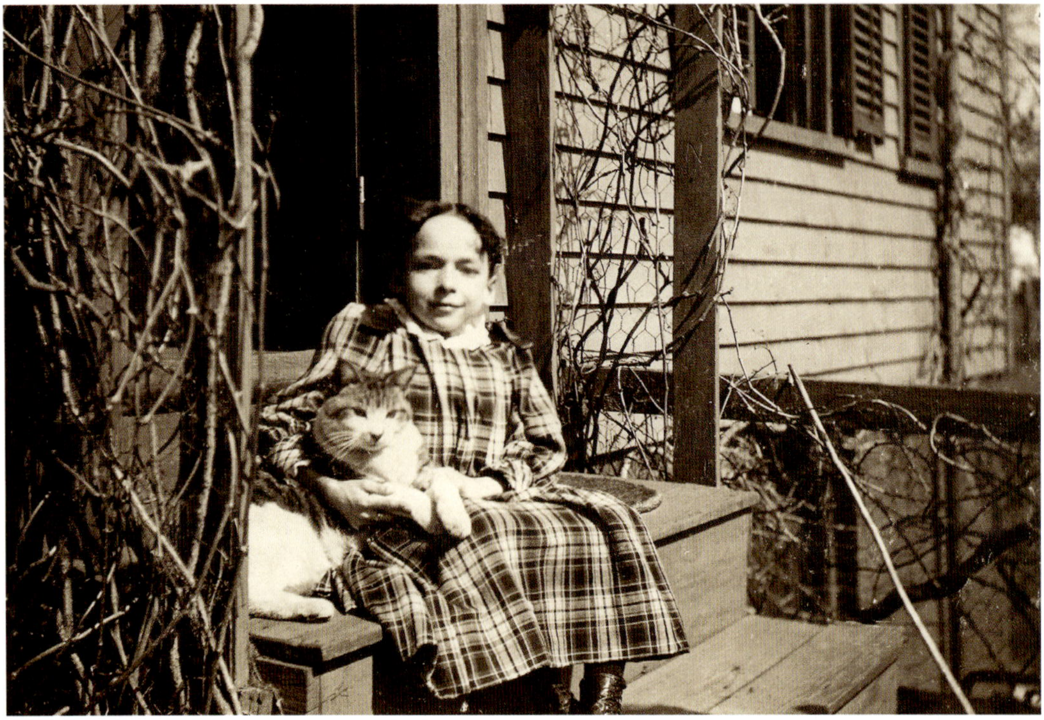

SITTING PRETTY: Seated on the porch of 45 Summer Street is Jessie Burdett with a well-fed feline. Her plaid dress could be worn today, but as Sophia shows us, comfort is more important these days and slacks are now permissible. She displays her stuffed animals and remote controlled car atop her fashionable bed.

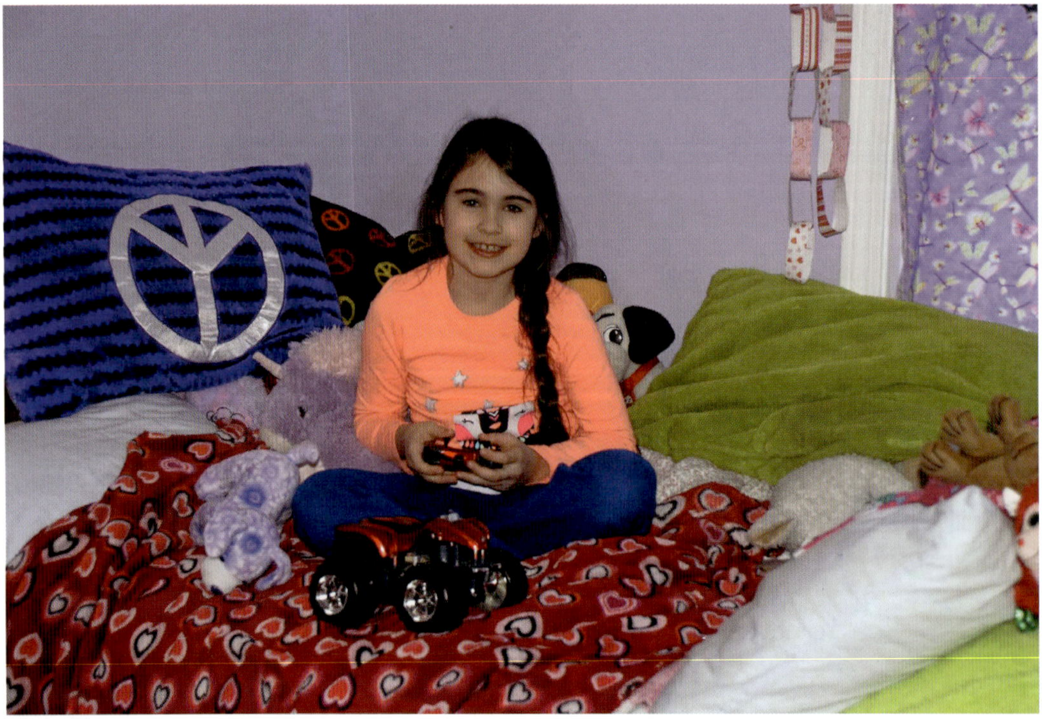

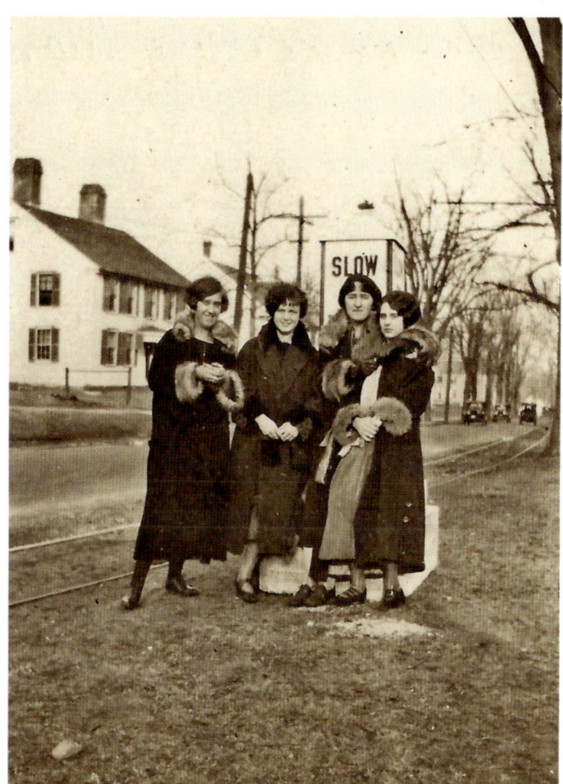

Some things never change: Four fashionable young women are enjoying a social outing in downtown Northborough, perhaps waiting for the trolley. Some eighty years later, long-time friends Jane Fletcher and JoAnn Sullivan, are exchanging stories at Applefest at the Northborough Historical Society's building on 50 Main Street.

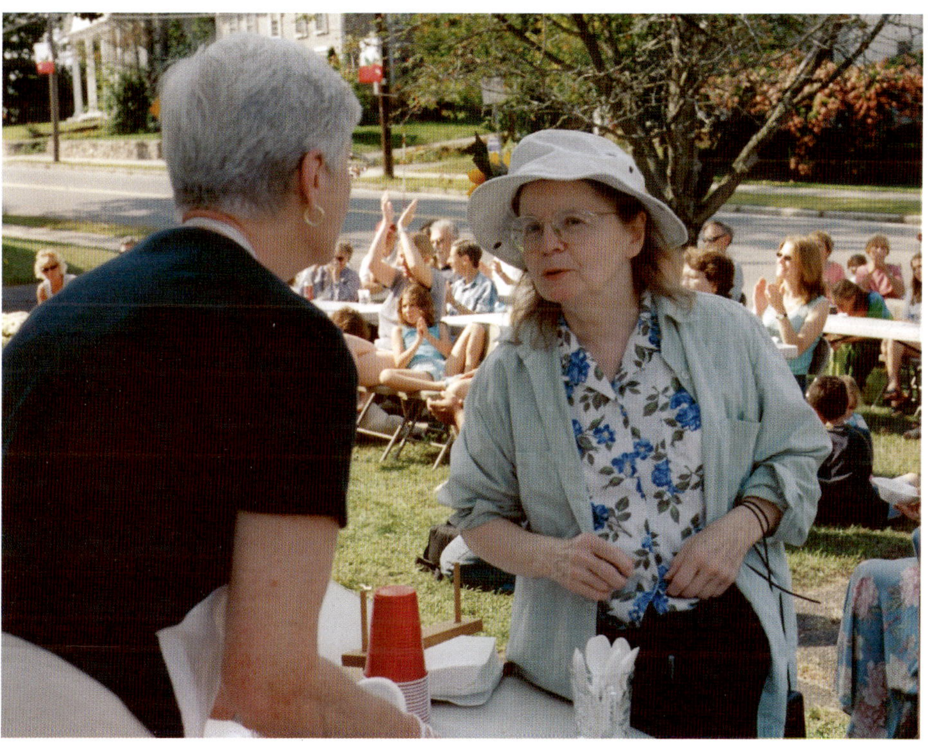

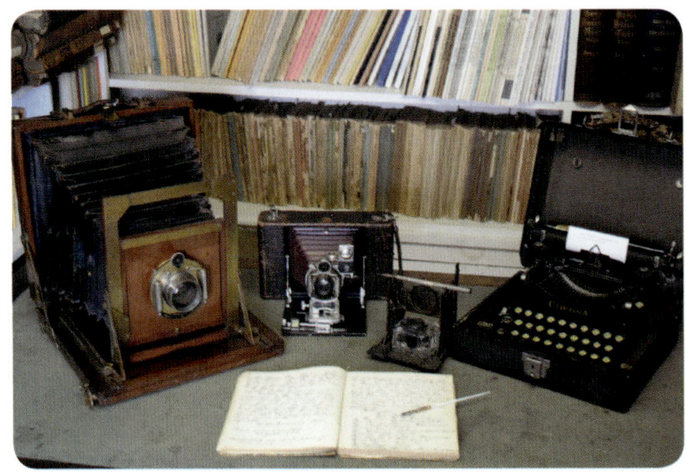

ACKNOWLEDGMENTS

Although a seemingly straight-forward project of selecting photographs and writing captions, many hours were consumed with this fun project. Historian Bob Ellis spent much time researching and writing many of the captions and I am indebted to him for all his work. I traveled about the town photographing the current views. Foliage, weather, traffic and bright sunny skies were variable and fleeting, so several trips were necessary to capture an appropriate shot before winter set in.

The majority of vintage photographs are from the Northborough Historical Society's Archive and author royalties will benefit the Society. Oke Olson photographed the town in 1966 for the Bicentennial and many of his shots are included in this publication. Rick Nieber, Bunny Rogers, Carolyn Squillante, Eugene and Carol Bostock supplied several photographs with some from the 1930-50s.

In 2006 Forest Lyford sponsored a photography contest for the Historical Society's 100th anniversary and four of those entries are used: Geoff Wilson, Skip Doyle, Betty Tetreault and Ellen Racine. JoAnn Sullivan and Kendra Owen dredged up photos of Girl Scouts while Rob Pike provided us with a current Boy Scout photo. Barbara Hogan's photo of the Jolly Ranchers' Dairy Freeze in 1960 is on page 37 and Jennifer Lyford captured several shots of the downtown area. Lastly, Cathy Cairns supplied photos of her grandchildren to provide the modern look of a new generation. My gratitude goes to all of them for contributing to this project. My special thanks go to Ernie Racine for writing the introduction, back cover preview, supplying innovative ideas, and his patience in finding his own dinner and no wife; or wife and no dinner.

Ellen Racine, Curator
Northborough Historical Society